This Time It's Personal

Teaching Academic Writing through Creative Nonfiction

John S. O'Connor
New Trier High School, Winnetka, Illinois

NCTE NATIONAL COUNCIL OF TEACHERS OF ENGLISH
1111 W. KENYON ROAD, URBANA, ILLINOIS 61801-1096

Staff Editor: Bonny Graham
Interior Design: Jenny Jensen Greenleaf
Cover Design: Pat Mayer
Cover Background: iStockphoto.com/PPAMPicture

NCTE Stock Number: 54304

It is the policy of NCTE in its journals and other publications to provide a forum for the open discussion of ideas concerning the content and the teaching of English and the language arts. Publicity accorded to any particular point of view does not imply endorsement by the Executive Committee, the Board of Directors, or the membership at large, except in announcements of policy, where such endorsement is clearly specified.

Every effort has been made to provide current URLs and email addresses, but because of the rapidly changing nature of the Web, some sites and addresses may no longer be accessible.

Library of Congress Cataloging-in-Publication Data

O'Connor, John S.
   This time it's personal : teaching academic writing through creative nonfiction / John S. O'Connor.
      p. cm.
   Includes bibliographical references.
   ISBN 978-0-8141-5430-4 (pbk)
   1. English language—Rhetoric—Study and teaching. 2. Reportage literature—Authorship—Study and teaching. 3. Prose literature—Authorship—Study and teaching. 4. Creative nonfiction. 5. Creative writing. I. Title.
   PE1404.O26 2011
   808'.042071—dc23
                                                              2011042004

This Time It's Personal

NCTE Editorial Board

As always, for Eleni, Alison, and Ted

Contents

Permission Acknowledgments

A version of Chapter 1, "Once More to the Ocean: The Case for Personal Writing," was previously published in *Schools: Studies in Education* (7.1 [2010]: 101–10) and was named a Notable Essay in *The Best American Essays 2011*.

Richard Hartwell's "Our Writing Lives: How I Evolved as a Writer" [*The Voice* 2(6)] is reprinted with permission from the National Writing Project (NWP). The mission of the NWP is to improve the teaching of writing and improve learning in the nation's schools. Explore NWP's resources at www.nwp.org.

"Middle Way" by Tom Clausen from *Contemporary Haibun: Volume 4*, reprinted by permission of the author.

"Facing the Wall" by John J. Dunphy, published in *Old Soldiers Fading Away*, Columbus, Ohio: Pudding House, 2006. Reprinted with permission.

"Green, and more green" and "Black on black" by Lidia Rozmus from *My Journey*, reprinted by permission of the author.

"Birthday Haibun" by Michael Ketchek from *Up Against the Window: American Haibun and Haiga, Vol. 1*, reprinted by permission of the author.

"On Visiting the DMZ at Panmunjom: A Haibun" from TIME AND MATERIALS: POEMS 1997–2005 by ROBERT HASS. Copyright © 2007 by Robert Hass. Reprinted by permission of HarperCollins Publishers.

Excerpt from "Why We Tell Stories" by Lisel Mueller from *Alive Together: New and Selected Poems* © 1996, reprinted by permission of Louisiana State University Press.

"For Mohammed Zeid of Gaza, Age 15" by Naomi Shihab Nye from *You and Yours*, reprinted by permission of the author, Naomi Shihab Nye, 2011.

Excerpt from "The Racial Politics of Speaking Well" by Lynette Clemetson from The New York Times, 4 February 2007 © 2007 The New York Times. All rights reserved. Used by permission and protected by the Copyright Laws of the United States. The printing, copying, redistribution, or retransmission of this Content without express written permission is prohibited.

Excerpt from "Corsons Inlet". Copyright © 1963 by A. R. Ammons, from COLLECTED POEMS 1951–1971 by A. R. Ammons. Used by permission of W. W. Norton & Company, Inc.

Acknowledgments

I am especially lucky to have worked with many brilliant teachers over the past twenty-five years. Each has made me a better teacher and a better person. Within this group, though, I must single out Spiro Bolos, Julie Johnson, Dan Lawler, and Sherry Medwin. They are not only great friends and extraordinary teachers, but they also helped to shape the ideas in this book by reading drafts and sharing their insights through many enjoyable conversations about teaching.

I am deeply indebted to my University of Illinois at Chicago dissertation committee for their thoughtful suggestions and penetrating insights on my dissertation, which informed every aspect of this book. Specifically, I have to thank Tony Grosch, Kathy Ruhl, and Bill Schubert—and most of all, Bill Ayers and Dave Schaafsma, who are great friends, inspirational teachers, and unflagging believers in the power of narrative.

At NCTE I am grateful as always to Kurt Austin for his encouragement, friendship, and valuable insights into teaching and writing at every step of this process. I am also grateful to Bonny Graham for her careful reading and meticulous attention to detail in bringing this project to completion.

I am enormously lucky to have worked at the University of Chicago Laboratory Schools and New Trier Township High School—two schools that have given me the creative freedom to experiment with new ideas every year. I would like to give special thanks to my New Trier department chair, John Cadwell, for the faith and trust he has shown in my teaching.

Most of all, this book would not be possible without the love and support of my family. My children, Alison and Ted, always remind me of the importance of writing and story in our lives—in and out of school. And I cannot imagine having written this book without my beautiful wife, Eleni, whose intelligence and encouragement guided me every step of the way.

Finally, I would like to acknowledge the thousands—is it possible?—of students who have shared their writing and their lives with me over the past twenty-five years. Reading the personal essays in this book and in my classes each year reminds me how truly grateful I am for the generosity of my students and how lucky I am to call myself a teacher.

I

Examining Our Lives as Texts

Once More to the Ocean:
The Case for Personal Writing

The Ocean of the Streams of Story is made up of a thousand thousand thousand and one different currents, each one a different colour, weaving in and out of one another like a liquid tapestry of breathtaking complexity.... [E]ach strand represented and contained a single tale.

—SALMAN RUSHDIE, *Haroun and the Sea of Stories* (71–72)

Trying to create a coherent narrative of my high school classes, I often feel like the eponymous hero in Salman Rushdie's *Haroun and the Sea of Stories*. The multiplicity of stories is dizzying—each of my five classes deserves a story of its own; so too do each of my 125 students within these classes. Yet, impossible as it is to unbraid the narrative strands, to hear each voice distinctly within the deafening din of a school day, this search is essential if I am to claim any understanding of the most basic questions teachers can ask themselves: Who am I teaching? What is happening in my classroom? And what, in short, is the purpose of school?

Every education system I've taught in for the past twenty-five years answers these questions numerically—through ability groupings, IQ scores, test scores, state standards, demographic data, and the like. Yet such measures seem hopelessly reductive to me as an English teacher. These numbers are useful in sorting students but not in discovering who our students are. They leave us with answers but not necessarily wisdom.

What's the Story with School?

The short answer is that it's a folktale with little regard for character development or dialogue. But it doesn't need to be this way.

In *Making Stories*, Jerome Bruner distinguishes between two kinds of stories—the legal and the literary, or "the established and the possible" (13). Within the world of education research, these story types are derived from quantitative and experiential research, and the tension between the two story modes has been long-standing. Citing scholar Ellen Lagemann in a 2007 issue of *English Education*, Schaafsma and colleagues say that

> the history of educational research . . . can be summed up . . . [as an] ideological battle between Dewey [and his commitment to grounding research and scholarship in experience] and Thorndike [and his commitment to "hard science" with its focus on experimentally based, numerically summarized notions of "proof" and "validity"]. (Schaafsma, Pagnucci, Wallace, and Stock 283–84)

Examining education research over the past century or so, and the great preponderance of quantitative measurement, Lagemann concluded that, at the end of the battle, "Thorndike won" (284). The consequences of this victory for the kinds of stories that are told about school life are profound. To privilege the "scientific" is to privilege the scientist as collector and analyst of data and to reduce students to mere data, often in the form of raw numbers. What's missing is the student him- or herself. Consider this brief excerpt from a student named Alexa (her complete essay appears in Chapter 11):

> To the nurse's office I'm a red folder full of immunization records and my temperature from the one time I actually needed their services. To the IT department I'm 20060916. . . . To the Dean's office I am parking pass 224 with a '95 maroon Volvo license plate #6718748. To the College Board I'm 329-XX-2222 and 13 penciled-in computer-read bubbles that spell my name—as if it even matters. To the college counselor's office I'm a 5.26 GPA AP student on the Honor Roll—all of which turn out to be meaningless distinctions in the <u>real world</u>. . . . But I won't be forgotten. I'll be remembered as a hard-working student, a friendly face who always said hi in the hallways, . . . the short comedian who spent every waking minute trying to make people laugh. I won't let myself become a ghost, just a number in a file.

Alexa's voice in relating this information is as alive as the numbers are dead, ghostly in their emptiness. This piece, part of a longer reflection written at the end of high school, speaks volumes about the third dimension—depth—that is lost when students' stories are told only through numbers.

Bruner himself once privileged the scientific narrative. Speaking as one of the most forceful and articulate proponents of scientific positivism, Bruner argued that "the scientific method could tame ordinary narrative into testable hypotheses" (qtd. in *Making Stories* 101). Forty years later, however, he reconsidered this notion in *Making Stories*, admitting ultimately, "I think I was profoundly mistaken." Seeing the legal or scientific story as looking only to "the actual, the literal, the record of the past," Bruner, like Alexa, sees such "ordinary" narratives as incomplete. Instead, he turns to a literary model since "literature looks to the possible, the figurative" (61). This is an especially interesting narrative leap when considering the learning and lives of children in schools.

Out of bureaucratic necessity perhaps, schools rely on the reductive story—the scientific story in Bruner's formulation—that seeks to establish absolute truths. These stories, such as those derived from scores on standardized tests, are often instructive, but they are also simplistic. They are usually more interested in figuring out what students don't know than in what they do know. As Mike Rose puts it in *Lives on the Boundary*, kids always "know more than the tests reveal, but they don't know how to put their knowledge into a coherent pattern" (8). As a result, these stories often read like folktales or fables, with students represented as two-dimensional characters—caricatures, really—shallow representations instead of human beings.

Typecasting

I walked right into such a fable at my first high school teaching job, where I was immediately confronted with a rigid and implacable tracking system. Most shocking of all was the nomenclature used for the four ability groups identified at that school: Alphas, Betas, Gammas, and Deltas. Contrary to what some of my students might tell you, this was not the Late Mesozoic era but the early 1990s! Incredibly, this public school blithely borrowed the terminology from the satirical dystopia *Brave New World* to describe its students. Students were assigned to these "ability" groups based on IQ scores, and almost without exception these students remained in their tracks for the duration of their high school careers.

Even among the academically strongest of the "low-level" students, an incredibly low self-image was common, making it difficult for any of these students to imagine they could ever be "college material." One student named Frank told me that "his people" didn't go to college, a statement that has haunted me ever since. Students seemed to internalize their rank and quickly came to see their track as determining their fate. As Tobias Wolff writes in his memoir *This Boy's Life*, "It takes a childish or corrupt imagination to make symbols of other people" (178), yet schools do this daily as a matter of routine.

Reducing students by labeling them reinforces their marginal status. As a result, schools create a facile world of stock characters—like those found in folktales. According to Bruner, "characters and events in folk stories serve as mere functions in narrative plots: they do not exist on their own" (*Making Stories*, 79–80). Literary stories, in contrast, "require a cast of characters who are free agents with minds of their own" (16). This cannot happen if students' stories are told only by institutions through numerical shorthand.

Diagnosing

Salman Rushdie might as well be talking about the reductive nature of tracking and standardized testing when he describes the poisoning of the Ocean of Stories. When Haroun tries to untangle the myriad story strands—and rescue himself by taking control of the story of his life—he realizes that the waters have become polluted with poisons and that *"the poisons had had the effect of muting the colors of the Story Streams, dulling them all down toward greyness; and it was in the colours that the best parts of those Stories in the Streams were encoded"* (Rushdie 122, emphasis added). Validating only quantitative measures such as tracking and test scores mutes the brilliance of children by robbing them of their individuality and reducing them to mere numbers or labels.

I've seen the inadequacy of labels firsthand. My daughter has autism, but I'm afraid to introduce the *A* word too early in any conversation. I'm liable not to mention it at all if I sense any hint of a lack of empathy. I'm terrified that people will conjure up images of *Rain Man*'s Raymond counting toothpicks and stop listening right there. My daughter is a bright, beautiful teenager, a talented writer and artist who loves to sing and draw and read. She is good-natured and kind, and she desperately wants to please the people around her. And, yes, she happens to have autism. Wittgenstein knew that "the limits of our language were the limits of our reality." I weep at the thought of anyone perceiving my daughter solely as a diagnosis, or as a test score, missing the full story of the lovely human being she is. So, yes, this time it's personal.

Reducing

On beginning-of-the-year inventories at my current school, I once asked all my students some variation of this question: What is the point of school? Their answers roughly corresponded to their academic track. High-track kids not only enjoyed school more, but they also took it on faith that there would eventually be a payoff for their hard work. Low-track kids saw almost no connection between high school and post–high school life. It was, as one student put it, "just something you have to do."

Karen, a student in one of my 2-level classes (the lowest track the school offers since the term *1-level* somehow sounded pejorative) responded this way: "The purpose of school is to find out who is smart and who is not and to keep the smart kids away from the dumb kids." As a 2-track student, Karen likely considers herself one of the "dumb" kids. But worse, she feels segregated from the "smart kids" around her, quarantined from the real intellectual life of the school.

And it's not just the low-level students who are reduced in the tracking numbers game. Elaine, a high-level senior, wrote a chilling memoir (such as those described in Chapter 5) about the death of her "10 year long dream to be a National Merit Semi-finalist." Though her "selection index of 215 put [her] in the top .05% of test-takers in the nation," she felt compelled to recite the "mourner's kaddish for [her] dead dream." Perhaps the most disturbing part of her memoir is the moral value she assigns to her test score: "I thought I would be rewarded for my hard work, even just for being a good person. I had thought good things happened to good people [but] I wasn't even good enough to deserve His [God's] favor just this once. I just desperately wanted to believe that everyone gets what they deserve." Elaine even makes an ontological case on the final page of her essay, commenting that though she herself had been ignored most of her life, "No one could deny a test score or deny its existence."

This is one of the saddest essays I have ever read. If tests carry a moral weight, I wonder, what are the moral consequences for those at the bottom of the test-taking pool? Do schools make similar judgments when they assign kids to ability tracks? At every school where I've taught, I have regularly heard teachers make the same association: "I've got a good bunch this year" or "The class is a real mixed bag, but there are some good kids in there as well." This is pretty standard teacher-talk; I've made these kinds of comments myself. But reading the moral reductiveness in Elaine's essay makes me wonder if she's not on to something, if we aren't tacitly assigning a moral goodness to those students who think about school the way we think about school and condemning those who don't—not just as academically deficient but also as morally bereft.

This tendency to reduce students to a raw score may be one reason so many students see little connection between school life and their lives outside of school. At best, they see school as preparation for the *real world*, a term that about half of my students invoked on those initial inventories. If post–high school life is "real life," clearly high school is to them largely make-believe, artificial.

It is easy to understand why so many students hold this view. The overwhelming majority of evaluation in schools is "objective," requiring fill-in-the-blank or multiple-choice responses. This is particularly true of lower-track students, for whom assessment is often couched in the language of charity: "That's all they can handle" or "They really like to know exactly where they stand." Such work, however, is much more concerned with where the teacher stands, or where the students stand in relation to the teacher. On such measures, students are literally deprived of their own voices. They use other people's words—or mere letters—to show how much they've learned. When Csikszentmihalyi and Larson analyzed the affective states of thousands of high school students, they concluded that "the average student is usually bored, apathetic and unfriendly" (205). Given students' marginal and muted status within the ongoing drama of the classroom, boredom and apathy are hardly surprising.

Directing

> The thick, dark poison was everywhere now, obliterating the colours of the Streams of Story, which Haroun could no longer tell apart. (Rushdie 146)

So-called objective testing is, if anything, on the rise. As George Hillocks said in "The Focus on Form vs. Content in Teaching Writing," "For more than the last two decades, the demand for accountability of schools and teachers has increased" (244). Education professor Greg Michie sees the "renewed emphasis on standardized test scores as the sole measuring stick for its schools, teachers, and students [as] troubling" (180). What's most troubling to me about the precipitous rise in AP classes and standardized tests, and the increasingly numerical measures of academic achievement, is the difficulty in getting to know students as human beings, mainly because there are too many of them and not enough time in the day or week. Given overcrowded classrooms and limited class time, the first casualty is storytelling. But we must listen to the voices of students if we are to see them as human beings—if we are to see ourselves as human beings and not as clerks filling out accounts payable columns in our grade ledgers. It's not mere coincidence that the enemy of free speech in Rushdie's *Haroun*, Khattam-Shud, is a "sniveling, driveling, mingy, stingy, weaselly clerk" (155). This is not a condition I aspire to as an English teacher, and it's not one we should be willing to accept.

Another difficulty in hearing our students' voices is what commonly passes as classroom discourse. Within the ample dramatis personae of a crowded classroom, the odds are not with every student getting a fair share of lines. Instead, most of the conversation is teacher led. The teacher gets the "starring role" in the classroom drama, receives most of the lines, and is usually spotlit in his or her position at center stage. Often the teacher is the only person in the room with any sense of what the play is about. Furthermore, the script of the play is usually written—and even performed—by the teacher alone. Students are often left to fill the nonspeaking roles at worst, or the parts of secondary characters at best.

That classroom discourse reinforces the teacher-as-hero narrative is nothing new. Nearly a hundred years ago, John Dewey noted that

> teachers have a habit of monopolizing continued discourse. Many, if not most, instructors would be surprised if informed at the end of the day of the amount of time they have talked with any pupil. Children's conversation is often confined to answering questions in brief phrases, or in single disconnected sentences. (*How We Think*, 185)

This disturbing trend has remained remarkably consistent. According to John Goodlad's classic study *A Place Called School*, teachers on average do 75 percent of the talking, and at the senior high level discussion of any kind takes place only 5.2 percent of the time. Notice the theatrical language in Goodlad's account of classroom behavior:

> For the most part, the teachers in our sample of schools controlled rather firmly *the central role* of deciding what, where, when and how their students were to learn.... When students *played a role*, it was somewhat peripheral, such as deciding where they sat. At the elementary level about 55% of the students reported not participating at all in choosing what they did in class. About two-thirds of our secondary students said that they did not help make such decisions. (emphasis added, 109)

Shockingly, "students seemed to become more compliant and accepting of the teacher's role as they moved upward[,] . . . socialized into accepting the authority of the teacher" and hardly ever assuming a "decision-making role in their own education" (109).

Jerome Bruner warns that "motives for learning must be kept from going passive in an age of spectatorship" (*Making Stories*, 80), yet students still most commonly find themselves spectators in an ongoing story of classroom life that they have no part in writing. But the teacher's voice alone is insufficient unless he or she wishes to assume an omniscient voice and reduce the classroom narrative to the level of fable. As Michael Smith and Jeff Wilhelm argue, "The important thing [for educators] is to engage in activities with our students that allow us to get to know them as, and that communicates our care and concern for them as, whole people" (21). This, of course, cannot be done if students have no voice, if they are not invited to tell their stories.

The Anti-Story

"Every Stream of Story has a shadow-self, and if you pour this anti-story into the story, the two will cancel each other out, and bingo! End of story."

"But why do you hate stories so much," Haroun blurted, feeling stunned. "Stories are for fun...."

"The world is not for fun," replied Khattam-Shud. "The world is for Controlling."

"Which world?" Haroun made himself ask.

"Your world, my world, all worlds," came the reply. "They are all there to be Ruled. And inside every single story, inside every Stream in the Ocean, lies a world, a story-world, that I cannot Rule at all." (Rushdie 160–61)

When students do write essays in school, most often they write in a stiff, stilted academic voice that sounds nothing like their own. *Engfish* might sound like a fantastical creature from the depths of Haroun's ocean, but it is actually a term coined by education theorist Ken Macrorie to describe the "dehydrated tongue" found in a great deal of academic writing. According to Hillocks,

Research suggests that at most levels of schooling, the writing situations encountered by the great majority of students are of a single kind. The writer's audience is almost always the teacher, and the teacher almost always sets the purpose of the writing and responds to the writing with a grade. Even though there is an immediacy to this writing, and certainly consequences for the writer, the richness of non-school settings that comes through discussion, reading, and informal talk is usually, though not necessarily, missing. (*Teaching* 84–85)

Many teachers I've spoken with have despaired of assigning papers of any kind, citing the enormous burden of time required to grade and respond to a set of, say, 100 same-sounding essays. Instead, they resort to Scantron-based reading quizzes that avoid writing altogether and steer students toward CliffsNotes. When they do assign papers, the writing almost universally falls under Sheridan Blau's description of "the hegemony of the thesis-argument essay" (*Literature Workshop* 179). Most essays assigned in school are thesis-driven analyses of literature, often following the five-paragraph-theme model. Such assignments, Donald Graves argues in *Writing: Teachers and Children at Work,* are often so restrictive that they do not allow students to be successful. This is because there is precious little room for individuality within the thesis-argument form. Graves says that students—like professional writers and teachers—should have some say in the topics on which they write so that they can assume some ownership (i.e., care) about their writing. Robert Scholes argues that writing limited to technical aspects of literature, far from being benign, actually creates a wall "between the literature students read and their own humanity" (35).

Thesis-argument essays exact a toll on teachers as well: they are not interesting to grade. They all sound alike in argumentative substance and in academic voice, a generic voice far different from the polyphony of possible voices in any classroom. Such deadening discourse creates an additional wall between the humanity that teachers and students share. I, for one, never want to read another meaningless essay response to the question of whether Macbeth is a tragic hero. (Spoiler alert: he is.)

In fact, Hillocks argues that much writing done in schools is literally *meaning-less*. Writing that involves meaning, he suggests, consists of "writing that either (1) constructs a new relationship with an intended audience, as in an empathetic piece that attempts to generate an emotional response of some sort; (2) constructs a new relationship in the substance of the writing; or both" (*Teaching* 10). Most school writing falls short of this test since the teacher is almost always the audience, the generic limits of the assignments do not allow students to construct new relationships in the substance of the writing, and the academic voice of such essays eliminates the possibility of empathy.

The Anti-Anti-Story

I am grateful to the personal writing advocates who have come before me, people like Donald Graves, Stephen Tchudi, and especially the "vernacular intellectual," Peter Elbow. These authors have helped to blaze the trail for classroom teachers, but as I argued earlier, the increase in standardized assessment has reduced the impact of their powerful example. The research of Vivian Paley also offers a powerful counterexample since she extracts a great deal of her wisdom from mining classrooms that create and encourage stories. Paley, a MacArthur Grant–winning kindergarten teacher, reminds us that wisdom is always readily available within all our classes because "the storytelling instinct is always there waiting to be resurrected" (5). Sadly, the stories our students and our classes could tell are rarely heard because they are so rarely sought.

Having taught English classes for the past twenty-five years at every level from junior high to college composition, it's clear to me that personal writing is tolerated less the higher the grade level. Courtney Cazden, writing about lower school classrooms, calls this kind of writing "sharing time," and says this may "still be the only time when recounting events from personal, family, and social life . . . is considered appropriate in school" (11). This personal connection, when it is offered at all, is usually reserved for lower or middle school children. By the time my students reach high school, they are all too aware of the divide between their lives and the life of the school.

In fact, the most commonly proffered writing advice I hear from high school and college instructors is to avoid contractions and the personal pronouns *I* and *you* in formal writing (whatever that is). I am not proud to admit that I too administered that kind of advice earlier in my career, teaching the way I was taught. The fact that professional writers almost never follow that advice is apparently beside the point. High school English and college composition students write almost exclusively to the teacher without using *I* or *you*. No wonder so much of their writing sounds artificial.

I want to create a classroom that eliminates this artificiality. Selfishly, and out of self-preservation, I decided that I would assign only papers from which I too could learn. What I was especially interested in was learning about my students as *people,* not as empty piggy banks into which I might drop golden coins of wisdom. In other words, I wanted to become a student of my students.

So I abandoned all tests and quizzes. Instead, we focused our energies on writing about ourselves and making story-sense out of our lives alongside the lives of characters we read about in class texts. I use the plural here not only because I write all the assignments with my classes, which I do, but also because I try to model my willingness to share personal stories, as I have attempted in this introductory chapter.

As an experiment, I also decided I would give no grades. Instead, I chose animal stamps— value-neutral pictures such as turtles, flowers, frogs, fish, and moose. This way, I figured, students would have to read the comments rather than rely on the grade at the end of the paper. (I chose these stamps carefully, remembering a colleague years ago who tried a similar experiment after assigning a major essay on *Moby-Dick.* Rather than give grades, he wrote subspecies of whales in large letters across the top of each paper. Ingenious, it seemed, until some students complained about having been labeled Humpback, Killer, or Sperm.)

For many of my students, the stamps did the trick. Just as I had hoped, they smiled at the cheery pictures and read the comments to figure out how successfully they had handled the assignment. These students took the gradeless environment as a license to take chances in their writing. Others, however, grew anxious without the certainty of a clear-cut letter grade. Yet their anxiety produced some surprisingly profound questions: "What does a turtle mean?" or "Is a flower worth more than a frog?" "That's deep," I'd reply. "Better read the comments."

My dream of a classroom without letter grades exploded with first-quarter report cards, of course. Since I *had* to give letter grades, I decided to use the opportunity for another conversation with students outside of class. I asked students to name the grade they had in mind before I revealed the grade I had written down. We agreed in almost every case and were never more than half a grade apart in any case. This too became a chance to talk, and together we negotiated the grade. I'm no pushover, but sometimes students convinced me with examples of their effort and their progress. If not, I used the opportunity to talk more specifically still about the student's writing.

In a class on personal writing, I grade my students on (1) their participation in class—not only the frequency of their comments but also how carefully they attend to their classmates; (2) the completeness and timeliness of their drafts and warm-up assignments; (3) their willingness to try new techniques; and (4) their willingness to revise. In comments and in conversation, I focus on the skills I emphasized for the particular assignment. For example, when working on place essays (see Chapter 3), I prize concrete description and sensory detail above all else.

Making sure all assignments have potential audiences beyond me as teacher allows me to assume the stance of coach and not just arbiter. This enables me to stand on the sidelines with students rather than across the desk from them, helping them consider the best strategies for reaching their various audiences and writing aims. It also encourages artistic risk-taking (after all, *essay* comes from the word *essayer*, "to try") rather than concentrating solely on the "quality of the final product." I enlarge a bit on this subject later in this chapter in my "Note on How This Book Works."

I also decided to allow students the chance to revise every paper as many times as they wished, something students took as a token of faith in their abilities and not as a reason to slack off. Students seemed to work harder than they had before, writing out of a desire for self-expression rather than toward a grade. Many more students stopped by for one-to-one writing conferences, and we found that even without grades we had something to talk about: our writing and our lives.

Robbie, a deeply imaginative student and star athlete whose father abandoned his family when Robbie was small, considered how his life would have been different had his family remained intact. The full text of his memoir appears in Chapter 5, but I quote the final section here:

It is November now. Football season's over. I sit in my room at a white desk, room dimly lit by a small desk lamp at 12:30 am. Hunched over a spiral notebook, I wonder what to write. The room is completely silent except for the noise of the crickets outside the window, but so much is spoken. Each time I ink pen to paper I utter another concealed emotion. I haven't talked to my father in six years, and I've bottled up anger, sympathy, pity, even hate for him. Through the paper, I am having a conversation with my father, who stopped watching Packers games with me when I was eight.

> *How are you?*
>
> *What do you like to do during your free time? Do you still fish?*
>
> *Do you work? What is your job?*
>
> *What kind of music do you like?*
>
> *My hair is curly just like yours.*
>
> *Did you see when Brett Favre got a concussion during the Giants game and then came back into the game and threw a touchdown? That was awesome.*
>
> *What do you think of the Packers' record?*
>
> *I Love you Dad.*

How many times have we heard the cricket quiet in our own classrooms? But what a spectacular imaginative leap Robbie makes in this essay by hearing "how much is spoken" in this deep silence. Rather than treat the silence as a dead end, he creates a dialogue with his long-absent father. There is a present-tense urgency in this piece that could never be tapped into by a multiple-choice test or a generic thesis-driven essay. His father's absence, which he wrote about later as well, was clearly the most important event in his life, yet it would never have surfaced without the invitation to make story-sense out of his life. Robbie's story journey parallels Haroun's: both boys search for their fathers and save themselves by (re)telling the story of their lives. We teachers need to make a similar imaginative leap, listening to our students' stories and inviting them into the larger community of storytellers.

Even when students wrote about topics outside of their lives, I wanted them to find a personal connection to the topic and a reason to invest themselves fully in their subject. A student named Anne, for example, set out to write an exploratory essay (such as those found in Chapter 10) about school funding and educational values in communities from different socioeconomic classes. In amplifying her ideas, she added a powerful and honest personal story about the role of education in her own life:

From the time I was born on October 9, 1987, I have been molded like the ancient Terra Cotta Warriors of Xian China to become a "success." In 1995, my father with slicked back hair and shaved chin like Michael Corleone, the Godfather, said, "You must never get anything but an A." He brought out a piece of paper and wrote with a ballpoint pen, "I promise to work hard and get As." He rotated the pen towards me and with only slight hesitation [I] signed _____. The next year I received nothing but As and my father presented me with a trip to London, Rome, and Paris.

In 1999, I received my first B and my contract was re-written. "Now, you must never get anything but a B or higher but strive always for the A," my father said, knowing he had to be realistic. I had broken my contract, and instead of receiving a trip to Europe my father decided that I had to pick up a sport, which would serve as a replacement for the failure to uphold the contract. I can feel the echo of his words rumbling in my ears now: "You must learn discipline." I choose gymnastics. At this point, my brain's veins were spastic and on the verge of bursting. I was computer-like, and school was deathly: days of memorizing notecards and vocabulary words. Gymnastics was not much fun either, and my palms were sweaty, afraid of the vault … [but] my father always said, "Winning is more important than friendships that don't last. You must learn to want."

The perverse obsession with grades in this family obliterates any sense of who Anne is apart from her grades. Perhaps this is why school is "deathly" to her: in some sense, she feels *she* no longer exists; she has become her test scores. The historiography implied by the dates this author offers also suggests a sense of detachment, as if Anne is excavating her former self here and examining it as an ancient artifact. The terra-cotta soldiers are an amazingly powerful metaphor for what schools (and families) can do to children. The statues are life-sized and lifelike and utterly unanimated.

Inviting students to write about their lives alongside the literary texts they read—creating texts of their own—holds important implications for students' self-actualization as well. Just as Robert Frost talked of "believing himself into being" through poetry, so too does the personal essay hold ontological implications. "Stories," Tim O'Brien remarked, "make our lives present" (180), not merely artificial abstractions. Jerome Bruner goes even further, writing that "[i]f we lacked the capacity to make stories about ourselves, there would be no such thing as selfhood" (*Making Stories* 86). So vital is this enterprise to Bruner that he believes "[i]ndividuals who have lost the ability to construct narratives have lost their selves" (86).

Personal writing is especially important at the critical developmental stage of adolescence. As developmental psychologist Dan McAdams writes:

> Life becomes mythic in our teenage years. The formation and reformation of identity remains thereafter the central psychosocial task of the adult years. From adolescence onward we face this task of creating an integrative life story through which we are able to understand who we are and how we fit into the adult world. As our views of ourselves and our worlds change over time, we revise the story. (91)

The personal essay is perhaps the genre best suited to this task.

McAdams further endorses the importance of "selectively reconstructing the past" because in so doing, "We create a self that is whole and purposeful because it becomes embedded in a coherent and meaningful story" (92). In adolescence and adulthood, we begin to adopt a historical perspective on our lives and to craft "a history of the self[,] . . . an account of the past that seeks to explain how and why events transpired as they actually did" (102). The act of creating these stories helps us to forge identities and examine how we see ourselves and how others see us. Giving students the chance to voice their beliefs and views allows them, in Montaigne's phrase, to "make friends with their minds" (qtd. in Lopate 302).

The inclusion of personal writing in the classroom can also help create what Maxine Greene calls the "curriculum as possibility," in which students can "articulate the themes of their existence and . . . reflect on those themes until they know themselves to be in the world and can name what has been up to then obscure" (qtd. in Stock 17). In creating such a curriculum, I hope to emulate what Patricia Lambert Stock calls a "dialogic curriculum," a curriculum in which "students are inquirers" and which offers their "most powerful means of learning" since it "utilizes students' past experiences" (24). Students in such a classroom not only come to recognize and articulate their own identities, but they also recognize the identities—fuller, human identities—of their classmates.

Telling stories gives us the chance to understand who we are and to measure ourselves and our circumstances alongside characters who lead lives different from the lives we lead. As Mario Vargas Llosa puts it:

> Literature transports us into the past and links us to those texts that have come down to us, texts that now allow us also to enjoy and dream. This feeling of membership in the collective human experience across time and space is the highest achievement of culture, and nothing contributes more to its renewal in every generation than literature. (298)

Inviting students to share their stories, to make story-sense of their lives along-side the lives of characters they read about, is an invitation to the collective membership Vargas Llosa speaks of— the community of storytellers, co-inhabitors of the literary landscape.

When Haroun saves storytelling from the forces that seek to stifle humanity, he wins for his father the title of the country's highest decoration, "the order of the Open Mouth," and he ushers in "a victory for the new Friendship and Openness . . . over our old Hostility and Suspicion. A dialogue has been opened" (Rushdie 192–93). This is what I hoped I had started in my classroom: an open dialogue and a search for possibilities.

Becca, a student in a low-track class, said, "If there's one thing I know about myself it's that I can't write poetry" and then wrote this poem:

W

The letter "W," the first letter
Of my last name looks like two V's
Holding hands or kissing if flipped
Upside down. "W" is a pair
Of beautiful mountains with snow-
Covered hills.
The letter "W" turned on its side is a 3
Or a crazy-looking E, or maybe
Big black bats flying in the night sky.
"W" has a lot of power, but it goes
Unnoticed by people; it feels neglected
And alone. The sound of "W" is the wind
Whistling past city buildings. "W" is
A young yellow flower blossoming.

Isn't it amazing how much Becca found within a single letter of her name? Isn't it astonishing how many images and stories Becca possesses, this girl who was convinced she couldn't write a poem? I've been moved by this poem since I first read it, and I've come to read it as something akin to a prayer. I think this is because it contains my deepest hopes for my own children, as well as for all my students—that they never feel neglected, alone, or unnoticed; that they come to know they hold a lot of power; that we see in each of them all the beauty and potential of a blossoming flower.

A Note on How This Book Works

The general framework of *This Time It's Personal* consists of high-interest creative nonfiction topics that give students choice in what they write. Creative nonfiction, for our purposes (and here I defer to Lee Gutkind, editor of the excellent journal *Creative Nonfiction*), is "factually accurate prose about real people and events [told] in a compelling and vivid manner" (xiii). In other words, my students and I write about the events of our lives using the tools of literary writing. There has never been a more important time to teach creative nonfiction. Within the last few decades, the world has witnessed a "memoir craze" and "an explosion of first person narrative[s]" (Gutkind xiii). The Common Core State Standards initiative has also recently weighed in: "Fulfilling the Standards for 6–12 ELA (English Language Arts) requires much greater attention to a specific category of informational text—literary nonfiction—than has been traditional" (5). Literary nonfiction is the focus of this book.

The assignments you'll read about are real-world assignments—that is, they are essays and essay forms that professional essayists and journalists regularly use—and they are all directed at audiences beyond the classroom teacher. This not only reinforces the idea of writing as a social, meaningful practice, but it also allows the teacher to work as a coach, helping students to reach those audiences rather than merely acting as judge or arbiter. The assignments also build in writing as a reflective practice, giving students the opportunity to become more self-conscious writers and thinkers. As Peter Elbow and Pat Belanoff have argued in *A Community of Writers: A Workshop Course in Writing,* "The most important kind of learning in school is learning about learning. The most important thinking is thinking about thinking" (18).

With every assignment, my students invent, compose, and revise. While we work on prewriting and brainstorming exercises, we read professional and student models of each type of essay, offering a wide range of models to underscore the importance of individuality. Students then write drafts that we workshop in class. They revise those drafts and self-analyze everything they write.

Writing these essays in stages helps me identify areas in which my students are struggling, reinforces revision as a process that is second nature to professional writers, but most important, guarantees student success. By success I don't necessarily mean letter grades. Rather, I measure success on these assignments by how much students have grown, how much they have invested themselves in their subject matter, and how willing they are to try new styles and new techniques. Most of all, I want students to be proud of pieces they have written and to write essays that no one else in the world could have written. This last goal might seem lofty, but it turns out to be true. When we write about our lives with the specificity of our personal experiences, no one else—not Shakespeare, not Faulkner reincarnated—is capable of relating these experiences.

Grading and Revision

I'd like to offer a brief word on grading and revision. Since I promise my students that every essay we will work on is genuine, that we are undertaking the same writing challenges faced by professional writers, I try to conduct my class by an ethic that treats them like professional writers. In writing marginal notes, I try to limit myself to positive comments (e.g., Nice, Terrific comparison) and questions (e.g., Can you introduce this character earlier? Does this word set the right mood for your scene?). Because I'm asking students to experiment with language in ways they never have before, I don't want to do anything to discourage experimentation. And because students often write about their most important personal experiences, I want to honor the generosity of their willingness to share these experiences. I want to respond like a fellow writer—and a fellow human being—with words rather than a letter grade. As a former colleague once drily put it, "There's nothing worse than an end comment that goes 'Sorry to hear about your grandmother. C+.'"

Granted, report card grades are a reality for most of us, but that doesn't mean essays need to be reduced to a grade. In my experience, students simply stop reading when they see a letter grade on a paper. In a recent talk at my school, Ron Ritchhart, from Harvard's Project Zero, went even further, saying that once students see a grade on a paper, all other comments are irrelevant. And is there anything more depressing than spending dozens of hours lovingly responding to students' writing only to see those same students steal a peek at the grade before they let the essays parachute into the recycling bin on their way out of class?

Recognizing the reality of grades, I'd like to offer a compromise: on papers, I favor "grids over grades," if I may steal a phrase from Peter Elbow. Rather than anguishing over minute distinctions (Is this paper a B- or a C+? Or in the deeply neurotic worlds of many English departments, a B-/C+ or a C+/B-, distinctions so esoteric that students are left not only clueless about their performance but also troubled about the sanity of their teacher!), Elbow suggests three categories: Strong, OK, and Weak. This way a teacher can quickly discern which essays are *notably* strong or weak. With just three levels, teachers can spend more time responding *as readers*.

I suggest changing the criteria for these grids to suit each particular assignment. For example, when working on the place essays (Chapter 3), I prize concrete description, sensory detail, and organization above all else, so I make sure those three categories appear on the grid. A sample grid for this assignment might look like this:

	Strong	OK	Weak
Sensory descriptions			
Concrete details / objects			
Organization			
Active verbs			
Voice / attitude			
Mechanics			

New skills we are working on go at the top of the grid, and I create the criteria with my students as they are writing their initial drafts of each new assignment. I want to make sure our writing goals agree. This quick snapshot on a half-sheet offers many advantages: it frees me up to spend my time writing substantial comments on the paper itself; it supports my stance as coach since it encourages students to ask about how they might reorganize or improve their imagery rather than to ask if a paper was a C or a C-; and it looks to the future, suggesting skills students need to work on further and where they might concentrate their efforts as they revise. And, of course, it gives me a starting point when quarter grades are due.

Course grades seem different to me from grades on papers. While I don't presume to tell teachers how they should grade, it is important for teachers to be clear about grades for the course. Elbow, for example, has more recently made the case for grade contracts, laying out guidelines for students at the start of each term. He might say, "To earn an A, you need to show up on time every day (with one freebie per term), hand in all assignments on time and completely (again one freebie), faithfully complete each nightly assignment, blog weekly, and revise at least two papers per term. Your essays must, after revision, fall mostly in the 'strong' category on the grid sheets." While I shy away from contracts, I agree that course demands must be clear to students from the outset, and I especially like Elbow's distinction between guiding comments on papers versus letter grades for a course.

Students also quickly learn that the tone of my comments reveals how successfully I think they have handled the assignment. "This is fantastic. Put it on your refrigerator!" clearly conveys something different from "The first half of this piece is engaging, but the second half lacks specificity. How can you add more sensory detail to the ending?" Like an editor responding to professional writers, I always comment with an eye toward the future in case students wish to revise their essays. As a professional writer, I have never had a piece accepted without a call for revision. Once I wrote a five-word poem that was accepted only after two successive revisions! I pay my students the same courtesy.

Sometimes when I tell fellow teachers that I allow students to revise everything they've written, they gasp in horror. But the number of takers is actually very small. Partly this is because we have moved on to a new assignment and students don't want to fall behind. Partly it's because I insist on meeting students outside of class if they wish to revise. There I make sure they've read all the comments I've written, and I ask them what they'd like to work on. Since I don't assign grades, revision primarily gives students an opportunity to work on a particular writing challenge, although that effort might also boost a score into a higher category.

Personal Writing: Student Models

I have written professionally as a radio contributor to NPR-affiliate WBEZ, as a blogger for the Poetry Foundation, as a poet, as a writer of essays in education journals, and as the author of a book on teaching poetry writing called *Wordplaygrounds*. I say this not only because I hope it will bolster your confidence in the chapters that follow, but also to suggest that my personal essays can be found in a variety of places. It is my hope in this book to foreground the work of my students.

The student work in *This Time It's Personal* comes from classes I've taught at the University of Chicago Lab Schools and at New Trier High School outside Chicago (an elite prep school and an affluent public high school, respectively). While these schools are highly regarded because of their lofty test scores, I hope I have made the case that what is really important is who these students are as human beings. The student writing models are strong, the kind of writing I am always looking for as a classroom teacher, because they are honest and real and often deeply personal.

The first half of the book consists of personal essay writing, exploring students' lives as texts. The second half considers texts outside ourselves—literature, history, movies, politics, education, etc. Many of the essays work in conjunction with essays in other chapters, and the book as a whole can be followed in sequence as a design for a writing class, such as the one I teach. Individual chapters, however, also can be used discretely as a guide to a change of pace from the usual classroom fare. Friends and colleagues have used these assignments in classes outside of English, specifically journalism, history, and American studies. The assignments might work well in other disciplines, too, and I occasionally call attention to points of intersection with other disciplines.

I recently found a list of goals I had set for myself a few years ago at the start of the school year. These goals are also tacit promises I make to my students. I return to these goals in Chapter 11, and will leave it to you to determine how well I have fulfilled them.

My Goals from the Beginning of the Year

To offer assignments unlike any papers you've written before.

To offer assignments that insist on originality—assignments that no one else could have written.

To get to know you as individual people and fellow writers.

To reinforce the idea of writing as a creative process.

To demonstrate connections between writing and other disciplines (history, journalism, film, photo, painting, music)

To offer only "real world" assignments, those with audiences and purposes beyond the English classroom.

To bring in voices other than my own!

To welcome all views but also to insist that all positions (including my own) are supported by example.

To ensure that you will help determine the shape of the course (leading discussions, presenting projects and positions) and the direction of your writing.

To help everyone understand the importance of writing for its own sake, not just for the grade (since we are not reducible to a grade).

To allow everyone the chance to revise.

To ensure that you are genuinely proud of having written at least one piece of writing (maybe more!).

As a teacher, I can honestly say I look forward to reading every essay I assign. Since the assignments in this book prize individuality, no two essays sound alike. What's more, through these assignments I am able to understand my students better because I know so much more about their lives—their writing lives, yes, but also their hopes, fears, dreams, ideals, beliefs. These are not essays to fill up a grade book. They are works of art, attempts at understanding our lives and the world around us through writing.

2

Where Have You Been, Where Are You Going? A Writer's Autobiography

He started handling my exam paper like it was a turd or something. "We studied Egypt from November 4th to December 2nd," he said. "You *chose* to write about them for the optional essay question. Would you care to hear what you had to say?"

"No, sir, not very much," I said.

He read it anyway, though. You can't stop a teacher when they want to do something. They just *do* it.

The Egyptians were an ancient race of Caucasians residing in one of the northern sections of Africa. The latter as we all know is the largest continent in the Eastern Hemisphere.

I had to sit there and **listen** to that crap. It certainly was a dirty trick.

The Egyptians are extremely interesting to us today for various reasons. Modern science would still like to know what the secret ingredients were that the Egyptians used when they wrapped up dead people so that their faces would not rot for innumerable centuries. This interesting riddle is still quite a challenge to modern science in the twentieth century.

He stopped reading and put my paper down. I was beginning to sort of hate him.

—J. D. SALINGER, *The Catcher in the Rye* (12)

In this scene from *The Catcher in the Rye*, Holden Caulfield lives out many students' worst nightmare. He comes face to face not only with his teacher but also with his own spectacularly vacuous essay on the Egyptians. It's a hilarious moment in the book and one to which many readers can relate (I, for one, have "phoned in" a few gems in my day!). But *why* is Holden's essay so terrible? It can't be a lack of ability; Holden is clearly a strong reader and he speaks engagingly throughout the novel. In this excerpt, for example, consider the difference between Holden's academic voice in the exam essay (in italics) and the hilarious, sardonic voice that relates the scene to us.

Holden's academic voice is stuffy, pedantic, and hopelessly general (pure "phoniness" in Holden-speak). One reason for this is the profoundly artificial nature of the assignment. It is difficult to imagine an interested audience for this essay beyond Holden's teacher, Mr. Spencer, nor is it easy to believe that Spencer wants or needs to hear the sum of Holden's knowledge about the ancient Egyptians. By Hillocks's definition of meaningful writing (*Teaching*) that I mentioned in Chapter 1, Holden's paper is literally meaning-*less*.

This scene reminds me of an anecdote in Wayne Booth's *Now Don't Try to Reason with Me*. Booth, an eminent English professor and rhetoric scholar, confesses that he once taught an entire course on exposition without ever suggesting that students ask themselves what their expositions were for. As a result, he received writing like the following, from a graduate student's study of Thomas More's *Utopia*:

> In this theme I would like to discuss some of the relationships in the family which Thomas More elaborates and sets forth in his book *Utopia*. The first thing that I would like to discuss about family relations is that overpopulation, according to More, is a just cause of war. (Booth 27–28)

Because Booth was a master teacher, he was able to consider the writing difficulty from the student's point of view and found some of the problem in the nature of the assignment. Thinking about this student's essay, Booth writes, "Can you hear that student sneering at me, in this opening? What he is saying is something like, 'You ask for a meaningless paper, I give you a meaningless paper.' He knows that he has no audience except me . . . or an audience that could possibly care one way or the other" (28).

Holden, too, knows he has no real audience. Perhaps this is why he avoids using *I* or *you* in his essay; sadly, this is among the worst and most commonly proffered pieces of advice in writing classes. Holden in no way connects with his reader; he knows he has nothing to say. Yet he recognizes this, and he's so desperate to connect with his audience that he writes a note to Spencer at the bottom of the page: "Dear Mr. Spencer, That is all I know about the Egyptians. I can't seem to get very interested in them although your lectures are very interesting. It's all right with me if you flunk me. . . ." (Salinger 13). Even though Holden says he dreads having to spend time with Spencer, it was his choice to visit his teacher. Like any writer, Holden is desperate to connect with his audience; think of the opening sentence of Holden's narrative: "If you really want to hear about it . . ." Spencer's assignment, however, precludes any significant personal connection between author and audience.

More than anything else, what leads to the inarticulate drivel in Holden's Egyptian piece is the utter lack of connection in his writing to Holden's life. His brother died and his life has spiraled downward ever since. He's obsessed by his past, hence his desire to visit his history teacher and his (albeit superficial) interest in "the secret ingredients" the Egyptians used in preservation. He is unable to move forward without addressing his past, and while he has nothing of interest to say about the Egyptians, he has an entire book's worth to say about his feelings for his brother and himself. *That's* the story readers want to hear.

A Writer's Autobiography

The first essay my students write is a writer's autobiography, a chance for them to reflect on their own writing lives, both the triumphs and the failures, in what I hope is a less painful way than Holden's experience with *his* teacher. Students rarely think about their writing, and this essay gives them the opportunity to do so. "The most important kind of learning in school is learning about learning. The most important thinking is thinking about thinking" (18), claim Peter Elbow and Pat Belanoff. So I have students write about writing. This opening assignment asks them to think about all the thinking and learning they have done in school thus far—different assignments, audiences, purposes, organizational strategies, word choice, and stylistic techniques.

To help students become more self-conscious writers, this initial essay reinforces the importance of reflection in writing. It also provides a rationale for all the writing we will do in our course. Through students' responses, we discuss the kind of writing their teachers have most valued and the kind of writing they themselves most value. But more than that, this assignment gives students a formidable challenge—to write about their writing in an interesting and compelling manner. Here is the assignment I pass out:

A Writer's Autobiography

In a personal essay of 2 to 3 pages (typed), take your readers on a guided tour of the **most formative experiences** (the good, the bad, and the ugly) in your development as a writer. Identify those pivotal moments that made you love writing, or hate it, or struggle with it, or approach writing in new ways. Develop at least two of these moments into full scenes to help your readers understand how each of these experiences influenced your writing and/or your attitude toward writing. At least one of these experiences should be recent in order to show how your attitude toward writing has changed. Do not limit yourself to school experiences unless that is the only writing you've ever done.

You might also want to consider the following:

- The role writing has played in your home and your family's or peers' social, cultural, and occupational practices
- People who influenced your writing (both positively and negatively)
- Books/writers who influenced your writing
- Memories of particular pieces you regard as successes, failures, delights, or disappointments
- Your shifting attitudes toward writing
- What has confused you (what still confuses you) about writing, including, perhaps, contradictory guidelines and advice you've been given
- Your strengths and weaknesses as a writer

Make sure your final draft features a title that captures the essence of your paper.

First complete draft due: _____

Final draft due: _____

NB: Please do not mention teachers by name.

Prewriting

As a first step, I ask students to brainstorm for landmark moments in their writing careers. I have them take out their writer's notebooks and make lists, writing as quickly as they can and writing continuously without lifting the pen or pencil off the paper, in response to the following:

Name the three people (not necessarily teachers) who have most influenced your writing.

What books, what authors have most influenced your writing?

What pieces of writing were your most successful? How do you measure that success?

Most moving?

Least successful?

How have you come to think of these pieces as successes or failures—through grades, self-reflection?

What kind of writing have you done outside of school?

Apart from schoolwork, what writing do your parents, your siblings, your friends do?

What was the most frustrating writing you ever attempted?

What was the most surprising piece you ever wrote?

What was the best writing advice you've ever received?

What was the worst writing advice you've ever received?

What have you learned about writing?

What have you learned about yourself through writing?

What piece of writing are you most proud of having written?

After the final question, I wait a minute or so and then ask students to find a comfortable place to stop. I reassure them that it's not necessary to have answered every question; we are simply trying to generate some material from which we can craft an essay. If there's time, we discuss their responses as a group. Their answers are always extraordinary and revealing. Some students share favorite writing teachers; some offer contradictory opinions. Consider this exchange: "Ms. J. was the best third-grade teacher ever. She loved me." "Are you kidding? She hated me. I could never do anything good enough for her." These comments are full of emotional weight, the drama that accompanies many students' language. They also reveal how personally students take their own writing and the criticism they receive, even when the writing itself is impersonal.

Many students are surprised by the amount and variety of writing their family members do outside of school, such as plumbing estimates, prescriptions, and advertising copy. Students love talking about favorite books and favorite moments in their "careers" as students. But in every class, I have a few students who tell me they have never been proud of a single piece of writing. Many students (like Becca, from Chapter 1) have told me they know they "can't write" or that they've been told they are "better at math and science and shouldn't write."

One year a girl named Missy lamented her "inability to write." When I asked her how she came to that conclusion, she sat up in her chair and said, "Mr. Asbell. He sits at that half-moon-shaped table of his like a fat little leprechaun guarding his gold. One time the only thing he wrote on the paper was 'Unsatisfactory' in huge shaky letters like a lie detector machine." Everyone in the class laughed—not at the teacher or Missy but at the obvious power of her storytelling. Spontaneously, the girl who was convinced she couldn't write created several striking images and deftly used figurative language to reveal her feelings about a former teacher.

As students think about former writing classes, the advice they recall varies widely, but platitudes and rigid rules predominate in both the best and worst pieces of advice lists. Here are a few:

- Forget everything you've ever learned about writing.
- Never end a sentence with a preposition.
- Write what you know.
- Find a formula and stick with it.
- Writing is like a triple hamburger (the top and bottom buns are the intro and the conclusion and the patties are the body paragraphs).
- Never use *I* or *you*.
- Avoid clichés like the plague.

Characters and scenes, like the infamous Mr. Asbell squatting behind his table, emerge in all of their responses, and I go out of my way to point out features such as specificity of detail and dialogue. While some rules can offer good general guidance, I stress that there are exceptions to every rule. These early discussions not only provide students with fodder for their upcoming essays, but they also help students recognize the importance of writing to a wide range of audiences and for a wide range of purposes and genres. The National Council of Teachers of English's (NCTE) *Beliefs about the Teaching of Writing* statement underscores the importance of this practice: "Writing instruction must include ample in-class and out-of-class opportunities for writing and should include writing for a variety of purposes and audiences." Reflecting on their experiences, some students feel lucky that they have had such opportunities; others begin to see that their school writing has been rather uniform. All students can use this reflection as a time to assess their writing strengths and weaknesses and then to dramatize those strengths and weaknesses.

Once we've brainstormed topics together, I tell students to begin expanding their pieces into an essay. While they have plenty of starting points already, I also encourage them to find actual artifacts of their early writing life. This is a little easier in the computer age, but many students discover that their parents have also saved hard copies of some of their earliest writing in a special box or drawer.

The biggest challenge students face here is form. Even when they want to criticize the formal restrictions of the writing assignments in earlier classes, students often wish they had more direction to work with in their autobiographical essays. They can't very well critique the five-paragraph essay by writing their own five-paragraph essay in response ("There are three problems with the five paragraph essay: . . ."!). So, as students are composing, we look at models. I try to offer a wide variety of models, both professional and student writing, so that students won't think there is one correct form to follow. I also offer a variety of voices, encouraging students to find their own voice, apart from the generic, academic voice that does most of our talking for us in our academic lives.

We often start with professional models, particularly early in the year as we establish a safe environment in which to discuss writing. Using professional work right away lends currency and legitimacy to our work since we are engaged in the same enterprise as real-world writers. Further, the fact that the authors are not in the room, coupled with the sometimes exalted stature of such writers, gives students freer rein to criticize the work. Still, we follow the same guidelines in considering professional pieces that we will with student work: first we consider all the things the writer did well; then we see if we can find ways of improving the piece.

Excellent examples abound. I have often used Stephen King's *On Writing*, which features a number of very short scenes from his earliest writing; the opening four paragraphs of Salman Rushdie's British Film Institute's companion to *The Wizard of Oz*, in which he recounts his first short story, "Over the Rainbow"; and Paul Mandelbaum's *First Words: Earliest Writings from Favorite Contemporary Authors*. Recognizing these authors' writing challenges as different from our own—they aren't writing for an assignment and their audiences and length requirements are different—allows us to review the goals I have for the assignment: creating character; using dialogue; focusing on small moments that contain conflict, especially triumph and frustration; and creating a unified whole out of small episodes. (This early practice will be necessary as a prelude to tackling a more complicated series of episodes when we write memoirs [see Chapter 5].) Here's a piece from Richard Hartwell, a teacher with the National Writing Project.

"We were twelve days out of Auckland, New Zealand, when it struck. . . ."

This sentence was the opening line of a short story I wrote for a creative writing class when I was 12 years old. I went on to describe a storm of such fury that my boat was dashed to pieces on an uncharted South Sea island, and I had to make do, a la Robinson Crusoe. Defoe, it was not. Melville, it was not. Hemingway, it was not. But what it was, was me ... at 12. It was the first time I wrote dynamically, with a purpose, and for me. It was written in one sitting and then polished, if that's possible in junior high school, over the next two days. I threw myself into the process completely.

This sea tale comes to mind whenever I think about my evolution as a writer—mostly because of my teacher's reaction. If I recall correctly, he didn't think much of my story. He wrote "Nice" in the margin and then proceeded to correct the spelling, grammatical, and syntactical errors. I don't recall being very grateful for these editorial comments. In fact, if he wrote anything of greater substance than this, the nature of his comments—like his name and face—has long since passed from my memory.

I could have used this as a learning moment and improved my writing. I could have continued to write short stories. I did neither because I had encountered the obvious fact that my lack of mechanical skills was more important than what I had to say. Instead, feeling totally dashed by my teacher's insensitivity to what I was trying to do as a writer, I withdrew into myself and, like so many adolescents, became a closet poet.

Although I had always been a reader, I now became an absolutely voracious one and was often found hungrily prowling the shelves of the city library. I was fortunate to fall in with the part-time night librarian, Ms. Vera Swaboda, who was also the Latin teacher at the high school. Unlike my foggy memory of the creative writing teacher, my recollection of Ms. Swaboda is crystalline. After repeatedly thwarting my attempts to borrow books from the adult section (this was, after all, the late '50s and early '60s), Ms. Swaboda began to track my reading interests. She discovered my tastes were eclectic ... and exhaustive. But she must have approved, for she granted me license to check out books from the adult section, and, miracle of miracles, she allowed me to borrow five books at a time! With her help and suggestions, I read my way through the entire library holdings of each author I touched, or rather, each author who touched me. She allowed and encouraged me to be a reader, which, in turn, allowed and encouraged me to be a writer once again.

My reading became a Joycean stream of consciousness. As an example, I read all of Ernest Hemingway, including "The Snows of Kilimanjaro." Africa, right? That led to James Ramsey Ullman's *The Day on Fire*. Arthur Rimbaud in Africa, right? After reading all the Ullman in the library, I read all of Rimbaud. This led to Baudelaire, which led to Blake, which led to . . . Well, you get the idea: I was immersed. If you'll pardon the extended metaphor, since my shipwreck in seventh grade, I was awash in the glories of language—the twist of a phrase, the juxtaposition of words crashing against or melting into one another. To borrow from Rimbaud, I was drunk on words; Le Bateau Ivre, and I was embarking on my education as a writing craftsman.

I started to write again—mostly poetry but some short pieces as well—imitating authors I was reading. But it was not until the 11th grade that I would again share my writing with anyone. Finally, I decided to show some of my poetry to my English teacher, Mrs. Miriam Self. She asked to keep it overnight. She didn't mark it up. She returned it privately and praised it. She asked to see more and told me to write more. Don't misunderstand; I still had little to no command of the mechanics of writing (and perhaps I still don't), but I finally felt free to write, encouraged to write, and validated as a writer. So I continued to write.

I graduated high school, went away to have some life experiences (the usual: marriage, deaths, Vietnam, drugs, divorce, etc.), and finally made it back into school. On the G.I. Bill, I enrolled at Santa Clara University, a Jesuit liberal arts school, and among other classes, I had to take "bonehead" English. Our class was taught by Fr. Francis Duggan, a degreed Jesuit who, I'm certain, had survived the Holy Inquisition and, depending on your point of view, may have even participated. To open the class, he read John Keats' "Ode on a Grecian Urn" to us. He read it with us. We read it independently. Then he told us to write a paragraph describing the scene on the urn that Keats had described so poetically.

My paragraph got an F! It had mechanical mistakes, of course, but Fr. Duggan noted that I rambled. He suggested that I hadn't said anything new, that I wasn't descriptive, and that I needed to hone and polish my phrases. I felt terrible. This was my first quarter in college, and I was tempted to chuck it all. Instead, I made an appointment to discuss my grade with him.

Fr. Duggan had me rewrite the paragraph. He corrected it again. It earned a D. He told me to focus, refine, and rewrite it again. I did, and again he corrected it. This time, I earned a C-. And so on and on until—and this will sound like an exaggeration—I had rewritten that paragraph seven times. The paragraph finally received a B+, but what I had gained, besides an excellent grade, was some inkling of what it means to be a writer.

Writing, like reading, is a process not a product, and it is a process of constant revision and refinement. Fr. Duggan didn't tell me not to rewrite the paragraph again (I probably could have gone on indefinitely); what he did say was that at some point a writer lets go and allows the piece to be "finished." I guess I still haven't let go of "We were twelve days out of Auckland, New Zealand, when it struck" but somewhere along the way, along with the detritus of failed marriages and career redirections, the manuscript of that story has been discarded. Interestingly, the final revision of "A Paragraph on 'Ode on a Grecian Urn'" is still among my papers.

Since my time with Fr. Duggan, I have been in and out of so many schools that I've lost count. I've earned an AA, a BA, an MA, and multiple teaching credentials. I have numerous rejection notices from publishers but have yet to be published for money. I write. I teach writing. I study writing. Am I a writer? Insofar as a writer is willing to "let go," then, yes, I am a writer. Do I make a living from writing? Then, no, I am not a writer. But I have great difficulty in separating the reader from the writer anyway. I would not be the writer I am today if I had not become the reader I am. As well, I would not be the reader I am today if I had not become a writer along the way. Obviously, this is an unfinished autobiography of myself as a writer. However, it is time to let go. . . .

My students like that Hartwell opens with an example of his own writing. This avoids what Wallace Stegner called excessive "front porch," the throat-clearing introductory material with which students often start papers. Get right into the house instead! Because so many students survive in schools on a steady diet of thesis-support essays, they often write openers like this: "Human beings have been writing since the dawn of civilization" or "Looking back over my life I see several important ways in which my writing has changed. . . ." It's hard to imagine a reader who is eager to read more. Hartwell, on the other hand, opens with a sentence from his younger writing life that acts as an artifact of where he's been as a writer.

Hartwell also does a nice job of developing characters, notably Swaboda and Duggan. The first teacher never comes into clear focus since the author says he no longer remembers what he looked like or what his name was. Significantly, this teacher's marginal comments ("Nice," along with identified grammar errors) are bland and unmemorable, too. But the piece clearly comes alive as Hartwell himself comes alive, when he experiences the thrill of reading and writing deeply. The connection between writing and reading here is always an interesting discussion topic. "All writing is emulation," according to Saul Bellow, and many of these essays spring from students' emulation of their writer heroes.

The ethos, or trustworthiness, Hartwell creates is effective throughout the piece as well. By admitting that he has experienced failure in "bonehead English" and as a professional writer, Hartwell endears himself to his readers. Who, after all, wants to read about an author who has never struggled, who sails blindly and blithely from triumph to triumph? Since conflict is an essential part of good storytelling, such admissions also help to create tension in a story.

Here are a few recent models from my students:

Picturing Myself as a Writer

Nothing could keep Grandma awake that night. But that was just as well; no babysitter could have put me to sleep. I was busy drafting a takeoff on *There Was Magic Inside*. The real book was about a young fisherman. He basically pulled a Pandora's box from the sea and promptly destroyed his city. My story centered on a girl and her cat. They lived in the prairie, and one day a mysterious box came floating down the river. Grandma mumbled that once I finished, she'd love to see what I wrote. But my seven-year-old self had a curious definition of writing. Writing required a stack of pastel-pink construction paper, a battered box of crayons, and a set of glitter-glue pens. Writing meant sketching log cabins, bubbling brooks and the faces of *There Was Magic Inside*. Writing gave me an excuse to tap Grandma awake—to show off my pictures, not my prose.

Sixth grade was quite the opposite. I (oddly) recall one essay debating the pros and cons of cloth and disposable diapers. Although I was a shy student, I hesitantly volunteered to read this essay aloud, surprising Mrs. K. This was good writing, I naively thought. It boasted my neatest cursive, five paragraphs, and the ever-creative title: Persuasive Essay. The margins were clean and blank, absent of my usual stray doodles. While writing the essay, I had kept the grading rubric alongside my paper at all times. If I momentarily forgot the criteria, the stark-white list of checkboxes silently blared my reminder. I was confident "Persuasive Essay" was worth sharing. Besides, presenting papers earned Mrs. K's buck-toothed grin and scratch 'n' sniff stickers.

So I was a little confused when, on the second day of junior year, my English teacher passed out his syllabus. His class would not include grading rubrics, five-paragraph essays, or prompts. But that didn't mean it would be easy. There were assignments galore—reading, rereading, journaling, constructing arguments, and revising, revising, revising. The first week of school, his class alone pushed my bedtime into the wee hours. I resolved to chat with him about his expectations. How many pages should the journals be, and how much time should we spend writing them, I asked.

I probably appeared neurotic, chasing him down with petty questions, my eyes a little fearful, a little tired. He replied calmly, almost too calmly, that journals should be as long as they needed to be, and we should work on them as long as we needed to. The worry I'd felt all week evaporated, but something scarier replaced it: the realization that I was in charge. I approached English homework with dread. Another book, another journal, another draft? It wouldn't stop.

But after several weeks, something clicked. Although my teacher assigned the work, I still chose how to complete it. I picked my topics, for one. If I wanted to explore the meaning of independence, I could. And if I still wanted to argue about infant apparel—well, I had that option too. I could change with my papers, I could try out different tones. Pretentious language couldn't convey my feelings about losing a friend, but terse words didn't get my point across either. Although not in the Crayola-sense, I once again began doodling in the margins. The obscene workload became a stack of blank canvasses, of pastel-pink construction paper— an opportunity to experiment, a chance to grow.

My AP English teacher emphasized structure—his "claim, reason, warrant!" dogma is eternally ingrained in my head—but he also stressed style. He demanded that we put some personality into our papers. So when my writing gets dull and tired, I try to add something. Perhaps that sentence needs some glitter, maybe that paragraph could use some neon colors. Or perhaps that paper just needs a writer.

—Aviva, grade 12

This writer does so many things well. Even though she has regularly experienced success in school writing, she has come to see important differences between her current efforts and her previous pieces. She shows concern for her title and with effective understatement recalls the former title "Persuasive Essay." Here she avoids the five-paragraph mold she self-deprecatingly mocks in the second paragraph, and she recognizes the Holden-esque hollowness of the "cloth vs. disposable diaper debate" topic. It would be hard to invent a topic that had less relevance to her life at that moment, and yet she says she received enormous praise for aping the form.

Aviva organizes her writer's autobiography chronologically, but she doesn't just list events grade by grade (a student once offered an eight-page essay with a paragraph for each of his twelve years of school from kindergarten through eleventh grade!). Instead, she selects a few key scenes and within those scenes chooses to devote four of her six paragraphs to her junior year English class. She also concludes her essay with an elegant nod back to the beginning image of coloring.

Aviva also begins to establish characters, referring to her grandmother and her middle school teacher, who gets a brief physical description. Curiously, though, she chooses not to develop the eleventh-grade teacher's character, even by giving him a name. More noticeably absent, though, is any actual writing from that grade 11 class even though her description of it consumes two-thirds of her paper. She offers a series of generalizations ("assignments galore"; "something clicked"; "[she] picked [her own] topics," used "different tones," avoided "pretentious language"). She talks about paper topics hypothetically ("If I wanted to explore the meaning of independence . . .") but doesn't offer any concrete examples of her actual assignments, specific writing techniques, or special word choice.

Very, Very Rough Autobio Thing

God if you could've seen her. This girl, Caitlin, was like, hell, she was like music. Intricate like a Monk piano line, and her face, *her face*, such beauty and purity that watching her in class it seemed like she should've had a red velvet rope surrounding her. It was seventh grade and I, I couldn't have told her that even if I knew she would have taken it the way she had in my dreams.

Writing came pretty easy to me back then you know, when I was young. Shit, I remember one day in fifth grade when I, incredibly bored in math or some other useless class, decided to write a poem in the style of "Edgar Alien." I tell you, when Mrs. Grant saw the dark, depressing, and raw emotions that lurked inside this 11-year-old's head, she had no choice but to call my parents and tell them that I had written the most f-ed up, yet beautiful poem she'd ever seen a fifth grader produce. That night, when my dad asked me about the poem, it only took me about two seconds to rip the raggedy square shaped piece of paper out of my pocket, unfold it, and present it like a golden straight A report card. I remember he was standing in his closet and I was sitting on the pink flowery ottoman of my mother's pink flowery dressing room chair, and the look he gave me …Well, he hasn't looked at me like that since that day. It was a look full of confusion, but with that little hint of pride, that same one that a father wears when he yells at his teenage son for having sex. It was beautiful.

I should get back to telling you about Caitlin. I had had a crush on this girl for the whole entire year and I, like any naive, self-conscious kid, had formed a friendship with her in the hope that she would someday realize that the perfect boyfriend was right in front of her face. I was so desperate for her that I could think of only one thing to do to get her attention: what had worked for Shakespeare would surely work for me, except that I would write the greatest love poem ever and then she would be mine. As anyone who's now reading this could probably have guessed by now, the poem didn't work, and I'll spare you the details of what happened when someone who shouldn't have seen the poem did indeed see it, but it's not like the whole ordeal didn't teach me anything, though. Let's just say that after the whole "love poem" thing was over I was well on my way to becoming a real live, bona fide poet. I still have the journals from seventh and eighth grade, each one filled with awkward love poems, my attempts at being *deep*, and my failures. In all honesty, though, those journals hold some of the truest writing I've ever done.

In the slide show that contains the memories of my personal writing history, there is no doubt that the next slide is the cover of *On the Road* by Jack Kerouac. After I read that book I became someone new. It was like I was Sal Paradise in my head, awaiting adventure, madness, and life as I walked the streets of the Maushop Village compound in

Cape Cod. That book taught me how to grow up, and one night, it was late, my brother and his friend Ryan were at the house, hogging my bedroom with a couple of the neighborhood girls. I remember lying on my aero-mattress in between the twin beds that lined the walls, thinking about how my brother was a pig, and how I felt betrayed in that strange way little brothers feel betrayed when their brothers stop being their best friends. I went on a walk because it seemed like what Sal would've done. I didn't have a bottle of wine, nor a cigarette, but goddamnit if I didn't feel like a real beatnik with real problems and real things to say. I wrote this poem "Sleepsounds," which was what I felt to be my first real poem. No bullshit, no mushy gushy love language, just me describing, in the most poetic words that I knew, what I heard that night as I let my knowledge of the neighborhood carry me to places I knew existed but had never bothered to visit. God I was good.

For some reason I don't recall writing all that much poetry after "Sleepsounds," in fact I don't remember writing anything at the start of freshman year. Maybe I was shook up, maybe confused, or maybe I was just lazy. It's not all that important, because I'll tell you what, I sure as hell remember the night I became a slam poet. Kelsey and I had been talking online like we usually did, me acting like she wasn't the love of my life, and her trying to ignore the fact that I'm not all that good at acting. Wouldn't you have guessed that at some point in the conversation I boastfully told her, "suuure, I'm a poet, hell, I write poetry all the time," and her, obviously intrigued by the aspect of a poet, asked to see something recent. I hadn't yet matched the glory of "Sleepsounds," so I panicked, knowing that my only piece of actual poetry was getting less and less real every time I read it. What other choice did I have but to start something new? What resulted from that panic was my first real two-page rant poem, and I'm not gonna lie, it was still speckled with the occasional rhyming couplet, and still written as if the left side of the page was superior to the right side. But good lord did she dig it! Not like, in the "Oh my god you're such a poet, kiss me you fool!" way of digging a poem, but in the "Damn, you should perform that sometime" way. And that's exactly what I did.

I've come a long way still from that awkward night when I rushed together that first slam poem. It's like my poetry has grown with me, except instead of getting bigger and bigger it has grown more and more to be a part of me. Poetry is my outlet nowadays, and instead of writing for girls, for slam poetry judges (the pretentious bastards), and for others in general, I write strictly for myself and the love I have for words. I write because I want to write those cool rhyming phrases that make people just stare at you, and snap their fingers at you if they can recover from the verbal onslaught quick enough. But in all seriousness, I write because I haven't found anything quite as therapeutic or rewarding as poetry. I'm not saying that everything I write is good, because that's just not true. I can honestly say though that I love each and every poem I write, not because it's perfect, or because it's written by me, but because it reminds me how much I love being able to experience things, people, anything and everything, and reminds me why I live each and every day of my life.

—Spencer, grade 12

This author clearly has loads of personality, yet the title of his piece reveals a lack of confidence or a preemptive defensiveness that many adolescents feel. But from the opening sentence, the essay is full of voice. It's almost Holden-esque in its combination of self-deprecation and self-aggrandizement and in the way the author interrupts the narrative to comment on his own act of writing ("I should get back to telling you about Caitlin"). The class loved the author's voice in this essay but wanted to hear some examples of his poetry—"Sleepsounds," of course, but also more recent work. The essay could focus more on key dramatic moments: the aftermath of Mrs. Grant's phone call and also the climactic moment of reciting a poem for Caitlin. Overall, though, this essay is engaging and brimming with attitude.

Forget It!

In the first two days of my high school career I was told to forget everything that I had ever learned about writing. After spending many laborious hours reading *The Hobbit*, my first New Trier assignment was to simply write an in-class essay—a five-paragraph essay relating the archetypal hero cycle to the book. Not impossible. But as the teacher's shoes high heeled around the tiled room and she slowly peered over everyone's shoulder, the clomping grew louder. After each sentence she read, the anger she felt shot right down to those heels. The next day, she told us all in such a tone you would think she was giving up on us at that moment, "You guys just need to seriously forget everything you ever learned about writing." That meant I should forget …

I couldn't wait to get to school; I mean I was writing my first real book. Yesterday, I asked Mrs. Butt if I could take it home to work on it, my chin barely reaching the edge of her desk, and she snapped, "No. You will lose it." Although that fazed me a little, I am still looking forward to having the opportunity to read "Amelia Bedelia Goes to the White House" (modeled after Peggy Parish's children's books). The light wooden chair in the corner where the blackboards meet shines so brightly. The minute I situate myself in this place of greatness, I try to imitate my mother as a first-grade teacher. I lick my finger before turning each page (although I did not seem to find it useful, I found it mature in some way) and turn the pages towards my peers so they can admire my perfect script. I really did not care for them to look at the drawings as I try to cover them up with the tips of my fingers. But those script letters and the cunning sentences and jokes I came up with in my writing were the parts I wanted others to see. The best work I had ever done. The smile I wear is so engraved that when I sit back down on the rug, I try to move my lips, with little success.

The feeling of failure plummeted deep into my stomach and swirled itself around as it fed off of my insecurity. I felt like a complete idiot when my eyes started to swell. I mean writing had always been a strength for me. Red pen never attacked my papers, usually it just left an "A" comfortably cushioned on top of my creative title. Well, I guess what I thought was creative....I looked around the room and no one seemed as bothered as I was, so I took out my planner and started to flip through the calendar to avoid making eye contact with my teacher. The teacher did not know us, so she read off our names, and with each one her tone became more painful, I feared the worst. C. Not horrible, but it was the worst grade I ever received up to that moment. The curved edges of the letter enclosed all my confidence about writing. I never wanted to write again. According to Mrs. Heel Click, everything I ever learned: wrong. All the confidence I ever gained: false. Sadly, for the rest of my freshman year I tried to completely restyle my writing, and it became dry, with no emotion or sense of passion.

Luckily, sophomore year my luck changed. My English teacher wanted each and every student to realize their individual talents and concentrate on not only what needed to be improved, but also what needed to be celebrated. The day I turned in my first paper about *Tale of Two Cities*, the tips of my fingers jumped nervously on my desk. For the past year, the only comments I received were either "good" or some lengthy explanation of everything I did wrong. But when this paper finally crept from the manila folder to my desk, the paper exploded with green bursts, and each one gave a specific reason as to why what I said might need to be changed, or he really liked what I wrote. And at the end of my paper, an entire page of green pen explained everything that I needed to improve on, but more importantly he let me know exactly what I did well, and how my written creativity greatly enhanced this paper. By telling me this, my creative confidence rose tremendously and concurrently my ability to write. The assurance in my writing before freshman year hibernated in fear of my teacher and now was finally ground-hogging back into the world. The smile I wore walking out of class that day was so engraved that when I tried to move my lips, it was with little success.
—Mandy, grade 12

This piece opens with some bad advice that came straight out of our prewriting work. The essay really begins to develop characters, two teachers who are identified by pseudonyms (Butt and Heel Click) that clearly reveal the author's attitude toward those teachers' classes. It would be nice to identify the final teacher by some sort of name, too. The essay also offers some sharp details, including the river of "green ink" that offers praise alongside constructive criticism.

With every assignment my students write, I ask them to write a brief self-analysis to accompany their final drafts by responding to these questions: How did you move from initial idea to rough draft to final draft? What new choices did you make in writing the essay? What were your greatest challenges in writing the essay? The following example from Sam is a fairly typical response:

> When I started the paper I tried to think of the first experience I ever had with writing. I kept adding moments that I remembered until I was done. I did not make any major changes while editing, but I made lots of small ones. A choice I made was to NOT have a formal introduction or conclusion. (That was the first time for me.) Instead, all the paragraphs were stories. In the first paragraph I made sure to outline what the paper would be about, but subtly without a thesis. I had never done this before. I really struggled with the last paragraph and I still think it needs much more work.
> —Sam, grade 12

These self-analyses are almost always striking in their honesty. Sam reveals a little trepidation about writing stories. He has never written a paper without an explicit thesis for school. His essay was ordered chronologically, a decision that seems to follow his prewriting strategy of "thinking of my first experience with writing." The absence of a formal introduction and conclusion also seems foreign to him, perhaps explaining his dissatisfaction with the conclusion. This self-analysis is a good reminder to me as a teacher of just how difficult a leap personal writing can be when students have dined almost exclusively on a diet of thesis-support essays in school. I'm thrilled with the early steps Sam has taken here. (His later memoir, reprinted in Chapter 5, shows just how much he grows in his willingness to use literary tools and to employ different organizational strategies.)

These writers' autobiographies are extraordinarily revealing for classroom teachers and help us understand where our students are as they enter our rooms. These opening essays shed light on students' attitudes about writing and school, but they also reveal many students' fragility. Like nearly all writers, students have tender egos. The essays also begin to develop ideas that will become the basis of future writing: character, ethos, dialogue, specific detail, scene. Here the greatest challenge many students face is the task of choosing which scenes from their writing lives to focus on. In the next chapter, you'll see how we telescope the action further by concentrating on a single scene as a way to explore even more carefully the physical world around us.

A Sense of Place: Writing Essays about Place

3

I belong there. I have many memories....
I have learned and dismantled all the words in order to draw from them
A single word: Home

—MAHMOUD DARWISH, FROM "I Belong There," *Unfortunately, It Was Paradise* (7)

Without a sense of place the work is often reduced to a cry of voices in empty rooms, a literature of the self, at its best poetic music; at its worst a thin gruel of the ego.

—WILLIAM KENNEDY

"What if the whole world were a Rorschach test?" I ask the class. "What you see is who you are." In the assignment explored in this chapter, I ask students to look at the world around them as a text of their own creation. Since all writing is, to some extent, autobiography, students can find themselves—their perceptions of the reality they're describing—even when they write about the landscape they occupy.

Where We Live Now

To illustrate, I have students write an on-the-spot description of the classroom for five minutes, offering no further explanation and not answering questions. "Just describe the classroom," I say. Their responses are usually not polished—how could they be with so little time to write?—but they are full of important discoveries about writing. Brian mentions seven colors in his paragraph, and his subjects range from the American flag to graffiti on the wall; Walker offers not only geometrical shapes but also estimated measurements ("There are 20 rectangular desks, each approximately 30" × 16""); Julia's description is full of feeling: "The blinds suffocate the light and tiny specks of dust ride helplessly on broken shafts of sun."

I ask students how their responses are different and how they are similar. Almost inevitably the class seizes on the fact that the viewer's identity determines the view. Walker has a well-known love of math and measurement, and Julia has a decided dramatic streak. But Brian surprises even himself with the descriptions he has recorded.

"Why didn't Julia describe the flag," I ask, "or Brian the blinds?" I ask some version of this question every time and the answer is almost always the same: neither was facing the object in question. Some students get defensive, complaining that I never said they could move around the room or claiming that they'd have described absolutely everything if given more time. I'm not so sure.

Where we stand, how we situate ourselves in relation to the world, determines our worldview to a great extent. Living in the suburbs now after a lifetime of living in big cities, I see many more trees and many fewer homeless people. My political stances position me toward people who care about the environment and the peace movement and away from people who care about the stock market. Aristotle used the term *topoi* (or places) to talk about such stances. Where we stand is closely related to what we stand for.

A few years ago, I visited the Garfield Conservatory, an indoor plant garden in Chicago, for a special exhibit by the master glassblower Dale Chihuly. Some of the pieces were exquisite: glass-blown tendrils in the shape of vines and tubers; vibrant glass saucers floating on the top of ponds like water lilies. I was moving briskly through the rooms when my son appeared from a room I had just left and said, "Did you see that star?"

I thought for a moment. "You mean the glass plants in the water?" thinking he might have mistaken a pond flower for a starfish.

"No, the *star*. It's huge."

I followed him back and looked around. When I still failed to see the star, he yelled impatiently, "Look up!"

There it was: a gigantic, neon yellow star, maybe twenty feet tall, hanging from the ceiling of the glass dome. I still can't believe I missed it—but I know I wasn't alone in this. A nearby couple also looked up in sudden astonishment. Thinking about this discovery later, I kept thinking about how fixed my stare is during the day. Like many people, I usually see things at eye level (think of the way art is hung on museum walls), but I rarely look up or down unless I'm gauging the weather or picking up something I've dropped.

It's worthwhile thinking about where we stand in our world, where we fix our gaze. This activity offers an opportunity for students to reflect on the way they see and organize their worlds and the way they stand in relation to the world. People almost never look behind themselves, which serves as a metaphor for memoir writing—writing the life behind us—that I explore in Chapter 5.

Maps of Our Existence

As a second warm-up exercise, I ask students to make word maps of the objects found in a particular place. What we're after here are nouns, the objects themselves. We look at the Campbell McGrath poem "Map of Dodge County, Wisconsin," a list poem of objects that earns its power through the specificity of its description and its surprising associations.

I have students start their "maps" in class and ask them to include a minimum of ten items so that they have something to shoot for. (I'm always amazed at the magic of minimum numbers. If I give students a number, they have a goal that seems to satisfy them.) We share these lists and talk about which items were most vivid and which could be expanded. I ask students how they have ordered their lists, and almost to a person they tell me they wrote down items as they occurred to them. Fine for a rough draft, but is that the best possible order for these items? How can you give the items shape? Consider this rough draft:

Gone Truckin': 1991 GMC

Ripped seats; faux leather;
bins of washers and screws; a box of matches, a nail clipper, a bundle of receipts,
a beat-up address book; outdated black stereo buttons;
my dad leaning to one side, one hand on the wheel, one on his phone;
my sister on the other side, her feet in the air, trying to avoid the light bulb;
rolled up blueprints stacked in a pyramid, piling above the back seat;
the rear-view mirror facing the black cap; bins bursting with paperwork
a gun rack with fishing poles; a garbage bag with Taco Bell wrappers;
the 350,000 mile odometer.
—Julia, grade 12

This list includes many interesting details, but some are more interesting than others. The "beat-up address book" and the "pyramid" of blueprint rolls are more resonant, more specific, than "a bundle of receipts." Sometimes these maps turn into discrete poems of their own, but they almost always serve as springboards toward longer essays.

A Sense of Place

Having taken students through a couple of quick warm-up exercises, I pass out the following assignment.

> For your next essay, describe a place that fills you with feeling—excitement, awe, dread, joy—and describe it in 1–2 pages. While you have surely written descriptive pieces in the past, I'm hoping you go even further in this paper. Your goal is to describe—show (and not tell)—why the place is so significant to you personally, mapping out the location with specific sensory detail. In so doing, you will reveal something of who you are, your attitudes, values, hopes, fears.
>
> In other words, you are creating a map of a prominent place in your life (a holy land, a sacred space). As writer Peter Turchi reminds us in *Maps of the Imagination*, "To ask for a map is to say 'Tell me a story'" (11–12). And any description of place inevitably tells a story, either through explicit narrative or implicit association. Plan on having a full draft of your assignment in one week.

If students struggle getting started, I ask them to identify a quintessential experience: not "the four years you walked past the old frog pond" but "the one day you fell in." They need to populate their essays with the *things* that make their space so significant (remember Walt Whitman's claim: All truths wait in all things) and the people they associate with the space.

Writers need to be both explorers, hiking into the uncharted lands within our minds, and guides, leading readers on another kind of journey, Turchi says (11–12). This essay allows students to practice both roles. If they can, I encourage students to actually visit the place they choose to describe, or they might review photographs or consider interviewing people to capture details of the space.

The shape their essays take is up to them, but I maintain a strict page limit for this assignment: two pages maximum, with normal margins and fonts that don't require the use of the Hubble telescope. This essay is also an opportunity to practice stylistic economy, so we don't have time for weak verbs or anemic adjectives. Every word counts.

When discussing this assignment with the class, I've also used Ian Frazier's "Take the F," Ted Kooser's "Small Rooms in Time," and Scott Russell Sanders's "Homelands" as professional models. Because this essay leads to such provocative discussions, I've created a closely related separate assignment—or a way to focus students' attention if they're having difficulty getting started—that concentrates on the notion of home, asking students to describe a space within their home or to describe the place that makes them feel most *at home*. Here are some recent classroom models of both varieties:

The Insect Hum

The insect hum, a pulsating buzz from the grasses surrounding the river, fades into the growl of thunder. Clouds ride down the sky from north to south, across the length of the Tetons, across the open fields where the cattle graze, and over the river. The giant hue dial in the sky adjusts itself to tint everything to shades of blue.

A pitter-patter sound picks up on the river, raindrops grow in size and persistence; they leave small rings on the water's surface. The trout go wild, knowing they can't be seen from above, and splay water around their bellies as they emerge to swallow drifting bugs and berries. A bit of fly-line droops around my calf, carried by the current downstream from the tip of my rod.

Silent lightning strikes from the north, through the cold clear rain it is only a bright flash of light. Following is the thunder, echoing off of the mountains to the east, rolling through the valley, interrupted by the nearing call of cattle and clod of hooves. I can feel the thunder shake me through my feet. I should pull myself out of the river and lower my rod.

The riverbanks melt to mud and slip into the stream. The grasses surrounding the banks bend and bow in unison like a great choir. Trees bend and creak, the wind howls through their branches and it looks like they're wailing for mercy. I can't see the riverbed anymore; the image is broken by the slap of raindrops. I have to feel my way with my feet. The wet slimy touch of algae-covered rocks, a nymph crawls over my toes. I shiver: the rainwater must be forty degrees.

And then the sky cracks. Blue light shines down onto the water, the raindrops slowly pitter-patter into nothing, the thunder becomes a faint rumble to the south. The river ignites with insect hum, a celebratory buzz to match the veracity of the thunder. A stonefly takes from the grasses; a grasshopper flips itself into the current. He spins in an eddy and cascades down along the bank. Then, I can hear his mistake: a sip and a splash from the lips of a trout. The moon appears bold and glaring in a calm pocket on the side of the river. The land is unmistakably alive.

The blue light fades into night. Stonefly spinners vibrate around the riverbank without direction, crickets strum their washboard legs, and the air is sweet with the scent of the river. The sun drops below the swaying grasses, and the insect hum rages on.
—Bo, grade 12

Bo said he never felt completely at home in big cities, enjoying instead the big sky and wide-open spaces of the American west. He tells a story here—fishing in a rainstorm—but the piece really reads like a prose poem with terrific attention to the sound of language ("a sip and a a splash from the lips of a trout"—all those percussive *p* sounds) and sharp sensory descriptions throughout. The last paragraph alone features sight (the sunlight, the grass); the smell and perhaps taste of the sweet river scent; and mostly sound (spinners vibrating, crickets strumming, grasses swaying, and the title drone of the insect hum).

The Little Beach, Duxbury, MA

I always walk barefoot to the little beach in Duxbury. The black asphalt of Somerset Road bakes in the summer sun, scorching the bottoms of my feet as I walk heedlessly over the rocks strewn across the road. By the time I reach the end of the street, the cool, rough granite steps down to the beach are a welcome relief. The summer breeze, laced with the salty taste of the bay, whips stinging sand into my eyes. I run my hands down the rusty pipe railing, set into the immovable granite as I walk slowly down to the coarse sand. The water dripping from the storm drain hits the sand quietly.

It is low tide in the bay with the water rushing out beyond the boats sitting at anchor in the shallows. They sit scattered around the mudflats like discarded **toys**. The **sand** shifts easily beneath my **feet**, cradling them, unlike the unyielding **asphalt**. I stride directly towards the **mudflats**, ignoring the discarded **seaweed** and overturned **dinghies** above the **tideline**. The **mud** squelches between my **toes** as I walk through the razor-sharp **sea-grass**, careful to avoid the **razor clams**. I scan the **mudflats**, searching for **snail trails** or **horseshoe crabs**. Intermittently, **water** shoots up my **calves** as **clams** burrow further into the **sand**. Gleaming black **mussels** lay in clumps or cling to the **slime-covered anchor** of the sailing boat, the *Shirley Anne*.

I taste the **salt** and **mud stench** of the mudflats, and the screeches of **seagulls** assault me. The **sun** beats down onto the **gleaming sea**. I pause at the water's **edge**, admiring the jeweled **blue waters**.
—Katherine, grade 12

Much of the power of this piece derives from the nouns and noun phrases. Sometimes I ask students to circle nouns in professional and student models we are reading. Here I've used bold font for the nouns in the last two paragraphs of the essay. Just as students practiced in their map list poems, the author brings the force of concrete objects to the place she loves most in the world. This piece features a family vacation spot where the author feels most at home. Her attention to specific details and species reveals her love of nature, a kind of seeing-as-a-naturalist observation that reminds me of Annie Dillard's writing.

Sweat Lodge

A shaggy wolf of a dog bounds towards me as I step past the wire enclosure. He nibbles my fingers as I look up to see a long backyard dusted with snow, a black-and-white striped eagle feather bound to each of its fence-posts. Directly ahead, along the trampled mud path, stand thirty of my classmates, chatting excitedly. They are all dressed to sweat; the guys are wearing just shorts, and the girls are wearing shorts and tank-tops. They are huddled around a blazing fire with bowling ball-sized rocks; the rocks sizzle and spit as red lines of flame shoot along the contours of each rock. Behind the fire stands a great bear of a man looking into the sky as a bird twitters on a branch overhead. The man, our guide on this journey, suddenly turns and says, "It's time," gesturing towards the lodge.

The lodge is less than I expected. Imagining an enormous log house, I am surprised to see a waist-high leather wigwam, barely 10 feet in diameter. I lift up the flap and crawl inside, scratching my knees on the stiff straw meant to keep us off the completely frozen ground. Once everyone is inside, the blazing rocks, known as Grandfathers to the Blackfeet, are placed inside a central pit with the help of two deer antlers. The flap to the lodge rolls shut, and full light of the outside world is replaced by the dull glow of the Grandfathers. Our guide sprinkles sweetgrass and tobacco on the rocks, and the air is suddenly thick with a musty aroma. Without warning water is thrown into the central pit, and steam billows up as the world becomes completely dark. Within minutes I feel the first drop of sweat ooze out of a pore in my forehead. Soon rivers of sweat pour down my chest and back, cascading onto my shorts. The sweat of the two bodies near me drips onto me and mine onto them. The Blackfoot tribe believes that the mixing of sweat is actually the mixing of thoughts; in the lodge, thoughts and prayers become real things in this way. The breath of the person behind tickles the hair on my neck. A collective dull hum rises as people begin to meditate and pray; the lodge is a grandfather mumbling to himself, lost in thought. The person behind me rocks back and forth. In the blackness I begin to see colored spots; I must be hallucinating.

Suddenly the flap is flung open and the wolf pokes his head in. The light temporarily blinds me, and I grope my way out of the lodge. As I step out of the lodge, I look down at my body, which is billowing steam like molten-hot iron once plunged in water. Silently, I put on a coat and begin walking. I wonder where I parked.

—Ravi, grade 12

This piece is decidedly different from the others in that it offers a clear narrative event. Initially after choosing this topic, the author thought he had made a mistake because he feared the darkness of the lodge might prevent him from offering sharp descriptions. But I like the way he uses the other senses (e.g., the musty aroma of sweet grass and tobacco) here to compensate for the lack of vision: instead of sight, he offers insight. The essay is also tightly structured (entering and exiting the tent). There is minimal lead-in material and an ending that offers not only unity but also humor. The last line lets us know the author doesn't take himself *too* seriously. He has learned the ethos lesson from the writer's autobiography assignment.

White Washed

Glossy white bathtub ledge— a perfect seat
For late night phone conversations.
The mirror stretches from wall to wall.
I watch the color drain from my face
When I ask,
"So you're saying this is it? We're over?"
Grazing the floor, a sheer shower curtain
Sewn with cascading clear crystals
Like falling moisture droplets.

The white tiled floor is always cold.
I grab a tissue; blot my eyes;
And shiver
Ivory sink with soap and water stains;
Its perimeter cluttered with toiletries and hair accessories.
Cool mint Listerine, Rave 4x mega hairspray,
Fresh fusion Lady Speed Stick, energy Aroma Therapy Softsoap.
Dust covered honeydew candle
With a crystal cornflower blue lampshade
Stands dangerously close to the edge.

Scattered brown and black bobby pins,
Lavender and copper hair clamps with barracuda-like teeth.
Tortoise shell, black leather, plastic, polka-dot,
Striped, plaid, and animal print headbands resemble horseshoes
Around the standing mirror handle.
Most are frayed from overuse
I only wore my favorites with him.

Soap dishes protrude from the bone colored wall—
One filled with green and clear sea glass
And the other with a decorative soap
In the shape of a blue martini.
Shiny metal towel rack with hooks underneath the word:
wash
Away the tears.

White wooden cupboard with glass windows
Displays my perfume collection;
Pink, Flowerbomb, Romance,
Ralph, Brit, Demeter,
Happy to Be, Falling in Love,
Heaven, Light Blue, Dream.

I bite my lip and smile.
The framed saying adorns the tea green wall
"Best friends are better than Boyfriends."

—Caroline, grade 12

I like to include a few models that challenge my students' notions of arrangement on the page. Since we are writing papers on the importance of space, it's an ideal time to consider spacing in writing. When this author finished, she said, "I'm not sure if I've written an essay or a poem." I'm not sure the distinction matters. What Caroline has clearly done is offer specific language of a specific place: the sanctuary of her bathroom. By highlighting the central position of the mirror, it is clear that everything she describes—the physical world around her, the relationships she is in, and her attitudes toward them—are all manifestations of her own self-image.

Bowl of Fire

The "Indians" spun in an improvised grass dance, each foot hitting the ground in rhythm with the pulse of the drum. The long fringe blurred the dancers' rotations and gave them a mystical aura. Each dancer had his own unique regalia. Most wore a shawl with long colorful threads hanging from the edges, and one wore a more colorful shirt with a large bustle tied to his lower back. The bells adhered to the dancers' ankles harmonized with the drum beat as they performed their dizzying waltz around the unlit fire.

The fire stood at an impressive twelve feet high, six tiers of *trees*, not just logs, but entire 22' sections of trunk, stacked in a triangular fashion. This formidable skeleton was stuffed full of branches, topped off a roof of straight branches and doused with kerosene, just begging to be lit. This stood in the center of the Grib Bowl, a large amphitheater-like fire bowl with seating for near five hundred. The spectators moved in one long chain, each gripping the next's shoulder with his right hand as they shuffled from the trail through the railroad-tie rows. Finally, once the crowd was complete, they dropped to their seats.

I stood out of the way in the corner of the bowl, hidden behind the trees. I had to piss again. This was the third time in 25 minutes. I shook with anxiety. I crept quietly past Derek to relieve myself on a bush while I waited my time. He looked composed as he watched the dancers. It was a cool July night and I was buck naked save for my breechcloth, a vest and my war bonnet but I was already dripping with sweat. I grabbed my moccasin and stretched my quads, preparing for my first time.

The drum sounded with two hard beats and the dancers sprinted out of the bowl. The crowd was silent. Someone made the whistle of the Whippoorwill from the trail, and the drummer responded from his perch in a tree high above the bowl. He began a drum roll that reverberated across the bowl, pounding in time with my heart. A young man in just a breechcloth darted through the bowl with a bow and arrow held in front. He ran down the trail, past the fire and over the sand paintings that decorated the floor of the bowl, and up the other side to a small fire, known as "the Chief's fire" that stood at the top of the bowl, just thirty feet from me. He paused for a moment with his arrowhead buried in the flames. Then, with the flaming arrow nocked in the bow at his side, he zipped back the way he came, making sure to steer clear of the juiced fire. With the drum still rolling hard, the runner reached the base of the exit trail and dropped to a knee. He cocked the bow, and in time with a final, hard beat on the drum, he let the flame fly deep into the woods. As the runner ran out after his arrow, Derek and I crept forward to my position at the top of a side trail into the bowl. The butterflies threatened to tear through my stomach. We stood solemnly with faces set and arms crossed. The three other pairs each stood in their corner, ready to go. The adrenaline rushed, and my heart felt ready to explode.

—Jack, grade 12

Jack's piece offers tremendous tension. Starting with a description of an American Indian tradition, the action telescopes to a sort of scouting ritual in which his anxiety is clear throughout. The specificity of details, and especially *things*—breechcloth, arrowhead, buckskin—places Jack's readers in the circle with him. The final line offers a great ending, one that signals a frozen moment rather than a "full" narrative.

Frozen in Time

The porch had been eaten by snow. Where there was once a wooden set of benches and railings there was now a giant, misshapen snowball. A small path was carved out in the snow, just as wide as the large, rusty shovel that sat up against the wooden, shingle-like panels that lined the secluded cabin. Right in front of the door was a two foot square small, grate-like metal patch in place of the floorboards of the porch. This was there most likely so that when the snow fell it would drop through the holes as to not block the door with mounds of snow-flakes. But the snow had already filled the gap between the grate and the ground. We couldn't wait to get inside.

I peeled back the flimsy glass and white aluminum storm door and grabbed the cold, silver door knob of the main door. It was heavy, wooden, and partially frozen to the frame. I twisted the knob and rammed the door with my shoulder and hip three times until we were finally able to cross the threshold. I made my way into the cabin, Danny following close behind. We wiped our feet on the old black beat-up plastic doormat even though we were still totally covered in snow. About four yards to our left we saw a mound of old scratchy orange blankets that we assumed covered one of the kids staying in our cabin who had fallen asleep on the couch. Even though it was at least three in the morning, an appropriate time to be asleep, we couldn't help but quietly snicker as the unidentified lump of fabric groaned and turned over, never revealing his face.

The front of the cabin was almost entirely windows, but some time over the course of the night they had been covered with the beige, cloth shades. The walls on either side were slanted inwards. It gave the cabin the illusion that it was really just a roof that someone had cut off of another house and relocated in the snow. The carpet was thick and lush, and just looked like the seventies. Every step we took was absorbed by the carpet and the only sound that could be heard was Danny half whispering, half snickering, "Look at that cheesy picture! How old do you think that thing is?!" The wall held a faded photograph of a skier jumping off a mountain in a flimsy metal frame that had been painted a cheap-looking gold. It was an action shot, but the man in the picture looked still and frozen in time.

We looked up at the balcony to see the two beds peering through the banis-ters, completely occupied. In front of us, we could see that the kitchen lights were on. The sink was piled with dirty dishes and stray bags of Ramen noodles lined the countertops. But there was no humming of the refrigerator. Not a single drip from the faucet. The cabin was asleep.

We crept toward the wooden dining room table set that looked like it would have been crafted by a Swedish family. We sat on the bench, away from the table and overlooked the living room and our mystery friend engulfed in the pile of old blankets. We put our feet in front of the heater built into the wall and just sat. The

only waking things in the house, we whispered quietly on the bench as if we were two kids waiting to catch Santa setting out presents on Christmas Eve. We talked for hours about everything that two strangers could until morning came but it felt like no time had lapsed at all. Although we were at least eight hours away from our houses, on a bench, in a cabin in Michigan, we couldn't have felt more at home.
—Margaret, grade 12

This scene lacks the drama of the ritual in Jack's piece, yet this winter cabin description still features plenty of tension. The opening line offers a lovely personification (snow-eaten porch), and there are effective sensory details throughout—"scratchy orange blankets," "dirty dishes," and "stray bags of Ramen noodles"—to ground the scene for the reader. This piece offers an interesting take on the "at home" assignment: here, the author feels most at home as a stranger in a strange cabin.

The final model I present recalls Matisse's dictum that "exactitude is not truth"; our sensory perceptions, however sharp, are mediated by our subjectivity. This is particularly true when viewing an event through the kaleidoscopic prism of memory. Here the specific memory of a place is inextricably bound to the author's relationship with his parents and grandparents.

The Dragon Coaster

"We are torn between a nostalgia for the familiar and an urge for the foreign and strange. As often as not, we are homesick most for the places we have never known."
—Carson McCullers

The Dragon Coaster is an old wooden roller coaster. It's painted like a giant dragon that twists and turns its way from start to finish. The coaster looks like it's about to collapse. The wood creaks and bends as the train breezes by on the tracks high above. It's warped from years of use; brown rust now covers the once shiny metal rails. The paint on the outside of the coaster is peeling off. Wood is exposed underneath the white and green of the dragon's scaly back. The wooden planks crisscross all the way to the top, as if the foundation of the coaster has been woven together rather than nailed.

On a hot July day, the line to ride the coaster stretches for half a mile. The dark asphalt floor is covered in candy wrappers and hot, sticky cotton candy that kids have dropped. The unforgiving sun burns the back of your neck while you wait for your turn to ride. When you finally reach the front of the line, you hand your bright neon pink ticket to the teenage girl running admissions; then you half-walk, half-run up the creaky wooden platform to quickly sit down in your favorite car. The front is most people's favorite. Painted with bright yellow dragon's eyes and a wide, smoke-breathing nose, it provides the clearest view from the top. But the last car, the dragon's tail, provides the best ride because you'll be whipped around the corners and steep drops. You grab the last car and settle in. You remember the feel of the seat. It's the same car you've sat in each summer since you can remember. A bar drops down, covering your legs. You can tell where people hold the bar from where the foam padding has been rubbed off. "Are you ready to tame the dragon?" asks a deep voice from the loudspeaker. People cheer in excitement.

The ride starts like all old wooden roller coasters—a rusted old chain pulls the train of cars to the top. The people below get smaller and smaller as you climb higher into the dry air. You finally reach the top and the coaster slowly rolls into its first turn. It's picking up speed.

Your stomach feels like it's full of Jell-O for just a second while you fall down the first drop and make a sharp right turn. The wooden boards that hold the coaster in place are only a few feet above your head. If you stand up during the ride, your head might be taken off. The daring teenage boys two cars ahead of you raise their hands and slap the boards as they fly by.

Suddenly, you're sent into a dark tunnel. Even though you've been on this ride a hundred times before, you let out a scream. For just a moment, the world becomes silent. The sounds of children laughing and bright carnival music disappears; you can no longer smell the hot dogs and bubblegum. Just as quickly as you disappear, you emerge again into the bright summer sky four stories high. After one final turn, the car halts to a stop. The ride is over. A group of girls towards the front cheers and laughs. The metal bar that's been digging into your legs for the whole ride lifts up. "Let's go again!" yells a young boy, pulling his mother by the hand. You walk down the same old wooden ramp that you used to enter the coaster. The sky is turning purple and kids' rides like the Merry-Go-Round and the Swan Swing have already closed.

You sprint to the back of the line so you can squeeze in one more ride before closing time.
—Nick, grade 12

In this piece, the author captures not only the sense of what it was like to ride on the coaster as a young boy but also the sense of the two-headed narrator we've discussed in class earlier—the simultaneous presence of the younger narrator experiencing the event and the older, wiser narrator looking back on those events. The length and specificity of Nick's self-analysis reveal how much this piece means to him and how much his writing, and his ability to think about writing, have grown.

Self-Analysis: The Dragon Coaster

Freshman year, I was lucky enough to score an extra ticket to see John Updike speak. One of the things he talked about was the power of the present tense in writing. He explained that not only does it sound beautiful, it can really change an entire piece. It can make the reader more aware of the action; it can let him become a part of a story.

I switched my piece into the present tense so that the reader could "take a ride" on the Dragon Coaster, so to speak. The present tense lets him connect with the piece better. Additionally, I tried to write about a specific ride, rather than just any ride. It makes it more interesting because I can include specifics. I don't know if this ride actually happened (though it probably did because I spent so much time on that coaster). But it really isn't important whether or not it happened. For example, when I think of my grandmother, she's always wearing a specific necklace that she brought home from China. She lost the necklace almost two years ago, but it's still around her neck when I picture her. This ride I describe in this piece is the way I remember the Dragon Coaster.

I tried to include details about the other riders because it makes the piece more fun. A movie is always better when there's a packed theater, a concert is always better if it's sold out, and a roller coaster is always better if every seat is full. One of the unique things about roller coasters is that they change depending on who is riding with you. The Dragon Coaster was different with my mother than with my brother, my sister, or my friend. My intention was to add personality to the ride and the essay as a whole.

I tried to make the part about the ride itself relatively short, because that's what the experience is actually like. At every amusement park, you spend a half hour in line for 45 seconds of fun.

I included the quote at the beginning because it describes the way I feel about the coaster. Thinking of the coaster makes me homesick. I can't say whether I'm homesick for my childhood, my old town, or a simpler way of life in which wooden coasters were the peak of excitement and didn't have to compete with Six Flags and reality TV. It's probably a combination of all of them. I'm homesick for a time when the dragon coaster was more than just a bumpy ride; I try to convey that in the essay.

Roller coasters don't age well. *Gone with the Wind* is as moving today as it was when it was first shown in theaters in the 1930's. Mozart's symphonies sound as brilliant today as the day they were written. But coasters only get worse as the years go by. The wood starts to bend, the paint starts to peel, the ride feels bumpier each time you ride it. Wooden coasters are far surpassed by newer metal ones. New coasters are safer, go faster and take you higher. The appeal of the wooden coaster is the simple history of them; it's essentially the same ride that

my grandparents rode more than sixty years ago on their first date, or that my father rode on his 7th birthday. It may not be as exciting, but the nostalgia makes it more interesting and adds personality. I tried to include a little bit of history to put my piece into perspective and explain that nostalgia behind the ride.
—Nick

Okay, I admit this student's reflection is a bit out of the ordinary. Incredibly, the self-analysis is almost as long as the essay. And would any other fourteen-year-old boy boast of scoring Updike tickets the way most of us would talk of a backstage pass to a Radiohead concert? But this self-analysis shows how much students invest in writing they care about. In fact, this author brought in a family photo of the roller coaster to show the class the day the assignment was due. Further, this response shows how much the student has learned about the craft of writing—the importance of revision, the selection of details. Nick mentions specificity three times, particularly focusing on a single event to generate sensory details rather than settling for a general feeling. Most of all, he maintains a keen sense of audience, expressing his desire to take his readers on a "specific ride."

One year I happened to talk about this assignment with a photography teacher at school. By strange coincidence, he was already working on a photography assignment in his class that used the same title: "A Sense of Place." So we decided to hang our work on the walls of school, both photographs and essays, the way art is hung in a museum. Then we combined our classes and had students curate their exhibits to one another, discussing the advantages and challenges each medium offered. Later in the year we met as a combined class one more time to listen to playwright Steve Feffer talk about theatrical space and to punk/country singer and painter Jon Langford as he discussed notions of space and place in painting and in the sonic landscapes of music.

In this essay, students concentrate on place, describing the world around them and thinking about how they orient themselves to their worlds. We consider the idea that where we stand determines what we see. In the next chapter, you'll read about students working on an even smaller canvas as they concentrate on the snapshot moments of little journeys that combine poetry and prose.

4

Journey to the Interior: Writing Haibun

Middle Way

At times it's hard to know whether to laugh or cry. The struggle
to be, just to exist requires each of us to be true to too many things
to make sense of which one of us is right.

> a few graves apart
> neighbors who had nothing to say
> to each other

—TOM CLAUSEN

"Middle Way" is typical of many modern English *haibun*, a fascinating hybrid of short narrative writing (often similar to personal diary or travel journal entries) and poetry (haiku). According to Bruce Ross, a noted haiku poet, editor, and anthologist, "A haibun is a prose narrative that is autobiographical . . . [but] that [also] includes haiku. The haiku act like little punctuation marks of feeling in the prose" (55).

In haibun, one or more haiku are interspersed throughout the prose paragraphs, and it is the tension between these two registers, these two textures, that accounts for the power of the form. Sometimes the haiku illuminate the prose like a light source in a snapshot or a painting; other times the haiku extend the meaning of the prose, hanging in the air like wind chime music even after the reader has moved on from the scene.

This chapter takes its name from haiku master Bashō's travel book *Journey to the Interior*, an account of his travels in Japan. But while haibun have their roots in Bashō's seventeenth-century Japan, many modern English language poets, including well-known American poets such as Jack Kerouac, Gary Snyder, and Robert Hass, have also written memorable haibun.

Bashō walked 1,600 miles as he traveled throughout Japan, but contemporary haibun writers cover many different types of travel, not only physical journeys but also mental journeys and memories. Since what we experience is always mediated by who we are, even external journeys are always, to some extent, journeys inward, shedding light on the intersection of where we are and who we are.

In Tom Clausen's haibun "Middle Way," there is an interplay between the prose section, a sort of offhand rumination on human relationships, and the haiku's sad irony that two neighbors, though close physically, were as distant in life as they are in death. Only the speaker's insight bridges these two lives, just as the haiku bridges the gulf mentioned in the prose section. The juxtaposition of these sections implies that being "right" may have brought about the reticence and the reluctance of these neighbors.

I love teaching haibun because the writing challenges are so different from anything students have ever done with essays. In fact, haibun help reinforce the idea of essay-as- experiment. The brevity of the form also offers great opportunities to teach economy. Every word matters. This is a great practical advantage for teachers. Since these essays are so short, it's a terrific time to zoom in on students' specific language and punctuation use.

Reading Haibun

Before I ask students to write haibun of their own, we examine a variety of models, some professional, some by students; some funny, some sad; some with several haiku, some with one; and haibun that vary the placement of the poem(s) within the larger essay. As always, variety is essential because offering a single model or a single type of model suggests a sort of orthodoxy to many students that is difficult for them to leave behind. I offer here some of the models I have used in class and explanations about the salient features of these models.

Facing the Wall

The polished black granite of the Vietnam Veterans Memorial in Washington DC—popularly known as The Wall—subtly reflects its visitors. While reading the names of over 58,000 Americans killed during that conflict, we suddenly realize that our images are transposed on those names.

This experience is especially poignant for 'Nam vets seeking the names of those with whom they served. They will never know a closer reunion with their fallen comrades.

                                        Vietnam Memorial
                                        aging veterans reflected on
                                        names of young men

—John Dunphy

This haibun is a moving tribute to those who died in Vietnam and to those who visit the wall to pay their respects. For me, the last line of the prose section is especially memorable. This visitation is the closest reunion possible, and the wall connects even as it reminds us of the immutable finality of death. From the first time I read this haibun, I was reminded of Yusef Komunyakaa's brilliant poem "Facing It." It might be interesting to pair these two as works that pay homage through very different forms.

Here are two haibun from Lidia Rozmus's book *My Journey*:

Green, and more green
A surreal forest covered with moss. Everything looks like big toys wrapped in green velvet and eternal dew.

Ancient spirals of ancient ferns. Rain in the air and this softness in everything—in the colors, shapes, sounds, and aromas. It is like a journey to the deep past.

                                        calm
                                        rain falls
                                        on moss

Black on black
                                        suspension bridge
                                        my heart sways
                                        over white waters
Storm approaching. First raindrops are heavy with the scent of cedar. They move the light green leaves of a young iris growing from the middle of a nearby pond. The surface of the pond is almost black from the dark clouds below.

The old cedar forest offers a little protection from the rain. Now it's pouring but still I can see. Between lightning and thunder, between the white wall of rain and the brownish forest, I can see the young iris growing straight, like a green arrow. The bud is still covered, not revealing the mystery of its color. I hope it is black.

These two poems are part of a longer sequence called "My Journey," Rozmus's journey from her girlhood home in Kraków, Poland, to her arrival in the United States. The poems suggest further variety within the haibun form since one opens and one ends with a haiku. Rozmus is an artist, and her imagination ("everything looks like big toys," the hope for a black iris), along with her obvious concern for color, make these scenes come alive. Both of these haibun are set in nature—a forest, a pond—but what is especially interesting is the way these locations are mediated by the speaker's observations.

Birthday Haibun

It is nap time at the day care center where I work, and have worked for thirteen years. The children are sleeping on their cots in this pleasant July afternoon. It is my birthday. I am forty-four years old, about fifteen to twenty times the children in my care. I am twice as old as my co-teacher. In two years, if we are both alive, I will be half as old as my father.

None of my fellow workers have remembered my birthday, and I have done nothing to remind them. In the quiet I can hear birds chirping through the open window.

> gentle wind
> ruffles where my wild hair
> used to be

—Michael Ketchek

In contrast to the "natural" scenes of Rozmus's haibun, Ketchek offers a scene inside a building. Note how this haibun is created without any special traveling and without any grand adventure in nature. He is at work, presumably where he goes most days, but the traveling here is mental—intellectual (the mathematics of age) and emotional. The tone is not self-pitying (the afternoon is "pleasant" and he has "done nothing" to remind his co-workers that it is his birthday), but he is keenly aware of time passing. Moments of insight, however, can stretch time, and I believe this is happening in this poem. By thinking about the past and the future, he arrives at the present, living fully in the moment of discovery. I like the humor of the poem that gently reminds us of time. The break between lines 2 and 3 is hilarious, pulling the rug out from underneath the reader (and the speaker!).

Haibun are also practiced by so-called mainstream poets. The next one is by Robert Hass.

On Visiting the DMZ at Panmunjom: A Haibun

The human imagination does not do very well with large numbers. More than two and a half million people died during the Korean War. It seems that it ought to have taken more time to wreck so many bodies. Five hundred thousand Chinese soldiers died in battle or of disease. A million South Koreans died, four-fifths of them civilians. One million, one hundred thousand North Koreans. The terms are inexact and thinking about them can make you sleepy. Not all "South Koreans" were born in the south of Korea; some were born in the north and went south, for reasons of family, or religion, or politics, at the time of the division of the country. Likewise the "North Koreans." During the war one half of all the houses in the country were destroyed and almost all industrial and public buildings. Pyong-yang was bombarded with one thousand bombs per square kilometer in a city that had been home to four hundred thousand people. Twenty-six thousand American soldiers died in the war. There is no evidence that human beings have absorbed these facts, which ought, at least, to provoke some communal sense of shame. It may be the sheer number of bodies that is hard to hold in mind. That is perhaps why I felt a slight onset of nausea as we were moved from the civilian bus to the military bus at Panmunjom. The young soldiers had been trained to do their jobs and they carried out the transfer of our bodies, dressed for summer in the May heat, with a precision and dispatch that seemed slightly theatrical. They were young men. They wanted to be admired. I found it very hard to describe to myself what I felt about them, whom we had made our instrument.

> The flurry of white between the guard towers
> —river mist? a wedding party?
> is cattle egrets nesting in the willows.

This haibun, from Hass's 2008 Pulitzer Prize–winning book of poems *Time and Materials*, concerns a trip the poet made to the demilitarized zone between North and South Korea. It starts with the speaker's incredulity—the numbers of dead, the vastness of the devastation. Numbers cannot help us comprehend the awfulness of war. The prose section talks about the artificial distinctions of geography, the reductive sides that are drawn. It is this reductiveness, perhaps, that makes it possible for opposing sides to forget the humanity of the "enemy." The final lines before the haiku offer a justification of the form. The speaker says, "I found it very hard to describe to myself what I felt." This attempt to understand, to come to terms with our experiences, is what haibun—and all art forms—attempt to do.

Writing Haibun

After discussing a variety of haibun, I tell students to go on a journey of their own, physical or mental. Since we usually spend about a week on this assignment, students can write about exciting trips they have taken, or they can focus on small journeys in their everyday lives that offer moments of surprise, delight, or frustration—taking out the garbage, feeding the cat, a trip to the attic—and to write a one-page essay (two if absolutely necessary) in which they relate a very short scene, a small journey, along with a minimum of one haiku. For students with wider artistic ambitions, I suggest they can also offer a picture to accompany the haiku (called a *haiga*), or they might even try setting the piece to music. All of these options reinforce NCTE's *Beliefs about the Teaching of Writing*: "In order to teach for excellence about purposes in writing, teachers need to understand . . . ways people use writing for personal growth, expression, and reflection . . . [as well as] aesthetic or artistic forms of writing . . . for the purposes of entertainment, pleasure, or exploration." Haibun writing is an effective way to marry the twin goals of encouraging personal reflection and fostering aesthetic appreciation.

Here are some recent student models.

Dreaded Destination

A smoky cough rises from the rusty exhaust pipe as the car patters into gear. The frost slowly diminishes as defrosters peel ice from the windows. Turning the knob to maximum, a warm new car stench fills my nose and warms my cheeks. The temperature gradually creeps towards the H that sits above it. I shift from P to R and carefully roll backwards towards the street, an icy layer between tires and pavement sliding the car along clumsily.

> Monday carpool—
> cold fingers
> grasp the wheel

—Al, grade 12

Not surprisingly, perhaps, many of my students write about cars when they think about travel. (In fact, driving is a memoir-writing prompt in Chapter 5.) Here the speaker offers some terrific verbs (*patters, peel*) and some specific details (the gear shift levels) as he braces to exit his driveway. The word *Monday* in the haiku intensifies the journey. Maybe the cold feels a little colder as the speaker "gears up" for another week of school.

Mount Masada

It was still dark when we left the hostel at the base of Masada. The cool air stung my cheeks and nose. My body, still groggy, struggled to keep up with my mind, eager to push forward to the top of the looming mountain in front of me.

> darkness
> outlining the mountain's
> darkness

I stop trying to count the rock stairs. We march single-file. Morning people made their way to the front of the line.

When I reach the plateau of the peak of Mount Masada, I drop to my knees and await the sun rising over the edge of the adjacent mountain along the horizon. I rest my head on my arms as I wipe the sweat from my brow waiting as the sky continues to get brighter.

> an orb of light
> appears over a distant
> mountain tip

—Noah, grade 12

This student spent part of a year in Israel and was clearly moved by his experiences. The prose paragraphs are especially short, but they also imitate the mountain climb. The two haiku offer a contrast of dark to light, suggesting not only the passing of time but also the speaker's sense of accomplishment and wonder.

Winter Orchids

"Be sure to *totally* warm up the car before you go. Keep these in the box to keep them from the cold. Tape it shut. Take them out of the water for the trip to her house. Wipe the bottom off so they are nice to give to her. Take out of box before she opens the door."—Aunt Debbie (your personal florist).

After reading the note taped to the cardboard box that contained my Valentine's flowers, I grabbed a pair of scissors and cut open the box. Inside were purple and pink orchids adorned with a pink ribbon resting in a Folger's Coffee jug full of water. They were perfect.

I re-taped the box and set it on the counter top by the back door until I was ready to leave.

Later that evening, car key in hand, I shuffled across my ice-covered walkway to my car. I started the engine and listened to Dave Brubeck's "Blue Rondo a la Turk" twice before shuffling back inside to grab the orchids. I gingerly picked the cardboard box off the counter top and wrapped it in my down coat for warmth.

Outside, I stepped as lightly as I could on the ice. With every skid and slip I gripped the cardboard tighter. I put the box in the passenger's seat, fastened the seatbelt around it and drove off, resting my right hand on my copilot.

I sat in her driveway until "Take Five" finished then gently peeled away the duct tape, lifted the flowers out of the box and carried them up to the house. The doorbell hadn't finished ringing by the time she answered the door.

light
from an open door—
winter orchids

—Drew, grade 12

Formal dances are another journey many high school students take. This piece offers more of a short story than a quick scene. I love the presence (in the note) of the speaker's aunt, offering assistance and advice as the big night approaches. The prose section is full of sharp details (the Folger's can, the song titles), and the speaker's tone seems just right, a mixture of jazz-cool and terror. Waiting for "Take Five" to finish (a song whose title might also suggest the speaker's wish to breathe a little easier!) is a wonderful moment. And the haiku at the end beautifully finishes the scene. Light is used as both a physical source and a sign of welcome and warmth, a contrast to the dark night, the way the tropical orchids contrast with the Chicago winter.

Three Blind Steps

I usually find myself watching the mouth. Ears pull my eyes toward the bouncing lips; my center of attention lies in the source of language. Occasionally, while listening to a speaker, my eyes will drift toward other listeners, and I will watch them. See how they react. See what they're watching. Sometimes I'll check out my surroundings, taking in the artwork and furnishings. But I usually just watch the mouth.

Eyes scare me. Eye-to-eye contact takes observational curiosity and spins it into a power struggle. Staring a person in the eye is playing "chicken" at 90 mph, and I'm usually the one who turns into the ditch, averting the returning gaze. Yet staring is love.

When Poppie and I talk, I stare at him all I want. Because he can't stare back. Blinded by macular degeneration, his pupils jump back and forth, side to side. For all I know, he could be looking at me from the only corner of the eye that still works. But we never lock pupils.

So every time I talk to Poppie, I get the chance to size him up. I can stare at him from head to toe. I see the Docksiders, the scarred knee, the "soccer player" in his belly, the wiry grin and his forty finely combed hairs. And the eyes. I can stare straight through his wire-rim glasses. I see the ten-year-old German boy, the American soldier, the oral surgeon. I see a father of three daughters, grandfather of seven. I see through his blind eyes—I feel the change from carpet to hardwood; taste awful mixture of fish and potatoes he scoops onto his fork during dinner; hear NPR, *Newsweek*, and the Old Testament on tape. I see his mental blueprint of the world and the way it works.

We sit in my family room together, watching Hillary Clinton on "60 Minutes," his favorite TV show now that he can no longer read the stock ticker on MSNBC.

"Poppie, can I help you fix your drink?" calls my sister.

"Sure, dear. Thanks." He lifts himself off the couch and waddles over to the stairs, slowing down as he approaches them. He sticks out the right foot until he finds contact perpendicular to the floor. "One, two, three," he mutters firmly as he glides up the three steps, completely self-sufficiently.

He can't see a thing, but he knows the whole house by heart.

> In my family room
> Three steps from memory;
> Son, father, grandpa

—Daniel, grade 12

This haibun breaks almost every guideline in the assignment. It's more a story than a moment, and it features more dialogue and character development than is usually found in haibun, which tend to be narrated internally. The haiku also features capital letters at the start of each line. But who cares about guidelines? I've always loved this piece for its humanity, the obvious empathy and love the author has for his grandfather. I guess that's why I wasn't too surprised when the author later told me he offered the haibun as a birthday present when his grandfather turned eighty. Because the grandfather had lost his vision, Daniel recorded the piece on a CD that was played at the birthday party.

Many students have likened haibun writing to taking a snapshot of a scene from everyday life. While this comparison is somewhat apt, the writing demands are great. Writing a brief and focused scene about a particular moment in time is difficult. Add to this the challenge of writing a haiku that responds to the scene, and students will be plenty challenged by what might be their shortest paper of the year.

But with this assignment, as with every assignment in this book, my primary goals are that students experiment with language and that they begin to make meaning out of their lives. So if students have created an effective title, if they have created a short scene that is clear to any reader, and if they have written a haiku that crystallizes a moment within that scene, they have, to my mind, completely fulfilled the demands of this assignment. More than perhaps any other assignment explored in this book or in the classroom, haibun force students to experiment with language. This is one reason why students have so much fun writing them, why students frequently include them as representatives in final portfolios, and why students frequently cite them as favorite pieces on year-end course evaluations.

Making a Living:
Writing Memoir

Because the story of our life
Becomes our life

Because each of us tells
The same story
But tells it differently

And none of us tells it
The same way twice

Because grandmothers looking like spiders
Want to enchant the children
And grandfathers need to convince us
What happened happened because of them

And though we listen only
Haphazardly, with one ear,
We will begin our story with the word and

—LISEL MUELLER, from "Why We Tell Stories"

This excerpt ends one of my favorite poems by Lisel Mueller. In these lines, Mueller makes a case for the power of storytelling. We all tell the "same story"—that is, the story of our common humanity—but each of us "tells it differently / And none of us tells it / The same way twice" since we are individual and unique. We celebrate our individuality by mining the particularities of our life. I love the way the poem ends with the word *and*, since stories always beget more stories. Writing is generative. As writing professor Tom Romano puts it, "We put down words and those words lead to more words" (21).

Mueller also makes an extraordinary claim about identity in this poem: that "the story of our life / Becomes our life." In other words, we *are* our stories. But this is not merely one poet's lofty sentiment; there is scientific support for this idea as well. Neuropsychologist Paul Broks says that "our identity is nothing more than a story the brain tells itself" (*Radiolab*). And neuroscientist V. S. Ramachandran goes even further, claiming that "the ability to tell stories about ourselves," what he calls "introspective consciousness," "is what separates us from the beasts" (*Radiolab*). There could scarcely be a more important, and more intrinsically interesting, topic for writing than stories about ourselves. Memoir writing allows students to consider the ways they have been defined and the ways they have defined themselves in order to arrive at their current self-identity.

In this assignment, we explore our past "selves" as a way to understand our present. This is the essential task of every writer. We begin with a series of exercises designed to help students explore their past for stories and then work toward unifying these separate stories into a coherent work of art: the ongoing project of our self-conception.

Memoir vs. Autobiography

A colleague once stood up at a department meeting to ask why memoir is ever taught in schools. "They're just teenagers," she said. "What have they really accomplished?" Apart from the accusatory tone, her question revealed a fundamental misunderstanding of the term *memoir*. The form we're after is not a set of memoirs, such as those written by heads of state or cultural icons like Henry Kissinger or Mikhail Barishnikov. As young people, my students are not looking back over the span of a lengthy life to assess the choices that led them to a ripe old age.

Nor are they trying to account for the sum of their life experiences thus far. We are not writing autobiography, which attempts to capture every significant detail of an individual's life. Instead, as William Zinsser writes in *Inventing the Truth: The Art and Craft of Memoir*, memoir writers "must manufacture a text, imposing narrative order on a jumble of half-remembered events. With that feat of manipulation they arrive at a truth that is theirs alone, not quite like that of anyone else who was present at the same events" (6). The "jumble of half-remembered events" is incomplete, but it is all we have, since, according to Tim O'Brien, "What sticks to memory, often, are those odd little fragments that have no beginning or end" (36). Our formula will be p(arts) + w(holes) = speaker's identity: in other words, we will find the art in parts and the whole amidst holes. There is no pretense to completeness, only snapshots of a whole that is still under construction.

So we start with memory. We do some exercises as a class and students do others independently. I rely on an exercise similar to one I use in my book *Word-playgrounds*. In fact, I use several of the exercises from that book in my creative nonfiction classes because there is considerable overlap between my poetry writing classes and my nonfiction writing classes. (And, for some reason, a great number of poets also write memoir: Nick Flynn, Mary Karr, Annie Dillard, Mark Doty, Donald Hall, just to name a few. I've often wondered if this is because poets who traffic in images are more comfortable with the snapshot shards of memory than with linear history.)

I start with Joe Brainard's *I Remember* as a model. Brainard's book is made up entirely of passages that begin "I remember. . . ." We read some sample lines of memory from his book, and afterward I ask students to write down ten of their most vivid memories, with the fullest possible descriptions. Models help enormously even with short exercises. After listening to some of Brainard's lines, a student who initially wrote "I remember my grandfather's weird clothes" revised to "I remember my grandfather's polka-dotted bow tie and those argyle socks which he pulled up past his knees." After everyone has a list of ten memories, we share the lists with the class as we listen for patterns of language and image.

One student was so happy with her memory list that she continued to work on it as a whole piece unto itself. It eventually became a section of her memoir:

Je Souviens

I remember how I first came to study French. My neighbor was a year ahead of me and taking before-school French class, and I was too young to walk to school alone. I tagged along, even though before-school language classes didn't start until the second grade. His name was Chip and he was my first friend I made upon moving to Wilmette when I was three.

I remember we would meet up outside his house and walk along Lake Avenue together. I remember one day passing a house between 6th and 7th street with dilapidated window shutters and an overgrown lawn.

I remember seeing a large German shepherd barking from behind the chain link fence. We walked up to talk to the dog just as its owner—a rotund, hairy guy—came out yelling at us in his boxers. I remember we ran away down the block laughing and gasping for breath.

I remember forever calling that house "Boxer Boy's house" and ritually doing a Macarena-inspired dance every time we passed it.

I remember the fallen trees obstructing our path after the great storm of 1998. Always opting for adventure, we climbed between the branches rather than finding an alternate route. I remember the leaf fights and the snowball fights.

I remember passing "Dead Man's Alley." According to the legend we invented, a man was once murdered in this alley between 8th and 9th. He was run over by a car that bore the license plate: "RVR VRV." Naturally, we chanted "R-V-R! R-V-R! V-R! V-R! V-R! V!" every time we passed the cracked pavement of the "crime scene."

I remember waiting at the crosswalk for crossing guard Dorothy to give us the go signal.

I remember waiting outside his classrooms at the end of school. I remember running home; trying to beat our best time.

I remember walking past motion-sensored Halloween decorations that would talk. A skeleton shook his arms at us singing his rendition of "Soul Man" by the Blues Brothers: "I'm a *bone* man, doo-da-doo-doo-doo-doo-da-doo!"

I remember one spring day we stalked a squirrel. Chip threw his red Bulls cap and it was a perfect shot. The hat moved around as the squirrel struggled to break loose. Chip snatched up the hat releasing the squirrel. He made me promise not to tell anyone; he loved that hat and did not want any adults taking it away from him for fear of rabies. I kept his secret because we were best friends. These were the days when he was chubby and I was afraid of the dark. I was convinced that Stephen King's "It" was waiting for me every time I walked to the bottom of my basement stairs. Nearly every day after school we would hang out at his house. I remember sitting in his father's office and watching the VHS of "The Lion, The Witch, and The Wardrobe" while eating a whole roll of Ritz crackers.

I remember playing basketball in his backyard on the wooden hoop he and his grandfather built.

I remember in 4th grade how all of this ended. He left me to take the bus to the middle school, and I had to walk alone.
—Julia, grade 12

This list is full of sharp, sensory details (the unkempt home, the fallen trees, the German shepherd's bark, the children's chanting, the taste of Ritz crackers), and some vivid characters (Chip, who appears more than once; the crossing guard, Dorothy) begin to burst from these lines as well. The piece feels unified by the last line that returns to the beginning detail of walking to school. But my goal with these exercises is not to create complete pieces. Here I am merely planting seeds with student examples of cohesion across memories, often with no conscious attempt to make them interrelate. Being aware of these patterns will be crucial when later we assemble segmented memoirs. Some students end up writing about sports or animals or food (especially in classes held around noon!). Many students make the critical realization that their lists of most important memories change over time, sometimes even day to day. After we have shared our lists and noted patterns, I ask students to expand any three of these memories into page-long scenes in their writer's notebooks. If students can't choose, I tell them to pick the three most emotionally significant memories. The three stories don't need to relate to one another, and we won't do anything more with these stories yet. At this point, we are simply trying to add ingredients to a simmering stew of scenes.

It is important to devote class time to writing and sharing student work in progress, not only as a way to help students get started writing, but also as a fundamental expression of the values of any writing class. So I frequently give students five minutes or so, encouraging them to write as quickly as they can without lifting their pen from the paper. These short, impromptu exercises are similar to what Linda Rief calls "quickwrites," and, according to Rief, such prompts "offer an easy and manageable writing experience that helps students find their voice and develop their confidence" (11). I have no expectation of polished writing here. These exercises are designed as extremely rough first drafts, early attempts at excavating material that may never find its way into longer pieces.

We work on some of these exercises in class, and I offer my students additional writing prompts to explore on their own at home. Some of these were suggested by students who read memoir models in and outside of class. Some of the prompts I've used in recent years include the following:

Memoir Prompts

Lie—One you told (preferably a whopper, but a "white lie" will also work).

Car Trip—The first time you drove, or a trip you were or weren't glad you took.

Music—A song that means something to you. You must associate the song with a place.

Haircut—A memorable haircut of yours.

Mirror—A time you posed in front of the mirror. Write about image vs. self-image.

Imitation—A time someone imitated you or a time you imitated someone else.

Song—A favorite song: what were you doing when you heard it? an anthem or a song you associate with a particular time or event or feeling.

Family pet—Why the pet mattered to you.

Prank calls—Made or received.

Shoes—A pair of shoes you bought that changed the way you viewed yourself.

Transformation—A time you represented yourself in a less than honest way (what you've done, where you live).

Money—A time you had or didn't have money.

Scared/Scary—A time you were frightened or a time you frightened someone.

Religion—A time you were forced to confront your own beliefs or someone else's.

Playground—A strong feeling from a playground—a time you felt confident, left out, victorious, defeated.

Toy—A favorite toy of yours, the games you played with it and the feeling it gave you.

Dolls/Action figures—Your attachment to a particular toy character.

Man/Woman—A time you were judged as acting like a man or a woman; could be the first time you were ever called a man or a woman or ever felt like you were.

Hiding place—Where did you run (where would you run) in an emergency?

Favorite food—Where did you get it, when, who made it.

Moving to a new house/Going on a vacation—How did you feel being away from home/a former home?

Alcohol/Drugs—A time you or someone you know drank or took drugs.

Prayer—A time you found yourself praying or were asked to pray.

Underwear—Yours or someone else's!

Gun/Weapon—This could be a toy or a real weapon. How did you use the weapon or how was it used on you?

Death—This could be a person or a pet; how did you hear?

The color pink—Any time you were aware of this color in nature or on a person.

Teeth—Any time you focused on your teeth or someone else's.

Handshake/Hug/Kiss—Some memorable point of contact: who initiated contact? How did it feel? What went through your mind?

Dancing—What was the occasion? Was there a partner? What were you (or the partner) thinking?

Holiday—Where was it held? Who was there? How was it out of the ordinary?

Hot/Cold—A time you were aware of the air temperature—or the emotional temperature of a scene.

Rumor—Who spread the rumor? How did it start? What were the consequences?

Questions—I stole this idea from Scott Russell Sanders. I ask students to name the ten questions that are most on their minds and to write them down without answering them. We look at these questions later in the year. According to Sanders, if the questions change, this should tell you something about yourself, and if they stay the same all year long, that should also tell you something about yourself.

Future me—To reinforce the idea of personae, I have students write letters (or sometimes those questions) to their future selves. A website started at Yale University stores and sends these letters as emails back to the sender in whatever amount of time you suggest. For the sake of class discussion, I ask the whole class to agree on a date and then we talk about the degree to which our concerns have stayed constant.

While I certainly don't attempt to solicit such information from my students, there have been occasions when students volunteer information about abuse. If a student tells me he or she drank a beer a couple of years earlier, I do not feel compelled to call a substance abuse counselor. In those cases, I act only as a reader. But as a state reporter, I know it is my obligation to refer clear abuse cases to social service agencies. My first step is always to talk with students, to let them know I am concerned about their welfare, to make sure I haven't misinterpreted what they've written, and to let them know that I'm attempting to help them by making my referrals. I'll never forget what one student told me a few years ago. Stephanie was being physically abused at home by a parent with a drug and alcohol addiction. Even though she clearly had loads of talent, her grades were poor and she was filled with self-loathing. How could school assignments possibly compete with her harrowing home life? Writing about her situation, she later told me, allowed her to be the hero and not the victim of her troubled family situation. I don't know if writing saved her, but it certainly gave her a new perspective on her situation.

Sometimes these story-scenes come from memories that have long remained dormant; other times they are stories that, as Tobias Wolff describes in *This Boy's Life*, "are recounted until they become legend. The Time Danny Got Hit in the Wallet. The Time Patrick Got His Shoe Shot Off" (11). Whatever the story's source, here we are after *scenes*—expanded, dramatic moments occurring in a particular time and place—like those we practiced in earlier essays.

The ingredients of these stories will come from sensory description such as that found in the sense of place essays, vivid characters like those in the writer's autobiographies, and specific moments such as those found in haibun.

Most important of all, perhaps, is *voice*—the attitude of the writer toward his or her subject. Researcher Don Graves calls voice "the imprint of ourselves on our writing" (*Writing* 227). Voice is the quality that makes our description of an event unique, distinct even from those of other witnesses to the event. It is critical that students have the chance to speak in different voices. In writing, as in life, we are severely limited if we speak in a monotone, with a single attitude toward the world. People who are relentlessly sunny are often boring; people who are unceasingly negative are usually too gloomy to tolerate. These pieces should encourage students to explore the full palette of their emotions and to adjust their attitudes to the topics at hand.

As we share responses in class, I encourage students to remember all the storytelling tools we've worked on and to keep them in mind as they write. Here are some examples of student stories that grew out of these early exercises.

Mistakes

"Lamb number one, get over here!" screamed Mrs. DaSilva.

"I'm here. I was using the washroom," I said.

"We don't have time for your potty breaks, Miss Lavinia!"

"I'm sorry; I'll hold it next time."

With only three weeks left until the Christmas play, Mrs. DaSilva, my music teacher, was on the edge of a nervous breakdown. I was not her first choice to be "lamb number one" but her rule of "first come, first serve" came back to bite her in the butt. I had chosen to be "lamb number one" simply because I wanted to be

Number One. I had not realized that I would have the most lines in the play out of all five lambs. Mrs. DaSilva tried to contain her annoyance while helping me memorize my four lines but soon gave up. She passed me over to Mrs. Araujo, my second grade teacher, who was more experienced and who actually liked me.

All I cared about was my costume, an oversized sack of white cushiony fluff with a hood and ears and white tights. During long, boring dress rehearsals I would curl up in my costume and sleep in a corner. Only to be awakened by Mrs. DaSilva's deafening voice screaming, "Lamb number one! Do you think this is a game?" I never understood why I had to watch the whole play. My part was over right after scene one. How did my being up benefit the other kids rehearsing?

I was able to amuse myself during the painfully long hours in which everyone perfected their parts. Some of my wanderings led to accidents. I once got a splinter in my hand so I went up to the nurse's office and asked Mrs. Sheffield to take it out for me. Her soft voice welcomed me and she painlessly removed the splinter. I tried to delay going back down to the rehearsal by complaining that my hand still hurt. I found myself purposely running my hands along the wooden stage to get a splinter so that I could go and visit Mrs. Sheffield. Mrs. D caught on after I acquired a third splinter that same week. She told me to stop hurting myself because my hand would soon be poisoned by the splinters and could turn into wood. Not wanting to look like Captain Hook I stopped having "little accidents" and I endured the dreadful rehearsals.

On opening night Mrs. DaSilva was more aggravated than usual. I stayed as far away from her as possible so that I would not cause the destruction of the play. It was seven o'clock when the performance began. Blinding lights filled my eyes and I started sweating. The orchestra started to play and I waited stiff as a doorknob to say my line. Then I yelled out, "Where is the baby in the manger?" during what I thought was the end of the song but turned out to be only a pause. With an evil smile on her face Mrs. DaSilva shook her head and mouthed, "Not yet!" My face turned beet red and I tried to hide my face inside the cushions of white fluff of my hood. After that moment I only looked at Mrs. DaSilva and waited for my cue. Besides my mistake everyone was "perfect." The play was a success, even though Mrs. D never produced or directed another school play again.
—Lavinia, grade 12

This essay offers a strong voice and a great sense of character. The central conflict is with Mrs. DaSilva, a memorable villain who supplies the author with some terrific details, such as the gothic description of the threat of a wooden hand. As in the earlier essays, this story also offers another trademark of effective memoir scenes: the presence of a two-headed narrator, the younger voice (with a genuine fear of developing a wooden hand) and the older, wiser voice of the speaker (who uses the quotation marks around "little accidents"). Dialogue situates the action right away, and the story's focus—the tension of the "big" performance—is maintained throughout.

When students are having trouble focusing their stories, I suggest starting with dialogue to eliminate any unnecessary lead-up to the story. Again I remind students to avoid what Wallace Stegner called "front porch," or superfluous exposition, rather than jumping right in with the main event. Opening with dialogue occurring in the moment is the best cure I know.

While this next piece doesn't start with dialogue, the speaker avoids lead-up by opening with the main scene of the essay: a Jewish family attending a family Christmas party.

Christmakah

Here I am at yet another family Christmas Eve party. We celebrate at my grandparents' house in Kansas City. This may seem strange because my family is Jewish, as are most of the guests in attendance. Let me answer your questions now. Both of my parents *are* completely Jewish and we do celebrate Chanukah.

I've been attending this party for my entire life, and every year is exactly the same. The Kansas Cityans enter in Noah's Ark fashion: two by two. Patti and Leonard are always the first to arrive. Leonard is a tall man who always comes dressed in a very expensive holiday sweater with a crisp white shirt poking up around his neck. Patti is by his side and has wrapped her body in countless chinchillas to keep warm in the temperate Kansas climate. After Leonard tries to convince me President Bush is Jesus' best friend and Patti accidentally plants rouge on my face, we awkwardly smile and engage in small talk over the chopped liver loaf, struggling to keep our conversation afloat.

I greet the rest of the couples individually. Each year they all tell me I've grown another foot; which makes me 18 ft tall. Can someone say self-esteem booster?

After I shake hands and am roped in for hugs and polite kisses, I nod and smile while the guests confuse me with talk about Kansas City sports. During these conversations all of my attention is focused on trying to remember their names. One woman, whose name has surprisingly escaped me, let's call her Betty, tells me each year that she remembers me from when she met me when I was two and living in London. Every year Betty utters her lines, verbatim, "You were so young; it's ok if you don't remember me." This is extremely kind of her to not expect me to remember her name from the year I was being potty trained. I do, however, find it odd that she somehow forgets that she has re-met me every year since that infamous day in London circa 1991.

Once all of Noah's party animals have made their way onboard, the party is sure to get rockin'. This is done with a dinner full of contradictions. Let me remind you again, most of the guests are Jewish, but we all put that aside, sit down at the Christmas decorated table, many in Christmas Sweaters, and have our classic gentile dinner of: latkes, brisket and noodle kugel. The meal is being served by three gentile Kansas Cityans, one of whom is a Reverend who knows the true meaning of love. It's "commitment."

From the table we can see into the living room where the famed Christmas tree stands, or rather leans, alone. Even the tree seems to be a member of the Jewish tribe as it stands at a soaring 4 ft tall which makes it appear more like a Chanukah bush. And if you squint really hard in this room of contradictions you can actually see the Menorah in the corner crying. And we all know those tears are sure to last eight full days.

—Henry, grade 12

This hilarious essay reads to me like the work of a young David Sedaris. Henry, who went on to study improv comedy in college, also has a comic's sense of punch lines, puncturing the turgid words of his relatives with droll interior observations at the end of paragraphs (e.g., "self-esteem booster" and the true meaning of love being "commitment"). This is another species of the two-headed narrator, the public and private voices we rely on in uncomfortable situations. The essay is self-deprecating and beautifully recounts the sense of being a young captive at a family holiday party, bouncing from one adult to the next and always at their mercy. Yet this author recognizes life as performance, and he seems to have come to the conclusion that he is strolling among a wacky throng of street performers, each doing his or her own holiday schtick. The chopped liver loaf, a Jewish delicacy, seems to feel as out of place as the author; so too the weeping Menorah. The choice to write in the present tense is interesting and gives the piece an extra sense of immediacy. I think it's important to let students see funny essays as well as serious ones; it's a mistake to privilege confessional writing over comedy. (After all, Samuel Beckett once wrote that tragedy was only under-written comedy.) As teachers we should be open to multiple voices and we should encourage students to choose the voice that best suits the subject matter they wish to explore.

Ava

Patiently waiting, I sat on my fuzzy, pink rug changing my Barbies' outfits. Even at twelve, they maintained the same allure as they had so many years ago. As I secretly took the rest down from their proud display on my bedroom shelves, I contemplated the storyline for that particular day. Would I march them down runways? Drive them around in their convertible? Maybe they'd host parties in their Barbie Dream House? The options were limitless. But on that particular afternoon, I was eagerly awaiting a visit from my real life Barbie.

"She's here!" I yelled as I ran downstairs to open the door. The view of the sunshine yellow, Volkswagen Bug always brought a smile to my face. Getting out of her car with open arms, she exclaiming, "There's my teenager!" I ran into her arms and took in the familiar sweet, citrus perfume. Without a doubt, that smell alone announced the arrival of my favorite aunt, Ava.

Unlike other aunts, she never had me call her Aunt, or Auntie. Her name was Ava and that is what she wanted to be called. "Aunt just sounds so old!" she would complain if the name ever slipped out. Ava was a lot of things, but old she was not. Being sixteen years younger than my dad and nine years older than myself, Ava and I had always had a close relationship.

Like always, that afternoon Ava stood with a poise and beauty that not even Barbie could match. Unlike my curly, brown hair, Ava's straight, blonde locks would softly hit her back as she walked. Her blue eyes were accented by her long, mascara-ed lashes and her California glow remained flawless. Being at the peak of puberty, my pale complexion only glowed when acne creams were caked onto my pimpled face. When she smiled, her glossed lips slowly separated to reveal a blinding, white smile. At the time, my mouth glittered of thick, wired braces. Even with her model-like, tall and slender stature, Ava managed to have a great, perky bosom that jutted out of her low cut shirts. At twelve, I anxiously stuffed my training bras with tissues; but I never achieved quite the same effect. Ava was a goddess.

I could still smell Ava's perfume on me now even after I had hugged her. Before I could say another word, the passenger door of Ava's yellow Bug opened. A girl with a spunky short hairdo and artsy black glasses got out of the car. "You must be Alice!" she exclaimed as she opened her arms and gave me a big hug. This hug was not like Ava's. Her wool, turtleneck sweater scratched against my neck as I breathed in what smelled more like smoke than perfume. I smiled back and greeted her, excited that I would finally meet one of Ava's friends, yet disappointed that I would not be spending as much time with her. Ava finally announced, "Alice, I want you to meet Sarah...."

That night as the family sat down to eat dinner, Sarah's presence brought a clear, unspoken disruption in what was usually our time with Ava. After all, it was Ava that did most of the talking, telling us about the various equal rights protests that were going on back at school. Sarah just sat there, dazingly staring at Ava as she told her stories. Later, as I went around picking up the plates of scraped cheesecake remnants, I uncomfortably fixed my eyes on Sarah firmly holding Ava's hand under the dinner table. Although she had not said more than a few words that night, my stomach dropped as I began to question whether there was a greater purpose for Sarah's mysterious visit. Bringing the plates to the kitchen, I overheard Ava speak what shortly proved to be seven, deadly words, "There is something you all should know...."

My short legs now furiously ran up the same stairs that they had eagerly staggered down only hours earlier. I was finally able to silence my family's yelling and crying from downstairs by loudly slamming my bedroom door shut. This was un-lady-like behavior that I knew would have ordinarily been punished, however, at the time, I knew that my unruly behavior was the least of my family's worries. I wiped away my streaming tears and kicked over the Barbies I had been playing with on my pink rug. "A Lesbian?" I thought to myself as I looked at the marital Barbie beds inside my Barbie Dream House. They had never made a Barbie and Barbie duo, it was always Barbie and Ken.

At twelve, my parents had touched on the concept of gay people; however, I had never actually known a gay person, let alone been related to one. My image of a lesbian was a short, chubby middle aged woman with a buzzed haircut, dressed in men's clothing. Definitely not Ava.

Hearing the steady clicks of heels going up the stairs I dove into my bed and under the safety of my fuchsia, velvet covers. The door squeaked open and the angry voices from downstairs could be heard again. The door shut to a welcoming silence and a soft voice that said, "Alice?" I didn't even breathe. My quiet room echoed with every click of her heels as she made her way to my bed. "Please come out from under there," she gently urged as I felt her weight on my bedside. That was the last thing I wanted to do: look her in the eye. Her voice quivered, "You know, this only changes things between us if you let it."

"How dare she," I thought, "How dare she make it seem like I have control over the situation. If it were up to me, she would be normal again, like the rest of my family." My head darted from under my covers with my mouth open to fire, "If I let them? Things will only change if I let them? Ava, I don't even know you anymore." Her mascara had run down her wet cheeks, as she cried quietly with poise. Her watery blue eyes sparkled as graceful tears streamed down her perfect face. She seemed almost peaceful in this pain stricken silence.... I was not. "Say something!" I shouted, "You're supposed to make everything better!" She said nothing and instead embraced my sobbing body and calmed me with her sweet, citrus smell. We sat there crying in each other's arms, surrounded by my toppled Barbies.

—Alice, grade 12

This essay has terrific sensory details—the itchy sweater, Ava's "sweet, citrus smell," the visual descriptions of her aunt and her aunt's partner. The author deftly inserts her own age into the opening lines. The final detail here is especially wonderful. Not only does it end the scene, but it also beautifully represents the speaker's own crestfallen emotions over the collapse of her narrow and naïve childhood world. A more mature perspective emerges with the final description of her beloved aunt crying with "poise," her "graceful tears" running down her face. The author's admiration for her aunt is obvious.

This scene features a number of conflicts—family, femininity, independence, growing up, accepting difference, to name a few, which is why I use it in the Memoir Outline Sheet discussed later (see pp. 87–88). I comment on these early essays as individual stories, but I always have my eye on the ultimate goal: a segmented memoir.

The next example is interesting for its stylistic choices and for its comedy.

Welcome to the Nation's Capital

Glencoe, Illinois

I mean my ankle hurt, but I didn't need a wheelchair.

"Yeah, it's definitely swelling up." It definitely wasn't swelling up. Mr. Barry, my 8th-grade volleyball coach, had mistaken my fankles[1] (fat ankles) for swelling, a common error. Partly because I didn't feel like practicing anymore, and partly because I wanted the kid to feel bad, I sat out of the rest of practice. The kid who injured me, Edmund (not his real name, but he could be an Edmund), didn't show any signs of remorse; in fact, he said it was my fault and I shouldn't have stepped on his ankle. Denial is a weak defense mechanism—especially if you're dead wrong. Everyone knows you're not supposed to put your foot under the net when the person on the other side of the net goes up for a spike. Call it one of the unwritten rules of volleyball. Well, I went up for a spike, got all of five inches off the ground, and maybe much to your surprise allowed enough time for Edmund to get under my feet, and I landed there. Twisted ankle.

When practice was over, I got up, scratch that, I tried to get up, and then realized I couldn't. Mr. Barry and my best friend Todd, more commonly known as Beefcake, man-child, or Gilbert, slung me on their shoulders and took me outside to Mr. Barry's car. It was the middle of February, tail end of winter, but the tail end of winter in Chicago feels like someone is constantly holding a hair dryer to your face, shooting out 32 degree air.

So, I was a little cold. I had never been in a teacher's car before. It was kind

---

1. There has been a little confusion over my use of the word fankles. Many people have come up to me and told me I've used the wrong word here, that I should use the word "cankles." Let me clarify the difference, because there is a difference. Cankles occur when one's calf and ankles are impossible to tell apart, fankles occur when one just has fat ankles, but a definite break between calf and ankle.

of a surreal feeling. I was of the age when I was under the impression that teachers did not have lives out of school. Mr. Barry, driving his 1995-ish Ford Explorer, listening to Rage Against the Machine, tapping his hands to the beat, seemed anything but . . . teacherly.

After the two-minute drive to my house, Mr. Barry helped me out of the car and walked me up to my door. I'm only 14 and don't have a key to my house, so I ring the doorbell until someone answers. Much to my surprise, my two 80-year-old grandparents from Long Island come to the door. It shouldn't have surprised me; my mom and dad told me they were going out of town for their 25th wedding anniversary. I guess it just slipped my mind.

"Oh my god," my grandmother said.

Wait. To understand my grandmother, lovely woman that she is, you have to have, let's call them benchmarks. She's a mixture of Mike Meyers's character from "Coffee Talk" (there is actually an ongoing rumor in our family that she is the inspiration for the character, a claim she will strawngly deny) and George's mother from *Seinfeld*. My dad says if you put Nana Shirley in a room with anyone, you've got yourself a sitcom.

"It's nothing, grandma. How are you?" I give her my customary European-style greeting, two kisses on each side.

Mr. Barry is still standing in the doorway, and is either in shock from the inordinate amount of makeup on my Nana and the pound of hair spray which gives her a kind of Jew fro, or is just unsure about what he should be doing, probably the latter. I thank Mr. Barry for all his help and tell him I'll see him tomorrow for history. "Oh yeah, and is there any homework?" I know there's no homework, but I think it makes me look good in front of my grandparents.

"No," Mr. Barry said, as he walked toward his car.

My grandparents are happy to see me, and as you might expect, my grandmother is a little hysterical about my ankle, but it's nothing I can't handle for the weekend. Not this weekend, genius. You're going to Washington. How could I forget about the most anticipated event of my middle school career—the trip to the Nation's Capital?

Washington, DC

Our first stop was the national mall. Originally created around the same time our country was, it became a place for protestors to collect and for new ideas to be heard. About a 10-minute walk from end to end, the Mall is a beautiful National Park (actually a *National* Park), lined with 2,000 American elms and 3,000 Japanese cherry trees. Oh, yeah, and it's one kick-ass place to test out your new-found love of wheelchair racing. My wheelchair buddies and I raced the length of the mall. In retrospect a juvenile activity at best, and realistically a disgrace to the National monument. And if that offends you, please skip to the next section.

Arlington National Cemetery sees 4 million people walk through its gates each year to view various national figures. War heroes, former Presidents, and American visionaries like Thurgood Marshall. Not a place one would expect to see a wheelchair race. Well, to be honest, it wasn't a wheelchair race, it was more a wheelchair ride.

After seeing the changing of the guard at the tomb of the unknown soldier, a somber and elaborate ritual,[2] Gilbert wants to jump on the back of my wheelchair, just hitch a ride down the fairly steep and more than a little wind-y hill. After a few minutes of Gilbert's persistent badgering, persuasive aggressiveness and a few tries going down the hill myself, I give in. Without much of a warning, Gilbert jumps on the back of the wheelchair and almost tips the chair over backwards. Instead the chair starts moving down the hill, slowly at first but quickly picking up speed. I find myself going faster than expected, and having to avoid rocks and sticks (I don't know if all wheelchairs are like this, but mine had a lever brake on each wheel you had to "activate" to steer). After I nearly over-use the brake, lose control of my vehicle and tailspin out of control, the ride is over.

Gilbert rolls me up the next hill, all the way discussing our little ride down the hill, and despite his lobbying for one more ride, I refuse.

Just as I take in the beautiful landscape of Northern Virginia, the rolling hills and plush green trees, just as we can see the exit, and in the distance the familiar monuments of DC across the Potomac, Linda, an insanely gorgeous girl abruptly jumps on the back of my wheelchair.

"You got to get off. I don't think you realize what you're doing."

"Shut up. I saw you and Gilbert do it two seconds ago."

Gilbert and I did do it two seconds ago, but that path was void of people, this one not so much. All of our classmates and the six adult chaperones occupied the hill. Objects of mass I would soon need to navigate myself around at an ever-increasing velocity.

"Seriously Linda, this is something I think you will regret. . . ."

"What are you, a pansy?"

Here's what I remember:[3] So I'm flying down this hill. This hill, that happens to be surrounded by the bodies of some of the most important people in American history, holy land if you will. But to me at the moment, it's a hill. A hill with a slope steep

---

2. The Tomb Guard marches 21 steps down the black mat behind the Tomb, turns, faces east for 21 seconds, turns and faces north for 21 seconds, then takes 21 steps down the mat and repeats the process. After the turn, the sentinel executes a sharp "shoulder-arms" movement to place the weapon on the shoulder closest to the visitors to signify that the sentinel stands between the Tomb and any possible threat. Twenty-one was chosen because it symbolizes the highest military honor that can be bestowed—the 21-gun salute. http : / /www. arlingtoncemetery.orgkeremonies /sentinelsotu. html

3. There are about fifty versions of what happened but all seem a little too glorified to me. This is the least sexy version of the event.

enough that it's gonna make the wheels on my chair go faster, and in turn make me go faster. It's kind of fun, but really it's scary. I'm dipping and dodging everything in sight, from Mr. Rosenberg (whose voice I can hear calling "What the hell are you doing with that damned wheelchair!"), to rocks. Rocks the size of baseballs scattered across the road. It was a rock that did me in.

I veer a little right to avoid some kid, and bam—I am on a direct course for a head-on collision with a, let's say good-sized rock. I try to avoid it by quickly using my left brake; I used it a little too hard. At about the same time that the wheelchair started to tailspin and tip, the right tire hit the rock sending me out of the chair, launching me down the hill.

I've been told anywhere from one to five seconds. One to five seconds in the air that is, flying, arms flailing, and bracing myself for impact with the ever-approaching concrete. I stuck the landing like a pro, went straight into a body roll down the hill, and came away from it with a jammed finger and a gigantic bump on the head. [4] Linda abandoned ship as soon as she realized the impending doom we faced, and I don't think she had a scratch on her body, none visible at least (and I thought I should've been allowed to verify that fact, for all the damage she put me through).

Mr. Rosenberg, more commonly called Rosy, was pissed. Actually I would have welcomed pissed, I think it was more along the lines of extremely livid. Linda got the brunt of his tantrum, but I had a few particles of spit projected my way. After his ten-minute rant to us, with the whole eighth-grade class looking on, we received no punishment, just the title of "stupidest fucking kids on the earth."[5]

Dinner at the Hard Rock Café was generic. Everyone got cheeseburgers, fries and a drink for everyone (except for the kosher kids who got hamburgers, they can't mix meat and dairy). To make dinner a little less generic some of us guys armed with our 8th-grade maturity level thought it would be a good idea to buy condoms from the condom-stall in the bathroom. Some kids would take them out of their wrappers and toss them on the floor. Others would put the condoms over their mouth and blow them up like balloons. The bravest, or dumbest, kids would go up to a girl, give her a little nudge, hand her the condom and give a wink. The fourteen-year-old male does not have fully developed mating techniques.
—Eric, grade 12

This essay is pure voice—cocky, smart-alecky, and genuinely funny. In these stories, you can hear the literary influence of Dave Eggers, whom we'd been

---

4. Ask me and I'll show it to you.

5. I think I should add that Rosy was in no way verbally abusive, or physically abusive to any of his students. He just let one F-bomb slip in the heat of the moment. As he put it, "If you two numbskulls got hurt, it's my ass." So you can see where the guy's coming from. And I wouldn't be doing Rosy service if I didn't mention that he was a great teacher.

reading: the funny footnotes, the direct address. Part of the humor also results from the distance between the fourteen-year-old boy learning to speak what he calls "the language of men" and the older, wiser perspective of someone who can't save his younger self from the antics he carries out. It's hard not to find this author's voice charming, just as it's difficult to imagine a teacher who would want to accompany this kid on a class trip!

A final note with this piece: it turns out this author is the brother of the girl who writes an exploratory essay about a serious addiction in their family (see Chapter 10 for the exploratory essay). I have no doubt Eric could have written a moving piece about the addict in his family, just as his sister did. I also have no doubt that he cares about his family member just as much. But while certain issues may dominate our lives, they don't have to define us or the way we present ourselves to the world. It's important for students to choose their subject matter and their voice in all their writing.

I offer one last example of individual memoir scenes. This following essay was originally used by the author as a college admissions essay. It also ultimately served as the opening scene in her segmented memoir.

Mirror

Emily was sad. Suddenly Emily was very sad. As I sat quietly dissecting my memory for an instance, a moment, a sign, a paramedic sat down beside me. "Your big sister Emily needs to go away for awhile," he said. "Your parents will explain later, but your sister is very sad and needs help." He peered down at me, his eyes barely viewing the world beyond his enormous potbelly. He looked at me as if I didn't understand. But it was he who didn't understand, he who clearly knew nothing about Emily.

Emily was my idol. Always smiling, she possessed the patience and understanding required to sooth my many childish fears. I remembered the time I ran, crying, into her room only minutes after my bedtime. The monsters under my bed and inside my closet had scared me and I sought the one person I knew could help. Emily reminded me that monsters were afraid of flowers and seemed shocked by the fact that I had overlooked this widely accepted fact. We covered my room with flowers collected from all over the house. But there was one thing, Emily told me, that would for sure keep monsters at bay. Her pink and white, cloth, hand-held, flower-patterned mirror. A monster's worst nightmare. I fell asleep clutching this mirror. How could I have forgotten? Monsters hate flowers.

The words depression, suicide, and self-mutilation had been quickly integrated into my vocabulary. Emily was sent away where she was to receive the help she needed. I didn't understand why she needed help at all. Emily was smart, funny, pretty, and happy. She gave me advice, helped me with my homework, and was always willing to play another round of "Stuffties," a very complex game involving every single one of my 72 stuffed animals.

It was on the phone that I gradually came to understand that Emily was sick. Unable to mask her pain, she seemed angry and was always crying. She knew I didn't understand what had happened or why she was so far away which led her to repeat into the receiver, "It's not your fault.... It's not your fault.... It's not your fault."

I went to visit Emily one year for Thanksgiving. When she was not tired from her medication or scheduled for a therapy session, it was like it used to be. She was still my big sister and we interacted as if we were at home again, laughing and playing Stuffties. But there was something hidden. Emily often stared at the wall, deep in thought. She looked away when I spoke to her, not for lack of interest, but because something else was clearly on her mind. This something she explained to me the night before I left. It had lived with her as a child. She tried to hide it from all of us in her perfect grades, numerous boyfriends, and successful athletic career. But it was still there. Always. Her senior year of high school she began to lose control of it. It consumed her and eventually swallowed her which led to the night of her breakdown. It lived inside her, tormenting her like a demon. Like a monster.

When I returned home from that visit, I sent Emily that flower-patterned mirror. She called me later that week, crying, but not for the inescapable sadness she had felt for two years, but for the memories of a time when I, too, was haunted by monsters. We laughed for hours, remembering all the bracelets we made, the trips we took, the times we got in trouble. Though the monsters she fought could not be vanquished by clutching a flower-patterned mirror, Emily was reminded of a better time and the feelings she and her little sister once shared.

There is hope for those who struggle with monsters. And if I ever feel as if something lurks within my closet, Emily is always there to remind me that monsters hate flowers.

—Virginia, grade 12

The short, child-like sentences in this essay create an effective two-headed narrator: both the frightened young sister and the more mature perspective she gains later are present in this piece. This enables Virginia to show the terror and the gradual understanding she achieves of her sister's frightening and mysterious ailment.

In choosing a unifying theme for the memoir, Virginia might have focused on her role in the family or her relationship with her sister. But, when she later looked back and realized she had written several short scenes about divorce, she decided that family separation was the common thread in her memoir. She ended up calling her memoir "Separated." Emily, who leaves the author in this opening segment, turns out to be an anchoring presence as the author's family undergoes a divorce. Divorced families, a student once suggested, all lead segmented lives; often two houses and two different family stories emerge even as the families struggle to find unity and stability.

Before I show how segmented memoirs are constructed, let's consider how memoir scenes build on one another to form a coherent memoir. The next example features the opening two parts of a memoir called "Setting My Sights." The title is clever, suggesting both direction—the author struggling to see where he is going—and also gun sights, which are featured in both of these pieces.

Setting My Sights

Michigan

The porch creaked as I slowly made my way out the sliding door. My grandfather's two cats scurried by my legs, startling the congregation of hummingbirds gathered around the bird feeder. I loved watching the hummingbirds, trying unsuccessfully to count how many times their wings moved up and down in a minute. But right now I could not be distracted; something magnificent had caught my eye.

At the end of the porch, covered by young spruce trees, I saw my grandfather's "dog house." The little wooden building housed everything my grandfather truly appreciated in his old age: his guns and his tobacco. "What's in Grandpa's dog house?" I asked my mother. "Nothing that concerns a five-year-old boy." But I knew she was wrong. It was everything that concerned me. I needed to know what was in that room. What made my grandfather retreat to this building? I had to find out, so I crept slowly toward the door.

The giant red door was heavy. My little arms strained as I slowly forced it into submission. The odors of pipe tobacco and cigar smoke filled my senses as I entered my grandfather's forbidden room of solitude. On the far wall, immediately catching my gaze was a shining, polished oak gun cabinet which housed my grandfather's impressive arsenal. Smoke still rose from the ashtray in magnificent, pearly white curls as I made my way past the *Sports Illustrated* swimsuit calendar. I arrived in front of the gun cabinet, gazing at the beautifully polished Winchester rifle within. I imagined myself wielding this weapon, killing the villains I saw on Saturday morning cartoons.

As I delved into the endless possibilities, the red door slowly opened as my grandfather entered. I turned around and tried desperately to explain myself. "I was just, ah, I was just . . ." I began with anxious sputters. My grandfather just smiled, his checkered cabby hat covering his graying hair. "Come on, let's get you inside," he said, releasing a sweet smelling puff of tobacco smoke from his mouth. He scooped me up gently into his padded brown overcoat and carried me back to the main house and went back to smoking.

—Ben, grade 12

A two-headed narrator is clear here as the five-year-old narrator takes a masculine mystery tour of his grandfather's secret sanctum sanctorum. Yet the vocabulary (*arsenal, delved, submission*) is quite sophisticated. Even in a short scene, the characters come alive, the mother providing limits for the boy to transgress and the kindly grandfather acting as tour guide. Some terrific details populate this piece—the "pearly white curls" of smoke, the grandfather's "checkered cabby hat"—and Ben's ear for the sound of these phrases is striking. There may even be some unintentional details as well (those young spruce trees that mirror his own youth).

South Carolina

It was hot. And I hated sweating. But how could I say no to firing a real bb gun? Smyth's backyard was filled with potential targets. Garbage cans and discarded trash covered his dirt lot, spattered with dried patches of yellow grass. The long, worn-down wooden fence shielded the small enclosure from any overbearing neighbors who might protest to three kids firing bb guns around their houses. "Ya'll want me to go git it?" Smyth drawled with a devious smile. He already knew the answer. Steven and I were ready.

As he pulled the gun out of his garage, my eyes gleamed. I tapped my finger against the side of my leg, a habit which temporarily quelled my anxiousness. "Watch this," he said. He took aim at the dented garbage can and fired. A loud "ping" made me jump a little, though I was careful not to let Steven see. "Ya, one time I hit that trash can, came back, hit me in the leg," Smyth said.

"I dun wanna hit trash cans. Let's take it up into the tree and hit that stop sign I saw on the way over here," Steven declared.

"Ya," I said in agreement, wondering if I really wanted to fire the gun outside of our realm of privacy in the backyard.

But it was too late; Smyth scaled the tree, grasping the gun tightly as he maneuvered awkwardly up the twisted branches of the ancient oak tree which seemed to guard the entrance to his yard. "A perfect place to shoot intruders into our fortress," I thought to myself.

"Come up here, ya'll," Smyth said. Steven and I climbed up the tree, taking positions around Smyth. "Who wants to shoot?" he asked.

I grabbed the gun forcefully with a look of determination. I wanted to show that a "Chicago boy" could still fire a gun better than anyone in South Carolina. I leaned the gun carefully against the tree branch which twisted around in front of me. I pumped the bb gun forcefully and gazed down the sight at my enemy: the menacing stop sign across the street. I fired. To my relief, a loud "ping" signified that I had hit my mark. I looked down at Steven with a smug grin.

"That's not fair," Steven said, "You leaned it against the tree. A real man holds his own weight."

"Oh ya?" I quickly took aim once again at the stop sign, holding the full weight of the barrel in my left hand. I pumped and fired, waiting for the triumphant "ping." But it never came. As I surveyed the neighborhood, searching for my shot, I could just make out a fractured car windshield half way down the block.

Ben's second piece features a new cast of characters and the recurrence of some imagery found in the first piece (trees, guns). But, while the presence of a gun provides a nice transition between the scenes, it wouldn't be enough to hold the entire memoir together. The scene has changed, from Michigan to South Carolina, and none of the characters except the narrator has returned from the first scene. What theme will hold this memoir together: traveling? coming of age? It could have been either of these, but what ultimately gave this memoir cohesion, Ben said, was the idea of power. Each scene is set in a different location because Ben's family moved around a great deal. Ben felt powerless as the eternal newcomer, the pesky interloper. As he struggles to live within the new parameters of each location, he arrives at an increasingly sharp sense of his own identity. This yearning for power became the basis of his finished segmented memoir.

Building Segmented Memoirs

Rather than ask students to lengthen a scene they have already written, I ask them to make an imaginative leap at this point in writing *segmented essays*. According to Robert Root, segmented essays "juxtapose one item alongside another item so they comment back and forth. . . . [They are built] by accumulation, arranging a series of segments or scenes or episodes so that they add or enrich or alter meaning with each addition" (83–84). Anything students have written in class to date is fair game.

I start by asking students to list the scenes they've liked the most, the ones about which they feel most strongly, and to use this list as a starting point. Here is my assignment sheet:

Assignment: The segmented essay you will write will be 6–10 pages in length, offering several episodes from your life that work as stories unto themselves *and* comment internally on one another. Pay special attention to transitions between sections. These connections do not need to be explicit or chronological. In transitioning between sections, feel free to experiment with imagistic or linguistic connections, but there should also be an overall thematic connection that gives the entire piece unity.

Construction Steps:

1. Brainstorm topics. Reread all the entries in your writer's notebook and consider all the exercises you've written thus far. Do not limit yourself to scenes you've already written. Sometimes previously written scenes will suggest new scenes.

2. Think about why these memories are worth exploring; i.e., why they mean so much to you.

3. Consider the focus of each, telescoping the action to a central event. Make sure to think about conflict in each scene.

In brainstorming topics, I ask students to review not only the scenes they've written but also the fragments they created in shorter exercises as a way to find patterns. Just as we did after the "I Remember" exercise, I invite students to consider the topics and ideas that have preoccupied them throughout our course. Many students are shocked to see that they have written more about a friend or family member or a place than they had imagined. I let them begin to create these connections, making sure that each scene works as an independent unit and, most important, that the scenes interrelate and enrich one another.

At this point, I pass out a crude outline form to help students organize their ideas:

Memoir Outline Sheet

We're working on segmented memoirs, 3–6 scenes from your life that work as discrete stories and as tiles in the service of a larger mosaic. In the spaces below, list some of the scenes you are considering using in your memoir. At the bottom of your list, write down some of the connections you see between these scenes.

For example:

1. Playing with Barbies as a young child
2. The day my aunt announced she was gay

Countined on next page

---

3. Taking ballet lessons

4. My grandmother chasing off a boyfriend

5. Entering and withdrawing from a beauty pageant

6. Playing sports

Possible unifying ideas: Femininity, make-believe vs. the real world, afraid of being lonely

For example:

1. Finding a guitar

2. Playing "house" with all my cousins

3. Playing electric guitar for the first time

4. Car accident on an icy road

5. Playing in a Beatles cover band

6. Fishing with my father in the UP

Possible unifying ideas: Independence, control over my life, discovering who I am—what I care about saving and what I am okay with leaving behind

Now your list:

1.

2.

3.

4.

5.

6.

Your possible unifying ideas:

These scenes are merely tentative and can change as students write. But having students fill out a prewriting list gives them a concrete first step. It helps to have memoir ideas marinade in the writer's mind as he or she composes, and having a list sharpens the focus of writing conferences as well. Once students have a tentative direction, I remind them to think in terms of key scenes—*moments*. I often remind my students about the magical phrase "one day." If they list "camping" as a scene, the piece is likely to be general, but if they can think about camping on that one day when a bear pawed at a tent, or when a cell phone fell in the river, a scene is much more likely to spring to life.

Students have already written several scenes from the warm-up activities at the start of this unit, like those modeled earlier in this chapter. The richest of these usually make their way into the final memoir, though they are usually redrafted with the larger theme in mind. And once students settle on a theme, they usually decide to compose additional scenes to accompany the ones they have already drafted.

In the first example in the memoir Outline Sheet, the scene listed first—playing with Barbies—is too general at this point. The second scene—the one *day* the author's aunt came out—is a sharply focused event and became the scene titled "Ava." (In fact, the author ended up combining both of these ideas in the final version of this episode.)

The essay that grew out of the second example outline appears later in this chapter in a full memoir called "Hello, Goodbye." It's interesting to see which of the pieces in the final memoir survived the editing process. Some, it seems, were cut in deference to the theme.

While students are developing scenes, I remind them to use the story tools we've been practicing—character, conflict, dialogue, sensory description, fresh imagery—to convey these moments. Memoirists prize voice above all these tools. Each scene must work as a discrete unit by itself, but students will also need to find points of connection within the language they've used—recurring characters, images, words. We look at models in class, and I ask students to trade pieces with fellow students for different peer workshops in class, always allowing them to "pass" on public viewings of individual sections if they feel the scenes are too personal. I ask that students share at least one section of their memoir with the whole class or with another student. These peer checks are especially useful for discovering what wider audiences will struggle with and for determining how cohesive the discrete pieces are.

The interrelation of scenes is critical. If the episodes offer no apparent common characters or theme, the essay will feel disjointed and unsatisfying. The memoir should feature a central tension—a father–son conflict, sibling rivalry— or some suggestion of growth across common experiences, such as the dating world or gradually leaving home. In the earlier model "Mistakes," for example, Mrs. DaSilva, the draconian elementary school music teacher, will likely not return in the memoir (unless she appears as a character type or as a reference point, e.g., "my mother was as angry as Mrs. DaSilva"), but Christmas (or holidays more generally), performing, or gaining/losing confidence might be useful threads for braiding this story with others in Lavinia's experience. Creating titles for the overall memoir or the individual scenes can help students create cohesion. Several of the following memoir models came together because of their playful titles.

One other critical suggestion is to reveal the author's age in each scene. (The South Carolina episode in "Setting My Sights," for example, doesn't let readers know how much time has elapsed since the Michigan scene when Ben was five.) Since we are creating essays through juxtaposition rather than through a more linear form such as straightforward chronology, it is vital to let readers know the speaker's age within each scene. Readers are frustrated by an ambiguous sense of time and place, and, of course, we read a first kiss or a fall off a bicycle differently if we think the narrator is eight or eighteen.

Memoir Models

The following memoir excerpt contains three scenes.

This Small Boy's Life

I pointed the gun at the ground and pulled the trigger. Nothing came out. So I pointed it at his midsection and pulled again, thinking the gun was empty. No such luck. Two pellets released simultaneously and hit him square in the stomach.

I had been shooting the airsoft gun outside our cabin, sending tiny plastic yellow pellets at trees and into the forest. When I thought the last pellet had been used (according to the obviously flawed count I had been keeping), I shot at the ground to verify. Then I pointed the gun at one of my eighth-grade campers to see his reaction and have a little fun at his expense. It didn't quite work out the way I planned it.

At the instant of impact I felt that sinking feeling you get in the pit of your stomach when you know you just did something idiotic. But I tried to fight it, to rationally deduce how the situation wasn't as bad as it seemed and how it was going to be okay. I considered it a toy: closer to a Nerf gun than a firearm. I had taken shots from closer distances than that—on bare skin too—so a shot through the tee-shirt couldn't hurt that bad. It probably wouldn't even generate the temporary red mark direct hits left. No, I thought at last, don't kid yourself here, you're eighteen years old and you're a camp counselor. Some Jewish, North Shore mom entrusted her baby with you and this is what you did.

As I walked to lunch, I saw the victim lifting up his shirt to show his friends the mark he now had. They had to lean in and squint just to see it, but I called him over to talk anyway.

"I'm not sure that's the best thing for you to do right now."

He nodded as if he understood and returned to displaying his new war wound. By the time he was telling the third spellbound group, I was keeping a real gun at camp and he was lucky that the bullet only clipped him—it had just stopped bleeding and who knows what would have happened if it was a direct hit.

I still thought there was an outside chance for this to go unnoticed when my unit head called me over for a conversation as I was making my way back from lunch. In my naiveté, I honestly didn't put two and two together to realize what this meeting was about. I thought we were talking about that night's evening activity, which I was helping to plan.

But it soon became apparent that I had some 'splainin' to do. This was my 8th summer at camp. In all that time, I had never caused any trouble. I never skipped activities, was never out after curfew, and never violated the "nothing below the neck" rule pertaining to conduct with the opposite sex. So what was going on now? The camp director and assistant director soon joined my unit heads and me at the table. Both fatherly figures had looks of confusion and disappointment on their faces. They had fired 4 staff members the previous day, but never expected to have this discussion with me.

I couldn't speak. The small tears running down my cheeks grew until my eyes were like water guns spewing a consistent stream.

I said my goodbyes, packed my things while the boys were all playing basketball, and lugged 2 four-foot-long Eastpak duffels to my parents' waiting car. Twelve hours after the incident, I lay in bed at my house, stifling the tears to induce the sleep I knew I would never achieve.

I had felt almost as tiny as the pellet that caused that entire ordeal when I approached the wall. I was overtaken not only by the sheer physical size of the wall, but also by its implications to millions of Jews worldwide. I felt my entire body tingle as I placed the note into an available crevice between the chalkboard-sized bricks. "I pray for peace between the Israelis and the Palestinians."
I was only a seventh grader—a small seventh grader—and each brick seemed taller than me and wide enough that I couldn't jump the length of one, even with a running start. Although the Jerusalem stone had faded from its original golden color, it was the most beautiful sight I had ever seen, structurally and spiritually. My father put his arm around me: "Son, you'll remember this moment for the rest of your life."

"Yup." I knew he was right. I also knew what was coming next, and the terse response was a futile attempt to avoid it.

"I remember the first time I saw the Western Wall...."

After enduring the memory with a smile and apparent interest, I did my best to absorb and preserve the extraordinary scene around me. I wanted to bottle this moment and keep it in my pocket for all eternity. People of all ages from all walks of life gathered in front of the wall. Ultra-orthodox Jews in black hats and wool suits helped more secular Jews to put on the traditional yarmulke (head covering), tallith (prayer shawl), and tefillin (phylacteries) for the first time in their lives.

I watched them wind the leather straps around their arms one, two, three, four, five, six, seven times. And I promised myself that I would return to the wall on at least that many occasions. The next time I felt this small and insignificant was my sophomore year, when I was on the varsity wrestling team.

"New Trier, one-nineteen," came the voice of the opposing coach from inside the locker room.

I walked up to the scale, trying to appear comfortable and confident. I was neither, and it showed.

"You're OK."

I exhaled, I had made weight, and that was the first part of the battle. All I had to do now was beat the guy on the other team.

"Wheeling, one-nineteen."

I would have soiled myself when I saw him, except for the fact that I was naked for weigh-ins. This kid looked a lot like the original Terminator. His deltoids had deltoids. If that wasn't enough, when he stepped onto the scale I couldn't help but notice the huge eagle spreading its wings across his rippling back. Was it even legal for someone in high school to have a tattoo?

Sitting in the locker room changing into my singlet—the leotard that is our excuse for a uniform—my entire body trembled with fear. Sensing that the lone sophomore on varsity seemed nervous before his first match, our senior 130 pounder approached me. Mike was a prankster, and the sentence he uttered then was the most serious one I ever heard from him: "At first I thought I was going to have to wrestle that guy, but then I looked at him again and realized that he was way too big."

I couldn't concentrate on warm-ups because every minute or so I would catch a glimpse of the remarkable physical specimen I was about to wrestle and start shaking again. I bumped into one teammate as I was shuffling to my left while the rest of my teammates were shuffling right; when they were jogging backwards I was skipping forwards and tripped over another.

I talked to my coaches, my dad, and the other wrestlers on the team in the time before the match. They all told me the same thing. It wasn't a bodybuilding contest, and I should just go out there, wrestle my best, and have fun. What I expected was far from fun, probably a lot closer to a massacre. Since our team had no wrestlers in the 103 or 112 pound weight classes, my match was first. I lumbered towards the center of the mat and reached out for the customary handshake. It felt like my hand was being reduced to shards of bone and loose pieces of skin. He finally released it. The ref blew his whistle and I prepared for the beating of a lifetime.

The match met my expectations to the letter. After a few short moments wiping the mat with my face and generally having his way with me, the referee mercifully called it a pin, ending the match. "Welcome to varsity," my coach said as I peeled my lifeless body off the mat.

—Keith, grade 12

The title of this memoir self-deprecatingly plays off Tobias Wolff's memoir *This Boy's Life*. The scenes themselves are full of lively voice and clear conflicts. At times the author seems unsure of himself and adds explicit transition markers to ensure his readers will see how the scenes are related. At the beginning of the second section, for example, he writes, "I had felt almost as tiny as the pellet . . ." when he approaches the Western Wall in Jerusalem. But a description of the enormous wall would already lead us to that conclusion. The first scene is so resonant that the note of ignominy hangs in the air even as we move on to the next story. Or the author might have opened with the "prayer for peace," a direct contrast to the belligerence he shows in the opening story. But this is merely fine-tuning. The stories themselves are terrific and together convey a clear sense of the author's personality and persona.

Before moving on, I'd like to make a point about unity. I have included only three scenes from Keith's memoir here, but the pieces as they currently appear don't yet feel unified. Each includes a reference to size, and Keith's father appears in all three scenes (albeit largely as a background character), but the overall theme is not yet clear, partly because the third scene occurs three years before he wrote this memoir. Usually the final scene in segmented memoirs is closest to the present, where that older, wiser voice can offer some perspective on the preceding scenes. But even more, the lack of unity results from the absence of a clearly governing theme. Physical stature alone doesn't provide the cohesion that could be achieved by focusing on emotional strength and the responsibilities that must inevitably accompany power. This wisdom, later scenes suggest, is gained in part through the larger presence of Keith's father.

The next piece is one that appeared as an example outline in the Memoir Outline Sheet.

Hello, Goodbye

"I don't know why you say goodbye, I say hello"—The Beatles

My sister and I dug around the small attic-like space that lay in-between our rooms, our secret room. To get to it you had to crawl to the back of a crowded closet and through a small square hole in the wall barely big enough to fit a small child. It was full of fascinating junk. As I was fishing through the piles of photo albums, canes, and dusty files I saw something bright red shining from the depths of the junk. I pulled it out and dusted it off. It was a red VOX electric guitar. Besides being dirty, it seemed to be in good shape. I stared at the various knobs and switches in amazement. I didn't know anyone in my family had ever even played guitar. I crawled back out to the hallway with my new treasure.

"Dad! Dad! Look what I found." I yelled as I ran down to his office. He sat at his desk in his big leather chair. He turned and lowered his head to look at me through the top part of his bifocals.

"My old VOX guitar. I had completely forgotten about it." My dad took the guitar and tried to play something. The noise that came out sounded like a bucket of nails falling down a metal staircase. He then started to tune it. I stared as he masterfully turned the chromed tuning knobs and the pitches of the strings slowly stretched into position.

"Dad, how are you doing that? Can you teach me?"

"Hold on, I'm just tuning it."

The curves of the bright red wood and the silver accents in my dad's hands made him look like a rock star. Once it was in tune, my dad handed it back to me. I held the guitar but I had no idea what to do. The instrument felt alien in my hands. My dad told me that VOX was the company that made the amplifiers that the Beatles used. Suddenly, there I was: a Beatle. I was onstage playing. I was famous. My dad took the guitar back.

"Let's see if I can remember any songs." He played for a few minutes and then I started to recognize the guitar part to "Day Tripper." He was amazing.

"Show me!" I demanded. My dad showed me where to put my fingers and what strings to pluck but I could not do it. I could picture in my head what was supposed to happen but my fingers wouldn't cooperate. Frustrated, I took the guitar and went to my room. I sat in my chair with the door closed and practiced without stopping until I started to recognize the melody. I went through it time and time again until I had it down. I ran downstairs and gathered my family together in my family room for my recital. I waited until everyone was seated and all the attention was on me. I looked down at my hands to make sure they were where they should be. I plucked the open E string and began playing "Day Tripper" on that old red VOX guitar. I only knew the opening lick but I was doing it. I was George. I knew at that moment I was destined to be a rock star.

The local country station, "Hodag Country," played as my dad navigated our big blue SUV my family had nicknamed "Babe" after Paul Bunyan's big blue ox. Neither my dad nor I really liked country music that much, but it had already become part of our fishing tradition that we'd dare not break. I stared out the window as the sun rose through the maple trees. I wondered why I wasn't still in bed. We had had no luck fishing in our previous outings earlier in the week. My dad assured me that early in the morning the fish were so active it would be easy. I had my doubts.

When we arrived at the lake it was early enough in the morning that the water was still covered in a layer of haze. My dad and I loaded up the boat. We were the only ones on the lake. My eight-year-old body still wasn't fully awake. My dad was going to teach me how to fish for muskie, "the fish of 10,000 casts." The boredom already began to set in. We motored over to a suitable spot. The motor kicked out of gear and my dad tied on the lure, a giant orange and black spotted Hawg Wobbler.

"Here Sam, watch me. This is how you cast these big lures." His thumb was on the reel's release button. His arms brought the lure behind his head and swung the lure forward. It landed with a loud splash.

The clumsy lure started moving across the surface of the water in a way that resembled an injured fish.

"Now you reel in at this speed...."

He was interrupted by a muskie slamming the bait on the surface of the water. My dad raised the rod in the air to gain tension on the line. He wanted me to catch the fish, so he attempted to hand me the rod. Somewhere between my hands and his, the muskie shook the hook. My dad and I stared as the ripples from the brief battle spread across the calm lake. I breathed heavily and my heart pounded as the adrenaline started to calm down. My dad and I fished with new intensity. Muskies have a tendency to follow lures without striking them. For the next few hours our frustration grew as muskie after muskie followed but did not strike.

At we drove back from the lake I thought about what lures I might use to catch the muskies after breakfast. As I stared out the window I saw a bald eagle flying above the tree tops with a large fish in his talons.

"Mom, I don't think Genny looks so good." Our 12-year-old yellow lab that we had owned since I was four years old was lying down on her favorite rug. She was on her side and breathing heavily. Her stomach looked swollen. "I think we need to take her to the vet."

My dad walked in the room and said, "No, I think she'll be fine. We don't need to take her to the vet."

I looked down at Genny and knew something was wrong. My dad had already gone back to his office. I pleaded with my mom to take Genny to the vet, and she gave in. We pulled Babe up to the garage. Normally Genny was very enthusiastic to get into the car. It meant we were going on an adventure. Maybe to our uncle's farm or to the beach, but today my mom and I had to help her in the car. We started driving to the animal hospital. Genny knew exactly which turn meant we were going to the vet, and normally she would start a series of whines and whimpers, but that day she was completely passive.

We pulled into the parking lot and walked Genny into the office. The lobby looked exactly like any other lobby with white walls, some paintings of fish, a couple couches around a desk covered with old magazines. The veterinarians took Genny into the back room. As we waited I picked up a magazine. I don't remember what kind of magazine because I didn't read a single word in it. I began thinking about all the games of fetch we had played together and how my smooth baseball swing was at least partially due to her unending willingness to retrieve my practice balls.

The vet came in her white medical gown with her light blue mask over her mouth and told us that Genny's stomach was severely bloated and was beginning to twist. If they did not operate soon she would die. The mention of death echoed through my head. I looked at my mom. The beginning of tears formed in the corners of her eyes. She asked what it would cost, and the vet told us at least thousands of dollars. She also told us that Genny's quality of life would never be the same. I then knew that I would never play another game of fetch again. We called dad and agreed that we should put Genny to sleep. The vet asked if we would like to see Genny one last time. My mom was crying so hard she could barely get out the word, "No." I told the vet I would. As I walked back to the operating room tears began to flow down my cheeks. It was the first time I had ever lost something I loved.

Genny was lying on her side on a metal operating table. Unconscious. Two vets were on either side of her putting away the instruments they'd no longer need. Genny's tongue was out and she was panting. Her eyes were half open but she could not see anything. She stared blankly ahead. Her belly had been shaved in preparation for the operation. I scratched her head in-between her ears the way she liked it and leaned down next to her ear. "Goodbye."

"Hello," my mom shouted across the room of people to get my attention. "I am so glad you could make it. This band is excellent. They just went on intermission."

My mom had organized a Beatles night at the country club and booked a Beatles cover band called "British Export." When the band came back they started taking requests. They played "Let It Be," "Hello, Goodbye," and "Yellow Submarine." I requested "Day Tripper." They wore the suits the Beatles wore in the early sixties and sounded exactly like the real thing. Not very many people had turned out for the party at the country club, but everyone there seemed to be enjoying themselves.

After "Day Tripper," "John" announced in his phony British accent, "I hear there's a young guitarist in the audience. Will he please come up on stage?"

I had lost my ability to breathe as I walked up on stage. "John" came over and whispered to me without the accent, "What song would you like to play?"

The small library of Beatles songs I had learned since I started playing guitar less than two years ago ran through my head in an instant.

"Uh ... eight ... 'Eight Days a Week.'"

"Alright, sounds good. George, hand him your guitar."

"George" took off his Rickenbacker that was plugged into a VOX amplifier. I looked around at the band and they were all looking at me. Then I remembered that "Eight Days a Week" starts off with a guitar riff. I pictured the song in my head and remembered the tempo and played the ascending chord pattern starting on the 12th fret and the rest of the band joined in on the downbeat of measure two.

"Oooh, I need your love, babe," John and Paul began. Paul was waving over to me to join in on the microphone. So there I was, onstage with lights, a band, and my guitar. For a moment, I was George. I was a rock star staring out into the sea of lights and screaming faces.

I looked across the lake and saw a suitable place to cast. As I swung to cast I must have swung too hard because the line broke and my lure went flying through the air and landed with a splash. It was a Rapala X-Rap that I had used to catch a muskie with just two days before. With almost ten years of muskie fishing experience I knew where the lure landed, because the lure did not sink or float and should be suspended about a foot below the surface of the water. My sister, my dad and I were on "Bob" the bass boat. It was a warm, clear sunny day as I motored over to where the lure had landed. Wolf Lake was so murky it looked like coffee. I took my sister's pole and ran her lure through the water hoping to snag my lure. As the lure ran figure eights right under the boat, a smallmouth bass seized it. It was not a very big fish, but I was happy to have anything bite while I was fishing for a lure.

As I reeled in the bass, a muskie darted out from under our boat and grabbed onto the bass. It was a large muskie and he was trying to swim away with my bass. He started to take out line and the situation on the boat got more desperate.

"Dad, grab the net! Madeline, get out the camera!"

"Why doesn't he just let go of the fish?" my dad asked.

"He won't let go."

Once muskies had food in their mouth they would rather be caught than let go of their meal. There are muskies mounted in the fishing lodge with smaller fish in their mouth. I knew if I played things right I would catch both fish.

My sister's pole had on light line and this muskie was very angry about his lunch having so much resistance. I brought the musky close but once he saw the boat he took out line and began to fight harder. After a brief battle I brought both fish into the net.

Once the muskie was out of the water he let go of the bass and started flopping. To my surprise the bass started flopping too. After I unhooked the bass I held both fish up for the picture. The bass had a series of teeth marks across his back but was relatively unharmed. I put the bass back in the water and he swam back to the depths with an energetic splash. I gave the bass a head start before I put the muskie back in the water. The muskie was the biggest I had ever caught, being slightly over three feet in length. He looked like a prehistoric fossil that had somehow managed to survive the past few thousand years and certainly smelled the part. When I put the muskie in the water he was at first too tired to swim. He had put up a hard fight and was clearly exhausted. I held him by his tail in the water and pulled him back and forth to get water flowing through his gills. He slowly gained back his strength in my hands. I finally let go and he slowly swam away on the surface of the water before vanishing into the depths.

My family and I fished through our garage looking for what could be thrown out or given away. We cleaned in preparation for the refinishing of our bathroom. We would have to store all the tiles and supplies in the garage and we needed to make more space. I was sorting my old sporting goods into "throw away," "give away," and "keep" piles. A large pile of junk was already accumulating in the back of Babe that I would drive to Goodwill. As I dug through the pile of hockey sticks, roller blades, badminton rackets, footballs, and baseball mitts I found my old aluminum baseball bat. It was blue with gold lettering on it. Holding it in my hands brought me right back to the games of fetch I used to play with Genny.

I looked out across my backyard—5 points for hitting over the fence into the neighbor's yard, 10 points for hitting into their tennis court. I held the slobbery tennis ball in my right hand. I tossed it up in the air. As soon as the ball left my hand Genny started dashing across the yard in the direction the ball normally went. I let the ball bounce and at its peak I ripped through it. I hit a line drive straight into the fence and the ball bounced backwards into the air. Genny was there to catch it in her mouth before it even touched the ground. She turned around and triumphantly galloped back. She placed the ball at my feet and looked at me eagerly awaiting the next swing.

I reached down and put the bat back into the "keep" pile.

—Sam, grade 12

This memoir could almost have ended with the passing of the family dog, Genny. After all, that scene fulfills the promise of the title by ending with the word *goodbye*. Yet such a premature ending would rob readers of the pleasures the later scenes bring: Sam as rock star and the miracle catch of the double fish vanishing into the depths. It's also nice to see the familiar characters of the dad and the sister return in that scene. The final scene is especially lovely. Even though the author is alone, the last story relates to all the earlier pieces. As the author conducts his own "good will" hunting exercise, he finds a junky old bat that emerges as a trophy of memory, and it allows him to conjure happy scenes he had had to let go of before. The whole idea of a "keep" pile seems like a terrific metaphor of memoir writing. We don't always have access to all of our memories, and some are too faded and too tarnished to maintain. But we keep some and restore others because these memories are crucial pieces of our selves. A final note: Sam's self-reflection in Chapter 2 reveals a reluctance to trust stories because he had never written a paper in school without an explicit thesis. This memoir offers an emotional depth and a range of intellect that could not be elicited by a thesis-driven essay.

This next piece was written by Sam's sister in a different class a couple of years later. I offer only an excerpt here to make a couple of points about subject matter and style.

As I was climbing into the passenger seat of Babe, our ancient Chevy Tahoe, on our way to the church, I noticed there was a run in my black tights. I didn't care. Anyone who would look at my tights on a day like this and think, "Hm, doesn't that just ruin her outfit" must not have a heart. My mom hadn't driven Babe in years but she needed the extra trunk space for all the photographs and furniture left over from the apartment. Her braking was jerky and her steering was wobbly because she wasn't used to driving such a bulky machine.

We pulled into the parking lot of the church. It wasn't our church, it was the church. This one was more convenient for all of my extended family members to get to, not to mention easier on the eyes than the rented gathering room of a community center that normally houses our church.

I filed into the pew next to my parents and brother just as everyone was beginning to settle in. My dad nudged me and whispered, "After the second hymn, you're going to go read Psalm 23, okay?"

I froze.

"Why me?" I stuttered.

"It would be really nice. You're good at speaking in front of people. Plus, Grandma would have loved it," my mom said. I had at least ten other cousins there and even at sixteen I was the youngest out of any of them. Why couldn't one of them read it? And of all things, why a psalm?

"But ..."

"Uck, look at that. Why would you wear those tights?" she tutted.

As I was about to protest, the organ starting buzzing and the priest took to the lectern.

By the time the final chords of the second hymn were echoing through the church, my knees were shaking and all color had drained from my face. I was about to be exposed.

The church was silent except for the obnoxious clacking of my heels against the wooden steps up to the lectern. I was hoping no one would notice I was up there. My voice was quivering for all the wrong reasons. I couldn't think about my grandma or the wonderful life she had lived, all I could think about was how wrong it was that I was standing there in a church, in front of my family, in front of all of my parents' God-fearing friends reading from a book that I resented terribly for dictating the first fifteen years of my life. I was making a mockery of Psalm 23.

"The Lord is my shepherd, I shall not want ... He makes me to lie down in green pastures ... He leads me beside still waters, he restores my soul ..."

If God did exist, he must have been sitting on a cloud with his head in his hands or ready to send a thunderbolt down my way.

———————————

I gasped as suddenly the cool glass lake was shattered by a two-foot fish hurling itself against my orange and black striped Hawg Wobbler lure. I set the hook a second too late and watched the muskie scuttle away through the shallow water.

"Oh, bummer," said my brother, "That guy was big. You'll get the next one."

I wasn't too bummed. I knew that even if by some miracle I hooked a muskie, there was no way I could reel it into a tiny canoe without flipping it over or falling out. I wasn't here to catch a fish so I could triumphantly write my name on the chalkboard next to the lodge along with the impressive muskie measurements. I was just here to admire the pine trees along the shore, that bald eagle circling the dock, and the precise choreography of the minnows darting among the swaying weeds. Fishing also gave me an excuse to watch my brother doing something he loved.

"Let's paddle over to that inlet by the reeds," Sam said, placing his pole down and picking up his paddle. Water sloshed against the sides of the canoe and we drifted to the other side of the lake.

My line buzzed and the Hawg Wobbler flopped right in the middle of the reeds, the perfect place for muskies to lurk.

"So, are you excited to be a senior?" my brother asked, casting off the other side of the canoe. It was strange. Normally the only thing we would talk about on these kinds of excursions was the proper casting technique or the location of the pliers. In between those conversations, we wordlessly decided that there wasn't anything we needed to talk about.

"Yeah, I guess." I replied.

"Do you see the eagle?"

"Yeah."

"Isn't it amazing?"

"Yeah …" I said warily. I had a feeling I knew where this was going.

"I think it's amazing that, you know, God created the whole world and decided it was important enough to make eagles, or muskies. He could have done without those. But He made them just so we could enjoy them."

Sam wasn't leaping down my throat and there was not a trace of accusation in his voice. His tone was only of concern attempted to be masked by casual conversation. I don't know how he had found out, but he definitely knew that I was apparently on the road to eternal damnation.

"Hey! I have a follow!" I said, seeing a dark green shadow lurking by my lure. I jerked and tugged at the line to make my little imitation fish seem pathetic and all too easy to devour. The green shadow drifted away. I shrugged.

"I can't see how all of this could be an accident," he continued. I hated this. I had had this conversation with my parents. They were disappointed, I knew it, I could read it in their faces every time they saw my eyes glaze over in church, but I could handle their disappointment. All parents have to realize at some point that their children aren't going to be exactly who they want them to be. But with Sam it was different. He was the one who made me want to join his former football team because he taught me how to throw a spiral. He was the one that first exposed me to music other than *NSYNC. He was the only reason that, as a teenage girl, I still enjoyed fishing and canoeing. He had always guided me and he had always guided me well, but that wasn't the case anymore.

"I don't understand that, either," I finally said.

"So you think God made it?" he asked, turning around to face me. The hope in his eyes nearly killed me.

I exhaled and tried to choose my words carefully, "I don't understand how this can be an accident, but I don't understand a lot of things. I don't understand how some people's lives can be so easy and others are so hard, and I don't understand how God created the world in six days but the dinosaurs were around way before we were, and I don't understand why He would make people inherently bad, and I don't understand why He set the world up from the beginning that women are to serve men and I don't understand how someone who's supposed to be so loving can tell a person who tried their best to be kind all their lives that they aren't good enough. I just don't understand."

Sam had stopped reeling in. I turned and looked at his black lure bobbing with the soft current.

"Sam! You have a follow!" I said, pointing at the shadow inching closer to his lure. He halfheartedly jerked his wrist before the muskie had even bitten his hook, an amateur mistake for such a seasoned fisherman.

"We should probably go back now, I bet it's almost time for lunch," he said, swiftly turning the canoe around back to the dock. I watched my paddle disturb the still water as we glided back to the dock in silence.

—Madeline, grade 12

Some of the same characters occur across both memoirs: her older brother, Sam; their father; the Hawg Wobbler; even the old truck, Babe. I love the way author deals with the central conflict: religion. Sam is clearly very spiritual, yet religion is not explicit in his memoir at all. Madeline deftly uses a fishing metaphor to talk about how close she was to being his "[religious] follow[er]." All this may change, of course. For all we know, she may find religion, just as Sam might one day lose his. But what these sharply drawn memoirs give us is a vivid sense of two caring and searching people who are establishing their identities even as they recognize themselves as works in progress.

Home Games

As I ran down the stairs, I could already hear the shoulder pad hits from the blaring TV. I stormed into my living room and saw my dad stationed attentively on our ugly maroon, suede-like-fabric couch, his eyes glued to the TV. As I walked in, I was greeted by his usual welcome: "Robbie! Move out of the way!" I hurried out of the way and sat next to him on the couch.

Every Sunday my dad would plant himself on our couch and attempt to drown out the noise of the family. Sunday was his day with the Green Bay Packers. I didn't watch games with him for the love of watching the football—I was only seven and didn't really understand it—but I just loved to spend time with him and emulate his interests. My brother, Steve, wasn't very interested in football when he was ten, so football Sundays were my chance to be alone with my dad.

"Who are we playing this week?" I asked, feigning interest. The long hairs of his funny-looking mustache curled with his upper lip, and he pressed his interlocked hands together in frustration. He was annoyed by my question. "The Vikings," he tersely answered. He ran his fingers over that funny mustache and let out a big sigh. The Packers were in their green jerseys, so I knew that they were playing at Lambeau Field, their home stadium. It was clear that he wanted me to shut up and watch the game, so I did.

"Come on, Brett! Get it together, damnit!" My dad shouted at the TV as if he were Coach Mike Holmgren yelling at his star quarterback, Brett Favre. The Packers were losing to the hated Vikings, and my dad continuously stomped his foot on the ground; with every passionate pound the whole house trembled. My mom came down during a commercial and placed a steaming, porcelain casserole dish full of creamy artichoke dip in the middle of our maple coffee table:

"Here you go boys, dig in," my mom said. I smiled and thanked her while my dad raised his arm off of his knee, waving her away. He couldn't believe she would even think of disturbing him during the game. I built a beautiful cracker tower, and then I took each cracker off, one by one, and smothered it with gooey, cheesy artichoke dip. With every crack and crunch, my dad looked over in annoyance. He scratched his curly hair so much that it actually started to spring out in an afro-mold.

Suddenly, Brett Favre dropped back and fired a ball to star receiver Robert Brooks in the end zone. My dad sprung up in excitement and yelled, "Yessss! That-a-boy Brett! Good job!" He lifted his arm, fist clenched, and rocked it back and forth as if he was pounding on a locked door. I followed, jumping up from the couch and flailing my arms in excitement: "Wooooooooo! Yaaa!" I didn't quite know what I was cheering for, but I figured it was the right thing to do. Still munching on crackers and dip and jumping up and down, I turned and looked up at my dad.

He stuck his hand up. "High five, Rob!" I gladly swung my arm up and smacked my hand as hard as I could against his. Within seconds, he sat back down on the couch and motioned for me to do the same:

"All right, now, get ready for the kickoff."

———————————

"Is that Dad?" I leapt up in anticipation, questioning my mom.

"Nope, not yet" she would constantly answer in disappointment. My mom, brother, and I waited in our maroon Jeep Cherokee in the McDonald's parking lot. Hours earlier, we had arrived and my brother Steve and I were looking forward to spending Easter in Appleton, Wisconsin, where my dad lived. I was nine years old, and my mother and he had divorced when I was seven. They used to switch off holidays for time with me and my brother; my mom would drive half-way, to a Wisconsin McDonald's on the side of the highway. From there, my dad would drive us the rest of the way to his apartment.

Usually, my dad was already there waiting in the parking lot for us; however, this time he seemed to be running a little late. I ate Chicken McNuggets, and Steve devoured a Big Mac. After the meal, we went back to the car to wait for him. It would only be a matter of time before he showed up and we would enjoy another holiday in Appleton. I crouched on my knees in the backseat, eyes fixed on the entrance to the parking lot. Every time I heard a car, I would spring to my feet in the backseat, and my face would light up in excitement: "Is that Dad?" Over and over, the car pulling into the parking lot wouldn't be the gray, rusted Oldsmobile that my dad drove. A couple years later my mom would tell me that every time I asked her if my Dad was there, she could see the life drain out of my face. She will never forget that look, she says, and I will never forget asking.

My mom went back into McDonald's four or five times and tried to call my Dad's brother, Uncle Kevin, who lived close to my Dad's apartment. Steve sat in silence in the front seat while I tried to spark conversation with him.

I asked him annoying little-brother-questions about what we would do in Appleton: "Do you think Dad will take us fishing? Do you think we will have an Easter egg hunt at Grandma's?" I continued pestering him; after all, I had no reason to believe that he wouldn't show up.

"I don't know, Robbie" he would answer, obviously annoyed and angry. He was twelve and knew a little bit about my dad's problem. My mom got back into the car and told us that Dad wasn't coming and we had to go home. We had waited for four hours; if he didn't show up by that time, he would never show up.

I was crushed. Tears streamed down my face on the way home while I tried to tune out my mom's attempts to calm me. I was worried that Dad had been hurt in an accident or that he didn't want to have us for Easter. I didn't understand why he didn't show up or why we couldn't be with him that Easter. My crying only stopped when my mom told me that we could still have an Easter egg hunt.

Shortly after we arrived home, my mom answered the phone to my uncle's explanation to why my Dad didn't show up. He had gotten pulled over on the highway, only about a half an hour away from the McDonald's, for driving under the influence of alcohol. It was his third DUI. I would have to watch the Packers by myself from there on out.

"Right eye, waggle left, on one," Patch, our quarterback, shouted to the huddle.

Upon hearing the play call, I trotted out to the left side of the field, knowing the play was intended for me. I could see our blue and green fans in the stands waving their arms and leaping up and down, chanting, "Trevians, Trevians!" I approached the 27-yard line, digging my right foot forward into the soft, dewy grass. I turned and signaled to the line judge that I was supposed to be on the line: "You're on!" he screamed, trying to be heard over the rowdy fans. Sweat crawled down my face and my heart beat furiously. I grinded my teeth nervously into my mouth guard in anticipation of the snap.

Across the line, the defender squatted three yards away, staring at the big "42" on my green jersey. Man coverage. I cracked a smile, knowing that I could beat this kid with the post-corner route that Patch called.

"Green sixty-nine, green sixty-nine, set hut!" Patch yelled, taking the ball from the center. I sprinted out of my stance, running right at the defender to drive him off. Without contact, I made the first cut at ten yards, angling towards the goal post. I continued for another three yards, and once I noticed that the defender had turned his hips inward, I knew I caught him off-balance. I quickly shifted and crossed over, turning and sprinting towards the corner of the end zone. I turned my head and looked for the ball. Looking up, all other movement seemed to stop as I focused on the spiraling pigskin. After sailing through the air, the ball fell beautifully into my open, gloved hands at the ten-yard line. I felt as if I were my favorite Packers receiver, Donald Driver, grabbing a Brett Favre touchdown. I ran the extra ten yards across the goal line, and instantly flipped the ball to the referee. I had scored my first varsity touchdown, putting my team up 18 to three with four minutes and 26 seconds left. As I ran back to the sideline, my teammates mobbed me in celebration. I looked into the parents' section, and I could see my mom shaking the noisemaker she made by filling an empty Tide detergent bottle with dried lima beans.

Brett took the snap from the center and dropped back. The Giants' rush came. The play had fallen apart. Brett scrambled to the right, looking for any receiver that may get open. No one did. The Giants' defensive end got to him and dragged him down to the ground, his helmet slamming against the grassy turf. He got rocked, and he wasn't getting up. The trainers came out to look at him and hurried him off of the field. He was out of it, woozy, concussed.

"This doesn't look good. Brett Favre might be out for the rest of the game," the announcer said.

"Oh shit," I mumbled, my hands clasped tightly in nervousness. I ran my hands through my hair, making it spring out into an afro, and sat back on our new, tan couch. My mom came down from watching the game upstairs—I like to watch the games alone, uninterrupted—and asked what was wrong. I lifted my head up slowly.

"Nothing, nothing," I snapped at her, waving her to go back upstairs. Doug Pederson, the backup quarterback, trotted onto the field, ready to lead the offense. The camera kept panning over to Brett Favre, who looked as if he had little birdies flying above his head. I nervously paced back and forth, fearing that the game was going to hell. I was dressed in my green number 87 Robert Brooks jersey and the 1996 Packers hat I'd been wearing since my dad bought it for me when I was nine.

Doug Pederson took one snap and handed it off to Ahman Green. No gain. Then, without clearance by the medical staff or the head coach—as we would later find out from the announcers—Brett came running onto the field and called his own play. Ten years ago, as a newcomer to the league, he may have called it quits; but he was a savvy veteran now and knew he had to be in the game. He dropped back and looked downfield. Javon Walker, the team's best receiver, was running a go-route. Brett heaved the ball up. It was a jump ball. Javon Walker jumped up over his defender and snatched the ball out of the air. His defender fell, and Javon walked into the end zone. Brett pranced around the field, his arms in the air like a little kid. That's what I love about him; he still plays with the heart of a kid. He ran to Javon and tackled him in the end zone, then returned to his sideline, still cheering. It ended up being his last play of the game. He suffered a concussion on the play before and still threw a touchdown strike.

"Holy shit! Oh, Baby! That-a-boy Brett!" I screamed at the TV. I sat back down and covered my mouth in amazement at what I just saw. After I got over the initial shock, I ate a cracker with some artichoke dip and got ready for the kickoff. My hero Brett had just thrown a touchdown even though he had a concussion—he probably didn't even know he was playing football.

Pacing back and forth in the gym, I stare down at the glossy red and green lines of the basketball court and toss a football between my hands. It's an hour before the last game of my senior season, and I am dressed in my green football pants and my blue, sleeveless, worn-out shirt that I wear for all my games. My Ipod is clipped on to my pants, blasting my "football playlist."
The Foo Fighters song, "My Hero," starts playing:

There goes my hero
Watch him as he goes
There goes my hero
He's ordinary
He's ordinary

I think back to Brett Favre's touchdown pass to Javon Walker. Will I make a game-changing play like that? Will I play like my hero? I put on my shoulder pads, lace up my cleats, and strap on my helmet. It's game time.

It is November now. Football season's over. I sit in my room at a white desk, room dimly lit by a small desk lamp at 12:30 am. Hunched over a spiral notebook, I wonder what to write. The room is completely silent except for the noise of the crickets outside the window, but so much is spoken. Each time I ink pen to paper I utter another concealed emotion. I haven't talked to my father in six years, and I've bottled up anger, sympathy, pity, even hate for him. Through the paper, I am having a conversation with my father, who stopped watching Packers games with me when I was eight.

How are you?
What do you like to do during your free time? Do you still fish?
Do you work? What is your job?
What kind of music do you like?
My hair is curly just like yours.
Did you see when Brett Favre got a concussion during the Giants game and then came back into the game and threw a touchdown? That was awesome.
What do you think of the Packers' record?
I Love you Dad.
—Robbie, grade 12

First, consider the deft use of repeated images that give the essay its cohesiveness: the afro-mold, the cheesy artichoke dip, the way the author imitates his father's penchant for shouting at the TV. But there are larger themes at work here as well. The title is simultaneously playful and painful as the author explores the idea of home football games for the Packers as well as for his own high school team and the change in his home after his father moves out. Brett Favre, the Hall of Fame football hero, becomes a sort of surrogate father, even though the author's choice of music suggests he'd settle for an "ordinary" hero, a man who would simply stay by his family. The turn to the present tense in the final scene is inspired. The immediacy of the memoir is apparent here, and it brings the events to the present as well. What a spectacular imaginative leap the author makes in writing a letter he does not actually send but which encapsulates the enormous absence he has felt his entire life but never written about.

In *The Stories We Live By: Personal Myths and the Making of the Self*, developmental psychologist Dan McAdams writes that "from adolescence onward we face this task of creating an integrative life story through which we are able to understand who we are" (91). Memoir writing, particularly segmented memoirs, requires that students explicitly integrate some of their various experiences and feelings into a unified whole. I do not imagine—nor do I hope!—that students will have "solved" the mystery of themselves through this process. But many students, including most of those who wrote the models reprinted in this chapter, never get the chance to write about their lives in school even though their ongoing life story is clearly always on their minds.

This chapter concludes the first half of this book. In these early chapters, I have considered our lives as texts we create in order to be read, by ourselves and by others. In the next set of chapters, I explore reading the world as an unfolding text. It may seem as if we are moving away from personal writing, but as scholar Don Murray notes in an essay called "All Writing Is Autobiography," all reading is autobiography as well (74). Try as we might, we can never really get away from ourselves.

II

Examining the World-as-Text

Everyone's Got an Opinion: Writing Op-Ed Essays

[When we read literature] we become more intense, richer, more complicated, happier, and more lucid than we are in the constrained routine of ordinary life. When we close the book and abandon literary fiction, we return to actual existence and compare it to the splendid land we just left. What a disappointment awaits us! Yet a tremendous realization also awaits us, namely, that the fantasized life of the novel is better—more beautiful and more diverse, more comprehensible and more perfect—than the life we live while awake, a life conditioned by the limits and tedium of our condition. (303)

This passage from Mario Vargas Llosa's essay "Why Literature?" is perhaps the most eloquent defense of reading I have ever come across. Literature, and especially literary fiction, Vargas Llosa argues, helps us understand the world by bringing the issues of our lives into greater relief. Literature says nothing to the complacent, to the self-satisfied. Rather, literature offers model worlds and exemplary characters that invite us to measure ourselves and our environment against a set of ideals. Not even dystopian literature, such as *Brave New World*, makes us feel relieved that we do not live in a horrific world; rather, it reminds us how far we've fallen from our own former ideals.

In this chapter, I explicitly consider how literature helps us better understand our everyday lives. For the assignment at the center of this exploration, students write commentaries, modeled on newspaper op-ed pieces (essays found *opposite* the editorial page). These are short essays on contemporary issues that appear in almost all daily newspapers. I allow students to write on almost any topic as long as they are truly invested in it—and as long as their positions are grounded in factual detail. As Daniel Patrick Moynihan said, "Everyone's entitled to his own opinion, but not to his own facts."

Since newspapers are the dominant genre for this form, the paper topic must also be a current event. Like a newspaper editor might, I allow students to write about past, even distant, events, as long as there is a pressing occasion that makes the topic relevant again. For example, a former student once wrote about the American hostages taken during the Iranian Revolution on the thirtieth anniversary of their release. Without the presence of this momentous anniversary, the topic would not be immediately relevant (or *news*worthy) to readers.

Using literature as a lens through which to see current events more clearly is widely practiced in newspaper writing. A few years ago, Nicholas Kristof, a regular op-ed writer for the *New York Times*, wrote a fascinating piece on the Bush presidency called "Et Tu, George?" In this column, Kristof uses literature—specifically Virgil, Thucydides, and Melville—as ancient shades returning to cast light upon what he saw as the arrogance of the Bush administration. "At a time," Kristof writes, "when we hear the siren calls of moral clarity, the classics almost invariably emphasize the importance of moral nuance, and appreciation for complexity, the need for humility." The column itself is remarkable for asserting the timeliness of the timeless classics, but even more so for Kristof's sign-off. There, he asks his readers, "Are there other classics beyond *Moby-Dick* or *The Aeneid* that you think would be appropriate analogies for President Bush and Iraq?" Hundreds of responses flooded in within the next couple of days (including, I was thrilled to learn, *Oedipus the King* and *Antigone*, two works I was teaching that quarter).

It is critical to let students know that this sort of writing is found every week in newspapers and magazines, on radio and TV. And I encourage them to read additional op-ed columns as models during the two to three weeks we spend writing them. The only difference here is that we are commenting on current events through the lens of literature. As Thoreau wrote in *Walden*, "What news! How much more important to know what was never old" (76).

I have used the assignment with a number of different texts, but following is the assignment I passed out after my students and I studied *Oedipus the King* and *Antigone*:

> *Oedipus the King* and *Antigone* are plays about character, choices, and consequences. Through the challenges his characters confront, Sophocles raises questions about human beings and their relationships with the gods/fate, with authority figures, and with their families. While he may not have anticipated society's problems in all their technological complexity, he did recognize gender struggles, identity confusion, sibling rivalry, and the conflict between loyalty to ourselves and loyalty to our religion or to our country. In what ways do you see Sophocles's plays—written in the 5th century BC—still speaking to us today?
>
> Write a commentary analyzing a current or recent issue/event/trend that suggests a theme from one of the two plays. Consider the play to be an

ancient beacon—light from a distant star, perhaps—that sheds light on an issue we are wrestling with, illuminating an angle we may be too blind to see in our modern age. Provide only the necessary background for a well-educated audience already familiar with the play's plot. (Anyone who considers him- or herself to be well-educated knows these plays.)

Warming Up to Commentary

Right after passing out the assignment sheet, I bring in a stack of newspapers (local papers, *The New York Times*, *The Washington Post*) and magazines such as *Sports Illustrated*, *Time*, and *Newsweek* and show students where to find op-ed examples. It's important for students to become familiar with the form, but with these examples I also want to stress the range of possible topics and the currency of this sort of writing. People practice this writing in the "real world" on a daily basis.

Writers might approach the commentary in one of two ways: students might think about issues they care deeply about and then consider literary analogues, or they might use literature as a springboard to think about political issues. One year I started with this simple warm-up exercise featuring quotes from *Oedipus*:

> Read the following passages from our text and find contemporary parallels between the events of the play and current events in the world of sports, politics, entertainment, or even local/personal examples:
>
> 1. "Mock me for that, go on, and you'll reveal my greatness" (line 502)
>
> 2. "I never look / To judge the ones in power" (592–93)
>
> 3. "I don't know / And when I don't, I keep quiet" (635)
>
> 4. "When my enemy moves against me quickly, / Plots in secret, I must move quickly too, I must / I plot and pay him back" (693–95)

For the first item listed, for example, students mentioned deposed Illinois governor Rod Blagojevich, singer Kanye West, and star wide receiver Terrell Owens right off the bat. For the second item, students cited fallen US soldier and former NFL star Pat Tillman, head basketball coaches like Rick Pitino, and even local school board officials. The third item suggested in-fighting in the White House, sports clubhouses, and even feuding rap stars like 50 Cent. It's important to allow students to explore almost any area they are interested in as long as there is a potential audience.

One of the best features of commentary writing is that it forces students to think about possible publication venues. Who might want or need to hear what we have to say? As they read commentaries I pass out, as well as those they discover on their own in print or online, I ask them to think about the intended audience and the assumptions writers make about these audiences. This audience analysis then becomes a central feature in the proposals students write before drafting commentaries of their own.

Proposals

Commentary Topic(s): Feel free to list more than one so long as you find corresponding passages from the play.

Passage(s) from the text: What lines most clearly speak to the issue you wish to address?

Target Audience: Who might want or need to hear your commentary?

Purpose: What does your audience currently believe and how would you like to change their minds?

Genre: Who might be interested in publishing your commentary? What makes that source ideal?

After students hand in their proposals, I return them with comments designed to help them focus their ideas about the issue and about the passages from the play with which they hope to elucidate the issue. It has always paid off to hold these proposals to rigorous standards in order to guarantee that the papers will be successful. Here are some examples from my students.

Michael Phelps' Greek Tragedy

No, the title of this editorial doesn't refer to the mere 6 gold medals Michael Phelps won in the 2004 Olympics in Athens. Rather it refers to just how Michael Phelps made headlines once again this week, which wasn't due to one of those dominating swimming performances we have come to expect from the Olympic champion. Rather this time it was for something completely removed from the world of sports. He has confirmed the validity of a photo released by a British tabloid that pictures him smoking from a marijuana bong. To most, this headline is shocking. Phelps' accomplishments in the swimming world, including winning a record 8 gold medals this past summer in Beijing, have made him seem rather superhuman, a swimming god among mere mortals. But Phelps would do well to remember that he is not a God, not above the law. During his 3-month ban from the sport, he might consider reading up on the Classics, as he is starting to resemble Creon, a tragic Greek character from Sophocles' play *Antigone*.

Throughout most of this play, Phelps' fictitious counterpart, the newly crowned King Creon, is displayed as someone who has become drunk with power, believing that his word is law above that of the gods, who afford proper burial to family members. At one point in a heated argument, he even exclaims, "The city is the king's—that's the law!" Creon, just like Phelps, acts in an arrogant manner that shows an ethical and moral disregard for the laws that his society lives by. This behavior eventually costs Creon everything, stripping him of both his son and his wife. So far, Phelps' lapses in judgment have not affected his swimming, rather they have only threatened his pocketbook, as he has lost at least one endorsement deal over this scandal so far, but his public mistakes will have farther reaching consequences than risk to his income.

Phelps is probably the most dominant athlete of our time, and as such, he has become a role model to young kids everywhere. They look up to him as a model athlete, and his actions suggest to those with dreams of the Olympics that illegal drug use is okay. As much as he may believe that he has a golden ticket to do whatever he likes, including abusing the faith that kids have in him as their role model, he had better know that the public will eventually lose patience with him, regardless of his successes in the pool, just as Creon's son lost patience with him in the play.

To see this flaw in such a larger than life character like Phelps is even more surprising when his rigorous lifestyle of eating, sleeping, and swimming (and not doing much else) is considered. But it seems as though his relentless training probably caused this error in judgment, as this is not the first time he has made a stupid decision regarding drug use following an amazing Olympic performance. Though not many outside of the swimming world would be able to recall his arrest for drunk driving in 2004, shortly after his 6 gold medal performances in Athens, it, along with his latest foray into public drug use, reveal a disturbing character flaw developing in Phelps. Hopefully he will heed the dark warning given at the end of the play, "The mighty words of the proud are paid in full with mighty blows of fate, and at long last those blows will teach us wisdom." If he does take this lesson from ancient literature and change his ways, he can avoid a tragic downfall worthy only of the Classics, as so many other star athletes before him have failed to do.

—Michael, grade 12

The opening word of this essay, *No,* already shows the author's argumentative engagement with the audience. The word *mere* in the opening sentence is also nicely full of ironic attitude. The end of the first paragraph offers a nod to the play, cagily calling Phelps a "swimming god" among mortals. In the following sentence, the author scolds Phelps (a common op-ed tone) by saying, "Phelps would do well to remember. . . ." In the conclusion, Michael deftly borrows from the chorus to "pass judgment" on Phelps. In other words, the chorus speaks for the author here in condemning the "words of the proud."

Battle Against the Genders

"Woman once made equal to man becomes his superior"—Socrates

Last Thursday, President Obama signed a bill, the Lilly Ledbetter Fair Pay Act, requiring equal pay for women. Although Lilly Ledbetter, the inspiration for the legislation, will not receive the money she deserves for her years of substandard pay, she can look to a different kind of satisfaction: "Goodyear will never have to pay me what it cheated out of me. In fact, I will never see a cent. But with the president's signature today I have an even richer reward." As she enters retirement, Ledbetter, and every other woman in America, can enjoy her triumph over discriminating employers.

Lilly Ledbetter finally completed a very tiresome journey that proved in times of trouble, we often look to women. And let's be honest—most men fear this. It weakens their historical role in society as the dominant sex. So, perhaps it was not so surprising that Lilly Ledbetter discovered, after a 19-year career as a supervisor, that she was being paid less than her male coworkers at Goodyear Tire and Rubber Company. *God forbid* that women earn as much as men. This is not a new story. In discriminating against women, Ledbetter's stand against her employer recalls the misogyny in Sophocles' play, *Antigone*. Creon, King of Thebes, could not believe that a *woman*, Antigone, had disregarded his decree. Creon argues, "We must defend the men who live by law, never let some woman triumph over us." Goodyear has similarly cared less about fairness than about Ledbetter's gender.

Discrimination against women has been occurring since ancient Greek times and before. Women have traveled a long road to change their demeaning fate. Lilly Ledbetter is one of a long line of women who have come forth to fight against our "superiors" for equality. Ledbetter could have reacted as did Antigone's hopeless sister, Ismene: "Remember we are women, we're not born to contend with men." Instead, Ledbetter chose a much tougher route. She took her case all the way to the Supreme Court, battling a huge company that would rather fight to the death than pay a woman the same as a man.

In fact, our new President is happy that Ledbetter decided to contend with men. "It is fitting that with the very first bill I sign—the Lilly Ledbetter Fair Pay Act—we are upholding one of this nation's first principles: that we are all cre-

ated equal and each deserve a chance to pursue our own version of happiness,"
Obama proudly stated. This tangible equality is something that ancient Greek
women could never have dreamed of. Creon just wouldn't have it.

Lilly Ledbetter danced with the President at the inauguration. With a new
leader in office, her rights would be considered, and personal satisfaction ultimately granted. Antigone, unfortunately, doesn't win against Creon, and her daring and rebellious actions did not give any justice to women. Ledbetter similarly
lost (her money) to Goodyear, but she at least lived to see her persistence result
in a lasting future benefit for all women in the workplace.

—Margaret, grade 12

This author immediately establishes how current the event is by opening
with the phrase "Last Thursday." She succinctly relates the terms of the new
law in the first paragraph before establishing a link to the play. In that second
paragraph, she offers some nice editorializing attitude—"let's be honest" and
"God forbid"—to reveal her feelings on the issue of gender discrimination. The
second of those phrases also offers a way into the play, as Antigone chooses her
duty to the gods over her civic duty. The conclusion of this essay returns to the
opening, contrasting their fates and the effects Ledbetter and Antigone had on
their respective populaces.

Blind Truth

The American people and the international community have spoken and our
President has failed to listen. The signs have been clear: the mid-term elections,
the Iraq Study Group, retired generals, and National Intelligence Estimate; it is
time to end our occupation of Iraq. Despite the overwhelming support for a
troop withdrawal (65% of Americans) the President has announced he will
send 21,000 more troops to Iraq. His latest plan yet again shows his inability to compromise and listen to anyone but himself, much like Oedipus in the
Sophocles play. Like President Bush, Oedipus is ruling a country distraught
with the status quo, yet fails to listen to others' expertise that tell him he killed
Laius, which is causing the chaos in Thebes. They both discount others' wisdom
and trust their gut because the truth is too difficult to stomach.

These men were not always weak and close-minded leaders. In the days
following 9/11, President Bush showed the strength and courage needed to heal
a nation, and with formidable national and international support he fought to
keep our country safe. Oedipus too was revered by his people. Amongst the tur-
moil in Thebes he was summoned to help his people, "Your country calls you
savior now for your zeal, your actions years ago" (161). These men are capable
of great feats, but fail as Commander-in-Chiefs when they go it alone.

But to truly understand the gravity of both situations, one must look back to the root cause, the lies surrounding both the invasion of Iraq and the killing of Laius. They have been told so well, they were seen as conventional wisdom. Oedipus began to understand his actions when Creon explains why the truth has gone untold, "She [The Riddling Sphinx] … persuaded us to let the mystery go" (166). Vice President Cheney is this nation's Riddling Sphinx because from early on he moved focus away from faulty intelligence. Cheney reassured us invading Iraq would be like stealing candy or health insurance from a baby, there was nothing to worry about. On September 14th, 2003, on "Meet the Press" our Vice President reassured the American people that our troops "would be greeted as liberators" and he has continuously told us staying in Iraq is making us safer. Woops. Common sense and bipartisan research tells us both of Cheney's claims have been dead wrong.

Well Mr. President, Creon has arrived, the truth is clear. Your policy was flawed and your new escalation will be no different. The wisdom that lies in Creon and Tiresias has appeared in front of you in the form of the Iraq Study Group Report and the National Intelligence Estimate. Now it's up to you, George, will you listen? Your country hopes you will.

Like Oedipus you are currently refuting the wise men around you. The truth hurts, there's no doubt about it, but you must once again show your strength and leadership and employ common sense. The more you refute the truth the more it will come, and the more troops you send the more violence you will create. As we wait in the constant eve of the troop escalation, be like Oedipus, Mr. President, and accept the truth. Listen. Listen to the evidence, the international community, and your country. Accept responsibility for your actions and act now to end this crisis in the Middle East. This takes courage and strength, but our soldiers' lives depend on it.
—Henry, grade 12

This essay displays both a strong voice (phrases like "woops" and "dead wrong") and a clear sense of conciliation. The author applauds Bush's Oedipus-like strength of character in the chaotic period just after 9/11. He does this to project a reasonable and balanced position for his readers and so that he can take Bush to task for his subsequent failures. The final paragraph offers an important conceit in many op-eds: direct address. The author switches to a second-person address, admonishing Bush and encouraging him to swifter action in bringing the war to an end.

While reading plays about arrogant people in power, it is common for students to analyze the actions of current political leaders. The Bush administration was a common target for eight years, and disgraced Illinois Governor Rod Blagojevich came along just in time for some terrific essays. I don't want to brag, but my home state of Illinois leads the nation in jailed politicians. University of Illinois at Chicago political science professor Dick Simpson says that since 1970, more than 1,500 Illinois politicians have been convicted on corruption charges. Luckily, bad behavior is not solely local. Political leaders and celebrities nation-wide keep on obliging writers with fodder for terrific essays.

Because of this assignment's emphasis on publication and audience, I encourage students to send these commentaries out to local newspapers or to our own school newspaper. These pieces also make for great blog posts (more on that in Chapter 8). But I don't judge the success of the assignment on publication. Rather, I'm glad students have joined an ongoing conversation on an issue they care deeply about. Students are beginning to explore the world around them as a text they can not only analyze but also help shape.

7

Death Sentences: Writing about Inexact and Irresponsible Language

For Mohammed Zeid of Gaza, Age 15

There is no stray bullet, sirs.
No bullet like a worried cat
crouching under a bush,
no half-hairless puppy bullet
dodging midnight streets.
The bullet could not be a pecan
plunking the tin roof,
not hardly, no fluff of pollen
on October's breath,
no humble pebble in the street.

So don't gentle it, please.

We live among stray thoughts,
tasks abandoned midstream.
Our fickle hearts are fat
with stray devotions, we feel at home
among bits and pieces,
all the wandering ways of words.

But this bullet had no innocence, did not
wish anyone well, you can't tell us otherwise
by naming it mildly, this bullet was never the friend
of life, should not be granted immunity
by soft saying—friendly fire, straying death-eye
why have we given the wrong weight to what we do?

Mohammed, Mohammed deserves the truth.
this bullet had no secret happy hopes,
it was not singing to itself with eyes closed
under the bridge.

—NAOMI SHIHAB NYE

The speaker in this poem laments the distorted language used in news coverage—terms such as *friendly fire* and *stray bullets* that *gentle* the horrifying realities of war. The poet hears the awful gulf between fatal bullets in wartime and the candied language used to describe those events. By titling the poem with the name of an innocent victim, she humanizes the often dehumanizing portraits offered by the media.

War offers many examples of language abuse. In his book *Death Sentences: How Clichés, Weasel Words, and Management Speak are Strangling Public Language*, Don Watson notes that terms like *shock and awe* are sold as brand names; he correctly identifies the military's ambiguous use of language, such as reporting that it had *degraded* 70 percent of an Iraqi brigade; and he claims that the vast majority of journalists use the words they are fed instead of, for instance, saying "70 percent of an Iraqi brigade was killed." He talks of politicians who boast of staying *on message*, a term that connotes monologue more than dialogue, as when, for example, Robert McNamara says in Errol Morris's documentary *The Fog of War*, "You should never answer the question you were asked but only the question you wish you were asked." That's staying "on message."

But one need not venture into war to run into troublesome language. Fortunately, schools offer plenty of ripe examples, such as what I have come to call the "f" word—*facilitate*. You may also be familiar with *task analysis, mastery, benchmarks, self-advocacy, ownership of material, committee work.* Using these terms isn't a life or death matter (in most cases, that is—I've been on some near-fatal committees!), but they do obscure truth and can profoundly affect the way our schools run. NCTE's annual Doublespeak Award is also a good source to explore for possible topics. This award is "an ironic tribute to public speakers who have perpetuated language that is grossly deceptive, evasive, euphemistic, confusing, or self-centered." A list of ignominious winners and samples of their deceptive language are available on the NCTE website (http://www.ncte.org/volunteer/groups/publiclangcom/doublespeakaward). In contrast, NCTE also offers an annual George Orwell Award for "honesty and clarity" in public discourse. Students need to know that many people—and many public speakers in particular—care a great deal about honest speech.

Examples of inexact and irresponsible language abound. President Obama recently boasted of "spending reductions in the tax code," which comedian Jon Stewart rightly pointed out was itself "code for raising taxes," something no politician enjoys saying. Stewart compared Obama's language to saying, "I'm not going on a diet. I'm going to add calories to my excluded food intake!"

Leaving a movie recently, I overheard this conversation: "That was intense; what did you think?" "Yeah, totally intense." *Intense* suggests magnitude but nothing else by itself. Was the movie intensely sad, intensely disturbing? I wanted to ask. Helping people respond to art is what I do for a living, so part of me was glad that I wouldn't be out of a job anytime soon, but I wondered if pat expressions like this don't create walls to stop our feeling, our ablity to talk and think about the world.

Does this make me a snob, a stereotypical joyless English teacher who doesn't know when he's off the clock? I hope not. It's not as though I cringe every time I encounter infelicitous language—and I certainly don't want my students to become nitpickers, pouncing on the verbal miscues of others. But I do think it's important to be aware of imprecise and unethical language, because language matters and it can have a huge impact on the way we live our lives.

Death Sentences

In "Politics and the English Language," George Orwell, writing sixty-five years ago, warns of our "declining language," but suggests "the process is reversible" (157). He argues that language should be used as "an instrument for expressing and not for concealing or preventing thought" (170). As we read Orwell and contemporary opinion pieces that focus on language, I ask my students to start making lists in their writer's notebooks of words that obscure or distort truth. On almost a daily basis, op-ed writers write essays that focus on connotations they find disturbing, and students readily offer examples from television, newspapers, and magazines.

The first time I tried this assignment, Barack Obama had just announced his candidacy for president. Shortly thereafter, Senator Joe Biden infamously "complimented" Obama as being "clean and articulate." This language was so loaded with unpleasant—and possibly unintentional—connotations that it inspired quite a few pieces. The best one I came across was this unusually long op-ed in the *New York Times* by Lynette Clemetson, which I merely excerpt here:

The Racial Politics of Speaking Well

Senator Joseph R. Biden's characterization of his fellow Democratic presidential contender Senator Barack Obama as "the first mainstream African-American who is articulate and bright and clean and a nice-looking guy" was so painfully clumsy that it nearly warranted pity.

There are not enough column inches on this page to parse interpretations of each of Mr. Biden's chosen adjectives. But among his string of loaded words, one is so pervasive—and is generally used and viewed so differently by blacks and whites—that it calls out for a national chat, perhaps a national therapy session.

It is amazing that this still requires clarification, but here it is. Black people get a little testy when white people call them "articulate."

Though it was little noted, on Wednesday President Bush on the Fox News Channel also described Mr. Obama as "articulate." On any given day, in any number of settings, it is likely to be one of the first things white people warmly remark about Oprah Winfrey; Richard Parsons, chief executive of Time Warner; Secretary of State Condoleezza Rice; Deval Patrick, the newly elected governor of Massachusetts; or a recently promoted black colleague at work.

A series of conversations about the word with a number of black public figures last week elicited the kind of frustrated responses often uttered between blacks, but seldom shared with whites.

"You hear it and you just think, 'Damn, this again?'" said Michael Eric Dyson, a professor of humanities at the University of Pennsylvania.

Anna Perez, the former communications counselor for Ms. Rice when she was national security adviser, said, "You just stand and wonder, 'When will this foolishness end?'"

Said Reginald Hudlin, president of entertainment for Black Entertainment Television: "It makes me weary, literally tired, like, 'Do I really want to spend my time right now educating this person?'"

So what is the problem with the word? Whites do not normally object when it is used to describe them. And it is not as if articulate black people do not wish to be thought of as that. The characterization is most often meant as a form of praise.

"Look, what I was attempting to be, but not very artfully, is complimentary," Mr. Biden explained to Jon Stewart on Wednesday on "The Daily Show.""This is an incredible guy. This is a phenomenon."

What faint praise, indeed. Being articulate must surely be a baseline requirement for a former president of *The Harvard Law Review*. After all, Webster's definitions of the word include "able to speak" and "expressing oneself easily and clearly." It would be more incredible, more of a phenomenon, to borrow two more of the senator's puzzling words, if Mr. Obama were inarticulate.

That is the core of the issue. When whites use the word in reference to blacks, it often carries a subtext of amazement, even bewilderment. It is similar to praising a female executive or politician by calling her "tough" or "a rational decision-maker."

"When people say it, what they are really saying is that someone is articulate for a black person," Ms. Perez said.

Such a subtext is inherently offensive because it suggests that the recipient of the "compliment" is notably different from other black people.

"Historically, it was meant to signal the exceptional Negro," Mr. Dyson said. "The implication is that most black people do not have the capacity to engage in articulate speech, when white people are automatically assumed to be articulate."

And such distinctions discount as inarticulate historically black patterns of speech. "Al Sharpton is incredibly articulate," said Tricia Rose, professor of Africana Studies at Brown University. "But because he speaks with a cadence and style that is firmly rooted in black rhetorical tradition you will rarely hear white people refer to him as articulate."

While many white people do not automatically recognize how, and how often, the word is applied, many black people can recall with clarity the numerous times it has stopped them in their tracks....

Together, my students and I discussed the structure of the article, the way the author immediately sets up the context for the essay (Biden had just made the remark and she quotes him directly) and then develops a larger context. Had this been a one-time slip by a single politician, the essay could only safely allege that Biden's words were racist. But Clemetson's essay has larger ambitions—she's calling for a "national therapy session." To justify this larger reach, she catalogs a number of examples of similar language and she invokes the authority of scholars and media commentators to corroborate her claims. Her tone is impressively dispassionate (in sharp contrast to much of the commentary that followed Biden's press conference), and her points are persuasive and compelling in part because she maintains this even tone throughout the piece—even though her attitude toward her subject is never in doubt.

Having looked at some professional models with the students, including poems, essays, and newspaper pieces, I introduce the new assignment:

> In your next essay, write a 1- to 2-page essay in which you comment on a word, phrase, or idea that distorts language, corrupts speech, or obfuscates thought. Use the topic as your title (*On the Subject of Friendly Fire, Traveling Hopefully, Thinking about the Real World, It's All Academic Anyway*) and immediately ground the topic in a specific example. This way your reader will see right away that the problem exists.
>
> While you might begin by shuffling through a mental catalog of language you find upsetting, the topic you settle on should be more than just a pet peeve; your topic should implicitly answer the difficult "So what?" ques-

tion. In other words, you must consider why the dead or deadening language you are focusing on matters and why the reader would want or need to know your take on this issue.

Feel free to quote from an outside source to anchor your argument. This not only demonstrates that language is being used irresponsibly, but it also suggests an audience—the people who used the language irresponsibly or people who have heard that irresponsible language without noticing.

Brainstorm for three possible phrases tonight. We'll look at them together in class tomorrow.

Proposals

I treat these initial topics as paper proposals, and we consider at least one from each student in class. The distinction between trivial annoyance and irresponsible or unethical language surfaces immediately. Brandon says he hates it when people say, "Um." We agree we want to concentrate on actual language. Patrick says he hates the word *juxtapose*. "Why?" the girl next to him asks. "I don't know. I just hate the way it sounds." We all agree this is rather petty. So too are other suggestions (e.g., overuse of the word *like* or *totally*; beginning sentences with *And*; people who say "later" when they are leaving, since it's obvious it will be later than it is now when you next see them). Jessi, however, says she wonders why we call rich neighborhoods "good" and poor neighborhoods "bad." She's clearly on to something. We discuss the blurring of economics and morality and she's ready to write.

Caroline says she's been hearing the word *retarded* more around school. The word didn't use to bother her so much, but now she thinks of her friend whose younger brother has Down syndrome. What if someone were to refer to that little boy with a casual, cruel remark? "I don't think people mean anything by that," Charlie challenges. "That's just it," Caroline responds. "They don't think. Words can hurt." She too has a topic.

Drew is bothered by the word *unreal*—as in "Did you see that girl walk by? She was unreal." It's a potentially hilarious topic, but not everyone is convinced it's meaty enough. Drew argues that he has heard it in many different contexts: people's looks, sports highlights, classmates' math abilities. I wonder about the "So what?" question, too. I approve the topic but ask him to see me as soon as he has a draft.

A student in another class has an intriguing topic. The Memphis Tigers are in the NCAA championship game and the announcers keep referring to them as "unorthodox." This is a subtle topic: since their starting lineup consists entirely of African American players, it sounds as though the announcers are using some sort of code, but of what? If he can unpack this language and demonstrate that the word connotes something else—racism? class prejudice?—he'll have a potentially fascinating essay. But if he cannot take the essay beyond the level of a "strange description," his readers will be unsatisfied.

Here are a few recent topics my students have developed into essays.

Death Row

"That's so retarded." The last word resonates in my ear as I flip my head in search for the culprit. No luck. The surge of students carries on, pulsing through the hallway without the slightest delay. After one last squinting look over my shoulder I saunter into the AP Biology room. Today's lecture: Genetic Disorders. In class I think of Max, my best friend's younger brother who has Down syndrome. The thought of him overhearing such a degrading and pejorative comment makes my stomach turn. According to the Thesaurus, the word "retarded" is synonymous with the terms: backward, underachieving, stupid, slow, and dull. In my eyes, Max fails to reflect any one of those characteristics.

"Down syndrome or trisomy 21 is a genetic disorder caused by the presence of a superfluous chromosome on the twenty-first pair," Mr. C's voice booms over the classroom. Not once during his lecture did Mr. C use the word retarded to describe individuals with Down syndrome, Autism, or Cerebral Palsy. Unfortunately, Mental Retardation, characterized by an intelligence quotient (IQ) of 70 or below, continues to be an accepted clinical term. Just recently, however, in June 2006 members of the former American Association on Mental Retardation voted to change the name of the organization to the "American Association on Intellectual and Developmental Disabilities." Despite such small efforts to eliminate the offensive term in the scientific world, colloquial usage of the word "retarded" does not cease.

It's nearly impossible to go a day without overhearing even some of New Trier's "best and brightest" students use the term. Nearing the end of my eighth period AP Biology class, Victor asks, "Wait, don't we have a double period today?"

"Today's Wednesday. We get ninth free, idiot," Justin retorts.

"Oh, right. God, I'm so retarded."

Clearly, Victor, an AP Biology student at New Trier, would never be categorized as being mentally retarded. How hard is it for a gifted student to think of an alternative word for "retarded"? Apparently, very hard. But who is to blame for this disgusting and habitual misuse of a word? Some would say the music industry is partially culpable. In 2004, the Black Eyed Peas (a popular hip-hop group) released their new hit album: Elephunk. The album's most popular song, "Let's Get

Retarded," naturally created a stir. The phrase "Let's Get Retarded" is west coast slang that means to go crazy on the dance floor (synonyms are "Go Dumb" and "Get/Go stupid"). However, like many other inside phrases this one was easily misinterpreted. It is disturbing that a musical group with the power to influence millions of people worldwide would choose a title and lyrics that could so easily offend those who are mentally challenged as well as their families and friends.

The term "retarded" has waited on death row for years and it's time for the final sentence. In a perfect world, Max's peers would not ridicule him, but rather appreciate him as the outstanding human being that he truly is. This utopia is not idealistic nor out of reach. All it takes is a vocabulary clean of dead terms.
—Caroline, grade 12

The tone of this essay reveals the passionate personal engagement the author has with this issue. While she grounds her paper with a personal anecdote, she takes advantage of her own scientific knowledge as well, quoting her biology teacher on the subject of chromosomal differences. The contrast of her teacher's sensitivity to her classmates' apparent lack thereof goes a long way toward proving her point. The author urges her readers to be as empathetic as her teacher, Mr. C. The extended metaphor of death row, from which she takes her title, feels forced to me—and several students who read this paper as a class model have objected to her own "loose language." Great, I say. Go ahead and write that paper!

Bus People

Why were the bus boys left behind? In a society where waitresses became servers, mankind became humankind, and stewardesses became flight attendants, why has the term *bus boy* survived? We all know that many modern bus boys are, in fact, not boys. They are not young in age and some aren't even male. Each Sunday when I read the weekly schedule at Boston Blackies Bar and Grill I can't help but feel a sense of anger when I see the term bus boy.

To start, all the bus boys I know and work with are far from boys. Adalberto, a professional bus boy, is the father to two children. Each day he leaves home around 10 am, takes two busses to work, and may not return home until as late as 1 am. He feeds his family on about $12 an hour (if the restaurant is busy). If Adalberto's children, Josefina and Miguelito, want to attend college, scholarships are a must. Yet each day he arrives, usually energetic and charismatic, ready to fulfill his duties. Although he has a childish sense of humor, his work ethic proves otherwise. Regardless of the situation, he will drop everything to assist a customer or coworker. Ironically, his coworkers have been liberated from their former titles.

The waitresses have become servers; the host and hostesses, "Greeters." Each employee, from chef to server, does his or her part to keep the restaurant operational. No one job is easier than another, bus boys included.

Not only is there this radical age discrepancy, the title itself is misleading. Yes, bus boys "bus" the used plates and glasses from the table; however, the job doesn't end there. They are the first to arrive each morning, cleaning whatever didn't get cleaned the night before, preparing utensil wrap-ups for each table, cleaning the silverware, stocking the kitchen, the list goes on. The heart and soul of the restaurant, all would cease to function without the bus boys.

Enough of bus and enough of boy. Neither is accurate. Each day the bus boys like Adalberto work just has hard as anyone else and have nearly nothing to show for it but a lousy and inaccurate title. Man or woman, young or old: the bus boys deserve more.

—Al, grade 12

This is a remarkably sensitive essay. Not only does the author reveal a keen sensitivity to restaurant language on the whole (greeters, servers), but he also shows great maturity in how he approaches the offending term. Note that he never complains about his own status. Instead, he creates the character of Adalberto, filling him out as a married man with children he hopes will one day go to college. Further, Adalberto is shown as a man of enormous competence who is the "heart and soul of the restaurant." The personal and passionate tone here raise the essay to a higher level than a fussy parsing of words. This essay derives its power from Al's ability to distinguish his character's three-dimensional humanity from the inadequate label.

This assignment encourages students to think about language seriously, language that is bandied about in the media and in their everyday conversations. While we are all, perhaps, better at hearing imprecise, unfortunate, or unethical language in other people's language than we are in our own, this essay also encourages students to consider the implications of the language they use. These skills will form the basis of blog posts, discussed in the next chapter, and will be essential in conducting the interviews and research described in Chapters 9 and 10.

Writing Out Loud: Blogging in (and out) of the Classroom

8

Katie's post

My mom recently received an email from the superintendent regarding a civil rights data collection survey from the US Department of Education our school must fill out. One part of this survey requires the school to report the races of all the students. The email informed my mother that her daughter (me) has reported herself as biracial based on the school records. However, the survey does not offer this option. Which leaves me forced to answer the question: what race *am* I? I have never identified myself with one race or the other (black or white). If I choose white, I'm neglecting the fact my father is a black man and vice-versa. I found it interesting that the Department of Education found it fitting to call their survey a "civil rights" survey when they force students like me to make a decision on which race they are over the other. I was born both races, and I am proud to be both, as anyone should be of their own race. Why is it that the Department of Education has, for forty years, decided to ignore the more than 6 million Americans who identify as multiracial? (Census Scope).

The legal definition of the phrase "Civil Rights" is defined as many things, including the "freedom from discrimination." To further clarify, the dictionary defines discrimination as "making a distinction in favor of or against, a person or thing based on the group, class, or category to which that person or thing belongs rather than on individual merit." In my opinion, the Civil Rights Data Collection survey is doing just this.

Not only can you not choose more than one, but there are only 5 options:

- White
- Black
- American Indian/Alaska Native
- Asian/Pacific Islander
- Hispanic

Middle Eastern? Not an option. But I guess they could just be Asian for this survey, right? Multiracial? Not an option. Just choose one, it doesn't matter, right?

Do you think the civil rights survey is discriminatory? Why do you think they leave out multiracial as an option? Why do they only have five options and do not include an "other" option for people to write in their race?
—Katie, grade 11 (original emphasis)

This blog post encapsulates much of what I have come to love about blogging. The author, a young biracial woman in an American Studies class, writes about an important personal issue whose ramifications extend throughout US society. Katie had been writing an analysis of hip-hop culture and the depiction of African Americans in the mainstream media when she received a notice from school about the Civil Rights Data Collection Survey. For the first time in her life, Katie was forced to identify herself by a single category of race. So she decided to write about her own predicament and to explore the larger social dimensions of the issue. I believe blogs, which allow for pictures, audio, video, and links to additional sources, several of which Katie used in her online post, are an ideal medium to explore such topics. But I didn't always feel this way.

Blog Convert

For twenty years or so, I took part in the ritual that anthropologists will one day soon call the Ancient Practice of Journal Collection. You know: the ritual of hauling home notebooks from more than 100 students to see how they responded to literary and writing prompts designed to extend classroom discussions and to help students prepare for upcoming assignments. As I mentioned in the introduction, I try to offer only positive comments and questions to encourage students to probe further—but that was when I could read their writing! At best, they looked like the handwriting in Figure 8.1 (and believe me, this is one of the most legible examples I could find).

Dutifully, I'd carry each pile from my classroom to my desk, the stack of journals so high I'd often walk blindly from my classroom to my office, avoiding stairs. Then I'd overstuff them into canvas bags, the kind you might pick up for free from publishers in the Exhibit Hall at an NCTE Annual Convention. I'd teeter down the street on my bicycle like an inept circus performer, a clown on a tightrope, with a bag of journals drooping over either side of the handlebars, acting as counterweights.

All that changed five years ago when I discovered blogging. I'd heard of blogs, of course, but that year, Will Richardson, a technology consultant, Web guru, and former teacher, came to our school for Fall Institute day. He quickly made an impressive case for the rise in blogging and then demonstrated how

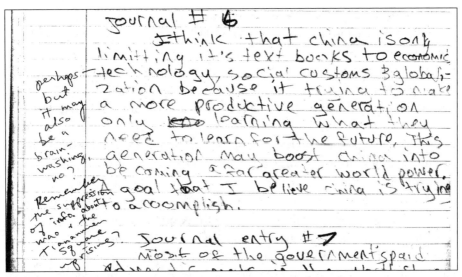

FIGURE 8.1: All too typical example of teen handwriting: Richie, grade 11.

easy it was to start a blog. Using a common tool such as Blogger, he explained, a new blog can be up and running in about three minutes. Richardson ended his talk by beseeching his audience to, if nothing else, start a blog that afternoon. I haven't talked with any other colleagues in attendance that day who took Richardson up on his plea. But I remember sitting in the back of that auditorium, picturing the pathetic spectacle of myself on that bicycle, and knowing right then and there that I had to take the plunge.

In about thirty minutes, I had not only started a blog but also written my first post, entitled "An American Studies":

> ***AN** American Studies (as opposed to American Studies or **THE** American Studies) suggests that this is just one attempt at making sense of a vast topic. Anyone who thinks they are covering everything essential to this enormous enterprise in a year long course—or perhaps over the course of their lives—is just kidding him or herself.
>
> *This blog will reflect the "**studies**"—gathering, questioning, and trading information with a community of scholars—of one American. Millions of people are approaching the topic of "America," but we don't presume to speak for them.
>
> *An American *[is a person who]* studies. While this does not happen always (maybe it is an impossibility), it is necessary for our country to achieve its highest ideal—that all of its citizens can achieve self-fulfillment. Studies—in the broadest possible sense of that word—must be part of this achievement.

That post from the blog, which is now called www.anamericanstudies.com, has had, in the past four years, more than 100,000 hits from more than 130 countries. Luckily, my—now *our*—current blog was designed with my team teacher, Spiro Bolos. In the interest of full disclosure, I should add that Spiro, in addition to being a terrific social studies teacher, is also a technology specialist at my school. But one of the important things I have learned from him is that starting a blog requires no special expertise. In our team-taught American Studies course, Spiro and I alternate posts throughout the year to extend class discussions, to relate major ideas in American Studies to current events, and to model effective posts for our students. Beyond that, we ask each student to set up his or her own blog, and we include a list of each student's blog on our homepage. Simple as they are, blogs have revolutionized my thinking about teaching, and I have come to see them as indispensable tools for any teacher interested in personal writing. In the rest of this chapter, I make a case for the value of blogging and talk about how blogs work in my classroom, specifically, in an interdisciplinary American Studies course.

Before hearing Will Richardson talk, I might have been one of the most unlikely converts to blogging. I admit I once held a view similar to that of American Library Association President Michael Gorman, who wrote an opinion piece in *Library Journal* titled "Revenge of the Blog People!" in which he called the blog "a species of interactive electronic diary by means of which the unpublishable, untrammeled by editors or the rules of grammar, can communicate their thoughts via the web." Gorman's title alone suggests a technological nightmare world controlled by a subspecies of cybergeek. I too worried that the barbarians were at the gate, but I was at least as curious as I was wary.

Even then I was aware of the overwhelming wave of information being transmitted electronically, especially through blogs. In fact, new blogs are currently being created at rate of more than one per second (Richardson 19). These numbers are especially robust among young people: "47% of teen bloggers write outside of school for personal reasons several times a week or more; 53% of nonbloggers think blogging is essential to later success in life" ("Blogging Helps Encourage Teen Writing"). This last statistic is especially noteworthy because it suggests that even nonbloggers are convinced of the importance of blogging. They are not alone. In a 2006 *English Education* article, Swenson and colleagues argue that "full participation in our globalized world also demands extensive experience with new literacies and the innovative thinking and flexible communication that grow from technological expertise" (365). Blogs help students practice these new literacies.

Like many teachers, I was also acutely aware of the amount of time my students spend online. "Young people today live media-saturated lives, spending an average of nearly 6☐ hours a day with media" (source qtd. in Swenson et al., 360). According to Lenhart et al. of the Pew Internet and American Life Project, 93 percent of American teens use the Internet, and of those teens online, 28 percent have created their own journal or blog (cited in Hurlburt). While it is true that a 2010 poll shows students increasingly migrating to social media sites such as Facebook and Twitter, blogs offer the best means of practicing essay writing in the online arena. Blogs can also help satisfy a major goal of mine as a teacher, as well as a primary goal of this book: to bridge the gap between students' lives in school and their lives outside of school.

A further key for me was the realization that blogging, as Danah Boyd puts it, is "primarily [about] communication, not publishing." That is why blogs are such a potent classroom tool. Yes, blogs generally allow for more leniency with respect to punctuation and stylistic conventions—but that's because they are really more about conversation than declaration. In fact, the influential journalist Andrew Sullivan, who has blogged for *Time, The New Republic,* and *The Atlantic*—says blogging is, in many ways, "writing out loud." The two-way street format of blogs, what Will Richardson calls the Read/Write Web, allows students to continue conversations with the community of teachers and fellow students outside of the classroom. (Think of the hundreds of responses—in less than a day—to the Nicholas Kristof op-ed I mentioned in Chapter 6. Online writing has revolutionized the relationship of writer and reader.) Contrast this dynamic with that of hard copy notebooks. There, only the student and I were engaged in a dialogue, whereas blogs allow participation from the entire classroom community and, indeed, the larger community of online blog readers.

The community building that blogs can promote makes them especially attractive to me as a classroom teacher. Blogs, Danah Boyd argues, have "tremendous potential for the classroom and this potential is in large part linked to the social network structure." The homepage of our classroom blog gives students a common base, a common text on which to focus our discussions. Reading and commenting on one another's blogs also builds community because students come to see one another as fellow seekers, fellow human beings with a wide range of interests and views. Many students have had conversations with classmates—online and in person—after learning of another person's interest in sports, music, politics, etc.

In the five years our blog has been up and running, we have had only a couple of instances in which students have responded inappropriately (with offensive language) to each other. And even then, those conversations became new opportunities to talk about tone and audience, issues that bloggers must always consider because of the immediacy of the audiences —the specific bloggers students are responding to—and the form of the comments, relatively short responses that usually address the tone—the passion, the outrage, the wonder—of the blog post.

The benefit of blogging for other types of writing has been documented outside of our class as well. Josh Keller, writing for the *Chronicle of Higher Education*, has concluded that "students who compose messages for an audience of their peers on a social networking site were forced to be acutely aware of issues like audience, tone, and voice." Rather than compete with the academic writing students do in other classes, Keller adds, "the out of class writing [such as blogs] actually made them more conscious of the things writing teachers want them to think about." An *eSchool News* article cites Bradley A. Hammer, who teaches in Duke University's writing program, as saying that "the kind of writing students do on blogs and other digital formats actually can be better than the writing style they learn in school, because it is better suited to true intellectual pursuit than is SAT-style writing" ("Blogging Helps"). Jamey Gallagher goes even further, suggesting that what blogs are doing is

> [f]undamentally . . . arguing in a more complex and more provisional way than a lot of other genres will allow. They open up a space in which thoughtful response is more important than thesis-driven essay analysis. . . . [W]e are not being asked to believe one thing and one thing only. The very temporary nature of the blog entry encourages thought instead of closure. (291)

Gallagher also makes an argument similar to the one I made in Chapter 1: writing is *not* a zero sum game in which your view or mine wins. Rather, writing—and blog writing in particular—can treat the reader as an ally, not an opponent, in the continuing search for understanding.

Classroom Blogs

Before assigning blogs, Spiro and I typically ask how many students have had experience writing blogs. The number of students who have tried blogging is clearly on the rise, but the first year we tried this, only one student had blogged previously. Rather sheepishly, Eli raised his hand and told us he had been blogging about baseball for a while. When he offered to show the class his blog online, I accepted at once, but secretly I was afraid we'd all be reading his online diary entries ("Today I saw a double header") or the random rants that fill most call-in sports shows ("The Yankees suck and Derek Jeter shouldn't make more money than I do"). Instead, what he showed us was a stunning, professional blog (now mlbdailydish.com) about baseball news—trade talks, strategy, and interviews he conducted with players he reached mostly online. It was immediately clear that this kid had a lot to teach his teachers. He's not alone in this respect.

A recent article in *The Reading Teacher* emphatically pointed out that "today's students possess knowledge about the Internet that we, as teachers, have not yet acquired. Inviting our students to play the role of 'expert' is not always comfortable because it means we must teach differently. We believe it is worth the risk" (Boling et al. 506). I'm never surprised by students who possess more technical knowledge than I do; what I care most about is their writing and critical thinking.

The assignment is simple: at a minimum, students must post once a week and comment on a different student's blog once a week. Anything students do beyond this is extra credit. Since there are approximately the same number of students in class as there are weeks in the school year—our team-taught classes enroll around forty to forty-five students—almost every student responds to every other student in the course of the year. Additionally, we invite students to comment on our homepage posts, which we also offer as models. This is a great way to encourage reluctant students who avoid the fray of large-class discussion. The number of comments on our posts offers built-in proof that our work matters to some people and that there is an audience for our ideas.

The form and length of blog posts vary widely, so we generally allow students to feel their way into the process. One year, to offer a little more guidance, I passed out the following tips on writing blog posts:

1. **Enter a conversation** the same way you would at lunchtime. You might remind people of a previous discussion ("Last week when we were talking about global warming, I remember thinking . . ."). If you're mentioning a topic for the first time, find a gentle way to bring up the topic ("I watched *An Inconvenient Truth* last weekend and it's got me thinking. . . ."). The most common ways of joining ongoing conversations is to listen to what other people are saying and jumping in when you have something new to add, some way of extending the points being made.

2. **Audience**: Ask yourself, *Who would want or need to hear what I have to say?* If you can find someone who sees things differently than you do, you have a built-in audience. But your posts can also extend discussions ("I agree with Tim, but I also think . . ."). Or, if you don't understand something or someone, you might write for the sake of clarification. Since we don't want to alienate our readers, make sure you consider your tone when responding to other people. ("The undying loyalty of Cub fans is fascinating to observe" is usually a better lead than "Why would anyone in their right mind root for the Cubs?"). Even if you are responding to one other person

directly, remember that the blogosphere is enormous and that you may have a much bigger audience than a single reader.

3. **Current events**: Like newspaper articles, blogs carry the burden of currency. They must be relevant. They must be *news*. This point is related to the previous two. It's difficult to bring up a topic from the distant past if the audience has no connection to it. Blogs for this class should comment on our current class discussions or current events in the world around us.

4. **Extend the conversation**: Once you find an interesting topic, make sure your post does more than merely restate someone else's position. What is *your* take on the issue? To what extent do you agree with the author / speaker of that position? Where, if at all, do you disagree with the position? What else can you add to the ongoing discussion?

Here is the blog post that drove me to offer these guidelines:

Danny's post: Seinfeld Reunion

I have seen many television shows throughout my 16 years of life, but none better than *Seinfeld*. *Seinfeld* is a sitcom about four people and their daily lives. It is one of the most popular shows in television history. I have [heard] many *Seinfeld* fans talk about a reunion of the cast and [Photo] maybe to do one more episode. Although this would very interesting to see as a fan of the show, I would highly advise against it if I were a member of the cast. I think that having one last episode would ruin the entire series. There is no way that the cast could come back and recapture the magic from the past. Especially because of the incident the actor that played Kramer had a few years back. I believe he was being heckled and then he made some racist remarks towards the heckler. I think that bringing back the cast and crew from *Seinfeld* would be just as disastrous as when Michael Jordan came out of retirement and decided to play for the Wizards. All of the *Seinfeld* episodes were so great during the 1990's and if they do one last episode, people will be expecting even better, and I just don't think that is possible.
—Danny, grade 11

I created the guidelines in an attempt to figure out why this post is so unsatisfying and how I could help Danny revise his post. As I always do when students' writing falls short of the assignment, I tried to determine where I had not been clear enough. Here the author doesn't seem to know of any ongoing conversations (*who* is clamoring for another final episode?); he doesn't consider his audience's views on the topic (no one is quoted, not even a casual friend); and perhaps most troubling, it's never clear why the topic was relevant to our class or to readers at large (the show had ended more than ten years earlier). This is not to say that students can't write on this topic, only that they have to identify the occasion for the post—Michael Richards's (Kramer's) much publicized racist tirade at a comedy club, say, the release of a new boxed set, or even someone else's blog post. Even then, the author would need to think carefully about the audience who might want or need to hear the post. If the demand exists, identify the ongoing conversation—quote it!—and then extend the discussion by offering a new take on the topic. I should add here that Danny became a much better blogger when the instructions were clearer.

Here's a philosophical post that still falls a little short of satisfying the preceding guidelines:

Basil's post: Controlling the Past

In [American Studies] class we have been talking a lot about how our views of the past as a society change over time. I've been thinking about how I see the meaning of the quote Mr. O'Connor gave us from the novel 1984, "He who controls the present controls the past. He who controls the past controls the future." The first section has an obvious meaning to me, that the present is constantly becoming the past so one who has control over what is occurring in the present subsequently controls the past as those events they controlled when they were present become past. But then I realized there was another meaning as well. The one in power during the present gets to control how past events are perceived. In this way, controlling the present gives one control over not only the history of their own time in power, but also the historical recollection of past events before their time in power. My initial interpretation of the second section relied on the assumption that past events and our present interpretation of the second section relied on the assumption that past events and our present interpretation of them dictate what future decisions are made. I point this out as an assumption because I have seen, many times in fact, that a society can be prone to making the same mistake twice. Because of this I sought a different way to interpret this piece of the quote. I believe it means that one who is in power in the present, and therefore controls the past, can use evidence from the past (which they control) to justify and rationalize decisions for the future.
—Basil, grade 11

Basil's post shows how much thought goes on in students' minds long after the bell has sounded. The author is genuinely wrestling with a philosophical paradox that makes him reevaluate his own thinking. Blogs offer students a chance to work out their takes on difficult subject matter, such as the Orwell quote he cites here. Ideally, this blog would move to the level of specific example, however. Basil says he has seen societies make the same mistake twice, but he never gives a concrete instance of such a mistake. A contemporary example would also likely help the blog post meet the requirement of currency.

I'm often amazed at the connections students make in blogs between their own lives and class texts and discussions. This next student makes a fascinating connection between *Harry Potter and the Goblet of Fire* and social class in America.

Harley's post: Fantasy to Reality

This past weekend I was just rereading one of the greatest fantasy book series of my lifetime **Harry Potter** and in the fourth book **The Goblet of Fire** they discuss an idea that I believe can be used to show a flaw in society. When Hermione is talking to Hagrid about the shocking idea that the school Hogwarts is in fact run by hundreds of House Elves, Hagrid the says that "You know a good house elf is around when you do **not even notice them.**" This caused me to think about the subject [from class] on how Americans try to build society so that the wealthy do not have to **see or acknowledge the poverty around them.** This led me to believe that J.K. Rowling has noticed how culture currently tries to separate the poor and the wealthy, the working class from the wealthy, and she displays this with the flawed system of house elves. People in the book believe that this is [the way] it has always been and do not want the change of having to pay for their personal slaves, just like how in America people are very adamant by keeping the lower class down with the funding of public schools being so unbalanced. For example, [our suburban] school has at least triple the funding of most inner city schools in the Chicago land area. By giving the wealthy even more education they are taking away the possible people from non wealthy areas chances of climbing the social ladder. The working class are the rich people's house elves and unless we take a stand they will continue to have a further gap between the two. At one point the working class will even beat themselves up for even thinking about reaching the next level just like Doby.
—Harley, grade 11

This post reveals an inquisitive mind as the author begins to develop a stunning parallel between the world of Harry Potter and our classroom discussion on social class. The post is a tad rough; it rambles a bit and consists of one long paragraph. I have also cleaned up some spelling errors just for the sake of clarity. But again, if we view this post as a communication tool rather than a monograph on sociology, it's easy to see how it might engender follow-up discussion in and out of class. The words in bold are the author's attempt to guide the reader to the most important points, but he has not quite learned to bold full phrases and sentences. For example, the second bold passage might quote the entire sentence: **Americans try to build society so that the wealthy do not have to see or acknowledge the poverty around them.**

Molly's post: Arizona's Immigration Laws

The news about Arizona's new law is all over the place, so I wanted to take the time to examine the situation. If you haven't heard about it, <u>here</u> is a link to a NY Times article providing background. Here's the summary of the law that this article provides:

It requires police officers, "when practicable," to detain people they reasonably suspect are in the country without authorization and to verify their status with federal officials.

This law also makes it illegal to be caught without papers such as a green card or driver's license for citizenship. This in itself has several implications—for example, a girl in the AIS day discussion told others that she, like many other people, often forgets things, and that it might not be fair to place misdemeanor charges on someone who is forgetful or disorganized. That being said, I'm not arguing that immigration reform isn't needed; it takes 15 years for some people to legally enter the country, and millions of people try to enter illegally every year.

The argument of people that disagree with the new law is that **it might encourage racial and ethnic discrimination** because border patrol and immigrations officers ("la migra") will only be looking for people who can't speak English fluently or look Hispanic. Now, I suppose that means that only a select group will be pulled aside. However, in my opinion, just because someone doesn't have my blond hair and pale complexion does not mean that they should be questioned by the police. This law has the potential to cause significant Hispanic discrimination.

My belief is that **the key to deterring illegal immigration is in better enforcing the law that prevents illegal immigrants from being hired. Some people think that making the borders impossible to cross solves the problem, but instead that creates thousands of horrible deaths for people who try to do it anyway.** Constantly checking IDs won't help either because not every illegal immigrant will be caught, or plenty of legal immigrants will be unfairly questioned. Not giving jobs to illegal immigrants will hopefully end up shifting those jobs to legal immigrants or other Americans. However, **I acknowledge that there is a lot I don't understand about the issue. What would you do?**
—Molly, grade 11

This author tackles a major story of the day, one we discussed in class and that she says was being discussed in her home as well. I like the way the author grounds the topic with a link to a news source, allowing her and her readers to share a common text. She also does a great job bolding key phrases from the post to guide her readers' responses. Best of all, her conclusion modestly and honestly acknowledges her limits in understanding this enormous topic, which politicians and judges grapple with every day. Her invitation to respond is not only a call for comments but also a genuine plea for help in understanding the topic more fully. Rather than foreclose on the topic by merely spouting her own view, Molly's post shows a desire to learn more.

Students often struggle to invent topics to blog about. In an age of declining newspapers, the source most teachers might instinctively rely on, where should students look? Again, Spiro and I attempt to model sources on our homepage: newspapers, radio, podcasts. Class texts and conversations also spark many blogs.

In the following model, the student discusses his struggle up front and takes up a thought from class as a point of departure.

Kevin's post: No Subject

I couldn't think of a subject for this post. I looked all the usual places: newspapers, TED [Talks], and NPR. But with all the tabs up in my browser, nothing was right for a post. I didn't want to write about something that was already in the news every day. I didn't want to rant about the people who use "common sense" to justify complex ideas. Finally, I thought of something Mr. B. talked about in class last week.

[Mr. B] talked about [how] it is hard to come up with ideas for your essay by just staring at it. Sleeping is when your brain is actually making the connections. I looked this up and found an interesting study on how distraction can aid in problem-solving. Three professors did a study (the raw data requires a subscription) in which 130 people were given a Remote-Association Test. This test was for the person to determine what 3 different words all had in common. An example are the words: cheese, sky, and ocean. The answer would be "blue" because it is commonly used with each of the other words. Half of the sample set, the "conscious" set, were told to study the questions for five minutes; whereas, the other half, the "unconscious," looked at the questions and then did something completely different for five minutes.

The results were that the conscious set did better on easy questions, but the unconscious set actually was faster at answering the difficult ones. The conclusion was that conscious thought produces linear results. It is very analytical because every new idea comes directly from the idea before it. Unconscious thought, the kind of thought that happens even when you are doing something else, is better at solving complex problems. This is because different parts of the brain are activated and actually help to manipulate the problem.

I think it raises an interesting question about teaching in school. For the most part, each day is broken into discrete parts that focus intensely on one subject. With the double period American Studies, we have time to come back to an idea from earlier in the class, but that isn't the case with other subjects. Do you think that school is arranged in the optimal way, or do you think there should be changes?
—Kevin, grade 11

Kevin's opening here is a metacognitive map of sorts. He reflects on his own writing process and admits his frustration at generating a suitable blog topic. By this point in the year, he had developed some go-to sites that had proven fruitful with earlier posts. Now, however, he was a little stuck. But thinking about something from class discussion gave him a search term that he pursued on his own. He has not necessarily come to any hard conclusions about this topic, but he has delved into the subject on his own. Rather than develop a thesis statement with support, Kevin is content to wonder.

Grading

Reading forty posts a week would be impossible, even split between two teachers. And, of course, we have other classes and responsibilities as well. So Spiro and I have developed a three-part grading system: the total number of posts, the quality of posts, and a self-reflection. We grade student blogs once each quarter. The number of posts is automatically noted on each blog, so it's easy to see at a glance how many posts a student has completed. The quality of the posts is a little trickier. We ask students to choose the blog post they are most proud of (see my class goals in Chapter 11) and write a reflection on their blog—what they have written on, how they have come to see their writing. We encourage students to write on a variety of topics, particularly in a course that attempts to address the broad spectrum of American culture. It's great to see that a kid loves basketball, for example, but if that's all she ever writes about, she's selling the course and herself short. In evaluating the quality of blogs, we mostly check to see if students are following the guidelines provided earlier. We also consider the following checklist when evaluating posts:

Blog Evaluation Checklist
1. Are the blog topics current?
2. Is the author in conversation with other thinkers?
3. How well has the author established the ongoing conversation?

4. Is it clear how the author has extended the conversation, added to it?

5. Is the post grounded in a common text (a class text, a presidential speech, a widely seen TV show)?

6. How clear is the author's voice, his or her attitude toward the topic?

7. How well has the author addressed his or her audience? Is the tone appropriate? Has the author avoided using references or language the audience may not understand?

8. Has the author used tools to enhance the post: links to relevant sources, pictures, audio, video, font choices for emphasis?

9. Has the author implicitly or explicitly invited the audience to respond to the post?

10. Is the post readable in terms of organization, punctuation, etc? (Here our goal is observance of the bare minimum of writing conventions necessary to convey ideas. Occasionally we see posts with so many typos, spelling errors, and abbreviations that the train of thought is hard to follow. Only when these errors are so numerous that they compete with the author's ideas do we mention this to students.)

By grading the blogs once a quarter, we ensure that students know what we are looking for and can offer them a chance to revise subsequent posts. It's important to comment on each student's blog along with any evaluation. Our primary goal is to validate each student's identity as a critical thinker. We try to comment on blogs more than once a quarter, but this isn't always easy to do given the pressures of the school year. The fact that students are commenting on one another's work every week virtually guarantees that each student is receiving regular feedback. It also helps to let students know of the so-called 1% rule: "Looking at statistics from Wikipedia and Yahoo, McConnell estimates that for every one hundred visitors to a collaborative online environment, only one will add content. That's 99 silent lurkers for every visible contribution, which means that even very successful and highly visible social networks have extremely low levels of direct participation from the larger reading (lurking) community" (Hurlburt).

As with the examples in Chapters 2 and 3, the student self-reflection is hugely helpful in learning what students value most, how they see their writing, and where they are struggling. Molly chose to use her post on Arizona's recent immigration laws as her "best blog post":

Molly's Self-Reflection

It's hard to believe that this year is coming to a close! I can fortunately say that I have enjoyed blogging and have learned a lot about the medium through my experiences. My favorite post for this quarter is entitled <u>Arizona's Immigration Law</u>. I picked this post because it demonstrates a better usage of the blogging style than some of my other posts. For example, I used bolding and included a source quote for my readers' convenience. I tried to focus on debating multiple sides so I can further analyze the issue and do not appear polemic[al]. That post is 380 words long, so it is more compact than my favorite post of the first quarter, which was 434 words long. Instead of shortening my analysis, I tried to shorten my source summary in order to make my posts more interesting and reader friendly.

An issue with my blogging in general is that I am afraid to post my own opinion. When reporting, showing opinions in writing is unprofessional, but blogging is more personal. In the Arizona post, I made the decision to put out my own opinion on the issue itself. By posting my opinion, my goal was to let my readers see inside my mind a bit, and offer them the chance to disagree with me.

Another thing I need to work on is putting voice into my blogs. Because blogs are more personal, I have the opportunity to be a little humorous and share personal anecdotes. At first I felt that my readers don't care about what I say about myself, but when reading my peers' blogs, I realized that posts with personal insight are far more interesting and entertaining. Although I haven't been entirely successful with this, I try to inject humor and personal stories into my blog posts whenever appropriate.

Whether or not I will continue this blog is unclear, but I know that I wish to continue the blogging style in some shape or form. I like blogging because of its conversational qualities—it's not a one way lecture or a serious paper, but a discussion about real-world issues with a general audience. This form of writing is more interactive than the other forms of writing we have done in class, and that is one of the reasons why I enjoyed doing it.

Whether this is the final post or just the beginning, to all of my readers, thanks so much!
—Molly, grade 11

This is an unusually well-developed reflection, and it is instructive in its specificity. Molly talks details about audience (shortening her summary and making the post reader-friendly) and explicitly mentions a "source quote" to ground the discussion she is joining. She has come to see that fewer words can be more powerful than a lot and that good bloggers spend more time on analysis than summary.

At the end of the reflection, Molly mentions the issue of voice. Helping students develop voice is a prime goal of mine as a writing teacher and one of the best reasons to use blogs in the classroom. Rather than, say, a *New York Times* article on immigration, in which one expects to find a series of facts, blogs offer the intersection of the personal and the factual. As Danah Boyd says, "when I read blogs . . . I expect to find the nuances, the backstories, the opinions, all framed in a self-critical, culturally critical, individual voice. In other words, I expect to read a different perspective, one fully grounded in the biases of the writer." Molly's post does just that.

Blogs still have plenty of naysayers. As I was writing this chapter, I came across an op-ed by *New York Times* writer David Brooks. In "The Medium Is the Medium," Brooks advances the now popular argument that "the dominant activity [on the Internet] is freewheeling, disrespectful, antiauthority disputation." Brooks fears, as I once did, that the choice is between the literary world and the boorish world of the Internet. But his dichotomy is false, as I hope I have demonstrated through the student examples presented here. Blogging does *not* occur at the expense of reading great works of literature. On the contrary, the conversations my students engage in, and the critical thinking they exhibit, often lead them to read more.

Though I was not an immediate convert, I have come to see blogging as an important 21st century literacy. In 2009–2010, I was asked to blog for the Poetry Foundation's Harriet site and wrote more than twenty posts for them. I have also started a second blog of my own called wordplaygrounds.blogspot.com that I hope will, among other things, serve as a forum for writing education. I have started blogs in other classes I teach as well. The format of this book does not do blog posts justice. Since the links and audiovisual material are not visible, I encourage readers to go to the blog sites mentioned in this chapter, as well as to others; Edublog and Edutopia might be good starting points.

Blogs allow students to voice their opinions on topics and texts from both class and outside of class and to do so in the spirit of ongoing discussion. Just as the last two assignments invited students to join the ongoing intellectual conversations of the day, blogs too help students find themselves within these conversations. The spirit of conversation will be key in the next chapter as well, in which you'll read about students conducting interviews and practicing oral history writing. Blogs are also extremely useful in research writing—but more on this in Chapter 10. For now, let me attest to the usefulness of blogs as their own ends, as powerful tools to help students discover themselves and the world around them by writing out loud.

Heard It through the Grapevine: Oral Histories and Interview Essays

9

> My moment of ultimate astonishment happened about 25 years ago. It was at a public housing project, a young mother, and I don't recall if she was white or black, because it was mixed. I remember her as young, as pretty, skinny, bad teeth, I remember that. The first time she'd ever encountered a tape recorder. These little kids are hopping around and about, they want to playback, a replay, wanna hear their mama's voice in the machine. So I press the button and they howl with delight, but she suddenly puts her hands to her mouth and gasps, "I never knew I felt that way before." Bingo. Jackpot. Not only was she astonished, but I was overwhelmed and astonished. And such astonishments have been forthcoming from the et ceteras of history ever since the year one. And there's more, much more where that came from.
>
> —ACCEPTANCE SPEECH BY STUDS TERKEL, National Book Awards, 1997

This quote captures the best features of Studs Terkel's legendary career as an oral historian: his ability to elicit surprise not only from his readers but also from himself and from his subjects themselves by their responses to his interviews. Like many people, I became interested in oral histories by reading Terkel's essays, and I have used the form to fascinate my students, teaching them a great deal about the academic subjects we are studying and also about the craft of writing.

In this chapter, I discuss the structure of oral histories and essays that are based on interviews. This technique has wide use across many disciplines. As with other essay assignments described in this book, I provide a combination of professional and student models. The student examples reprinted in this chapter represent the themes for which I have implemented this technique: the American dream, civil rights, Vietnam War literature, and race. Professional models of these themes can be found in works such as Terkel's *American Dreams: Lost and Found, Working,* and *Race: How Blacks and Whites Think and Feel about the American Obsession*; Ellen Levine's *Freedom's Children: Young Civil Rights Activists Tell Their Own Stories*; and Al Santoli's *Everything We Had: An Oral History of the Vietnam War.* I have organized this chapter around the component parts of writing an oral history: (1) choosing a subject, (2) interviewing, (3) describing the setting and the interviewee, (4) recording the interview, (5) editing the transcript, and (6) organizing and developing an essay (including conventions such as punctuation and paragraphs).

Choosing a Subject

As a first step, I ask students to identify three possible interviewees. It's critical to have backups since family or work emergencies occasionally arise and people are not able to be interviewed. This is all the more likely because we generally spend only a few weeks on this assignment. So students need to contact possible subjects right away and then schedule the interviews as quickly as they can. An early interview can often be rescheduled. As students set up their interviews, I urge them to be up front with interviewees about the topic and the time involved. If students ask, "When might you have twenty minutes to spend talking about the American dream?," their subjects are less likely to feel ambushed and therefore more likely to do the interview.

Depending on the topic, I have sometimes helped students contact subjects to interview. For the Vietnam War literature assignment, I have encouraged students to visit local hospitals, museums, and support groups. I also suggest that students have their family members and friends help them find possible interview subjects. Just about the only people I don't allow students to interview are those they already know well, which means I generally veto family members, close friends, and neighbors, especially if their stories are already known. I want students to experience the same "astonishment" that Terkel and his subjects did.

Interviewing

When students have settled on a topic, I distribute the following list of interviewing tips:

Interviewing Tips

- Choose someone who is comfortable speaking on this topic, someone whose story you are not familiar with.

- Choose a good (quiet, relaxed) location. Allow some time at the beginning of the interview to make conversation so that you and the interviewee can get comfortable. Remember, this is a conversation, not an interrogation!

- If at all possible, tape-record the interview. Remember to ask for permission ahead of time. If the subject refuses—which is extremely rare—take very careful notes so that you can gather lots of information, jotting down memorable quotes or startling pieces of information, without making the interviewee feel you're not paying full attention.

- Since your interviewee may not be able to spend an unlimited amount of time with you to complete the interview, make sure you have a list of ten strong questions and that you have considered possible follow-up questions.

- Avoid yes/no questions; they tend to yield short answers.

- Avoid leading questions. Lawyers, for instance, cannot ask questions that have already been answered, nor can they ask questions that offer no room for thoughtful response—and for good reasons. Imagine interviewing a subject on the Vietnam War with this question: "Why did you fire your gun in combat even though you know killing is wrong?" Such a question seems designed to elicit a certain response ("I was following orders" ?) and is likely to make the subject feel defensive. I would replace such a question with a more open-ended one such as "What were your greatest misgivings in combat?" Or "When your values were most in conflict with those of the army, how did you reconcile the conflict?" Questions like these, which contain superlatives (*greatest, most*), often yield the longest, most substantive answers.

- Try to get the interviewee to speak as much as possible. Feel free to refocus the interview if the responses seem too far removed from the main topic; on the other hand, this is the subject's life: try not to censor his or her thoughts or cut them off. Don't judge the interviewee's comments, attitudes, or values.

- Remind interviewees that your essays will be seen only by your teacher and possibly some other students in our class—unless they give their explicit permission to have the essay read by others.

- Offer to show the final essay to the interviewee before you hand it in. This might also be a good way of checking details or adding descriptions about key events.

Describing the Setting and the Interviewee

A key decision student interviewers will need to make is the degree to which the setting and the interviewer should be present in the final essay. If a student is interviewing a protester at the end of a protest march, the setting, the clothing, and the props the subject is holding might well become part of the story. But if the interview occurs in a generic setting, or if the writer finds that the setting has little to say about the essay topic, such descriptions can be ignored.

Just as with documentary filmmakers, students must decide to what extent they are present in the interviews. Michael Moore, for example, is often the leading player in his films, whereas Errol Morris is almost never on screen, though he occasionally speaks off-camera. Still other filmmakers, such as Barbara Kopple, are often invisible in the final cut of their movies. In general, I encourage students to be invisible in these interviews.

Recording/Transcribing the Interview

It's ideal to tape the interview with a recorder that contains an external microphone. The full interview should then be typed out. For a twenty-minute interview such as the ones we aim for, the final transcript usually comes in around ten pages. I don't require students to transcribe those parts of the conversation that clearly have no bearing on the interview at hand.

Editing the Transcript

According to Studs Terkel, there are no set rules for interviewing, and he admits to "shifting things around" and "adjusting the sequences" when sifting through transcripts, since "an interview is not written in stone." But above all, Terkel believes in "never altering the words [since] the words are the words of the person, that's clear" (Lenehan).

In editing an interview, it is appropriate to:

- Change verb tense to enhance uniformity or understanding

- Eliminate unnecessary repetition, digression

- Substitute words to clarify meaning. This type of change should be made selectively. For example, substitute a noun for a pronoun if the meaning is unclear: "They thought that then they could choose an assignment" becomes "Men who enlisted thought that then they could choose an assignment." Or substitute a word for another if you are positive the subject unconsciously used the wrong word.

- Rearrange text to group ideas or to improve flow, as long as meaning is not altered. As noted interviewer Studs Terkel says, "When I edit, I can shift the order in which a person gives a response. I'm not altering what the person said. That order was arbitrary to begin with. I want to get at the truth of what the person said. What I always try to do in an interview is highlight the truth."

- Create paragraph breaks. Look for natural breaks in the interview, such as shifts in time or topic.

- Consult your interview subject when in doubt about a change.

Organizing/Creating the Interview: Narrative Arc, Grouping Like Terms

Here is an assignment of mine for writing an oral history interview on the American dream:

Writing Oral History

For your first major assignment of the term, you will interview an older adult (though it kills me to do so, let's say this means "someone over 25") about their American dream. Your final product will look something like the Studs Terkel pieces we've read. In other words, your paper will look like one long quote, a monologue broken up into paragraphs, with your subject speaking in the first person about his or her life. But, just as Terkel does, you'll need to do some careful preparation to get the best results.

Hand in documentation of these steps with your final paper: Choose three possible subjects to interview. Prepare a list of 10 questions you plan on covering during the interview. You may not get to them all, but you should have a clear focus. Write down the questions you asked during the interview which followed up earlier questions, or which occurred to you only during the interview.

***Keep in mind the central issues we've discussed in class: How does a person's background affect their success? What expectations did they have

Continued on next page

---

for themselves? What expectations did others have for them? Why weren't they ultimately successful, if they feel they have not been? What sacrifices were made in achieving success? Was achieving their goal everything they thought it would be? How did they arrive at their definition of success? What additional responsibilities did success bring?***

DO NOT JUDGE THEIR LIVES AS SUCCESSFUL OR UNSUC-CESSFUL IN THE PAPER OR IN THE INTERVIEW. Not only would this be unthinkably arrogant and rude, but I also hereby remove myself from liability for injuries sustained during the course of said judgments. For this paper, let the subjects speak for themselves and let them judge their own lives; we'll have plenty of chances later on this term to consider the lives of other characters, both fictional and nonfictional.

The final draft (with notes) will be due in three weeks. The hardest part of this paper will be to shape your interview notes and your transcript into a coherent 2- to 3-page paper. Start early! I'd be happy to read over any rough drafts before the due date.

American Dream Essays

Let's examine an essay through the stages I've outlined.

Rough Draft: Hole-in-One

Edmund Rzepnicki was the second oldest in a family of 6 boys and one girl. Growing up he played sports, especially football, baseball, and basketball with the older kids. He and his wife Erma always call each other by the nickname Butch.

Football was always my first love. I visualized making it big. At that time (1920–1930's) football was played just one way, you had to play both defense and offense, you didn't have specialists like you do now. Everything we learned in sports we did on our own. There was none of these sports camps where these kids now learn the finer points of handling everything. We did it on our own, and we must of did okay.

She caught my eye from the very beginning. Butch was the cheerleader, I was the athlete. We kid each other about it, at that time too. I don't remember the first time I talked to her. She says we were at the library in school when she first started talking to me, and I think that's the area where they tell you to be silent, don't they?

My leg fractured my senior year of high school. My dreams were curtailed with my bad left knee. It hampered my style of play. I played as long as I could, but I never made the jump from just, what we used to refer as "semi-pro" type playing. If I had been injury free I think I would have been able to develop into something, but with bad legs you don't get far.

I had an athletic scholarship to go to Ole Miss. And I enjoyed every minute of it. During the summer vacation when I came home the Studebaker plant had semi-pro baseball.
—Erin, grade 10

This is an excerpt of a rough draft. When students read it in class, I asked them what they liked about the essay and then if they were confused about any aspect of the story. The voice is what immediately captivates here. It's critical to keep the voice alive even at the expense of conventional grammar. An interesting passage is found at the end of the first paragraph, where the author quotes the subject as saying "must of did okay." The *of* here is a mistake in transcribing rather than one of speaking; it must be changed to *have* for the sake of clarity. On the other hand, I wouldn't change the word *did* to *done*, because the sense of the phrase is still clear. The first paragraph of the interview also includes comma splice errors in the third sentence. This is a key point that all students learn in this assignment: people don't talk with punctuation marks, nor do they paragraph their thoughts. Writers must use these conventions, however, in order to speak clearly to an audience not immediately present.

In terms of organization, the author's essay turns too abruptly at times. The second paragraph jumps to the subject's wife, Butch, and then back to football. It might help, some suggested, to "group like terms" (in other words, group, say, "sports" information separate from "work" information). For that matter, the second paragraph opens with the word *She,* though the referent "Butch" has not yet been introduced. For the sake of clarity, the author can switch these two words. Even though the subject did not say them in this order, meaning is kept intact and clarity is enhanced.

Sometimes the author needs to offer parenthetical definitions of unfamiliar terms. For example, some students didn't know the meaning of *Ole Miss*. As a final suggestion, several students wished to know more in that introductory paragraph. How old is Edmund Rzepnicki? Where did he grow up?

Here is the author's final draft:

Final Draft: Butch

Edmund Rzepnicki, at age 80, is the second oldest in a family of six boys and one girl. He plays golf with his friends and brothers every day that he can and knows most of the modern baseball, basketball, football and golf athletes. His love for sports and competition was born with him in South Bend, Indiana. For the first half of his life he worked at the Studebaker plant, putting doors on cars. After Studebaker closed he had a job shearing steel at Buchanan, Michigan. He calls his wife, Erma, by the nickname Butch, which she also uses to call him. He speaks slowly and confidently and seems pleased to share his life story.

Football was always my first love. At the time when I was growing up football was played just one way: you had to play both defense and offense. You didn't have specialists like you do now. Everything we learned in sports we did on our own. There was none of these sports camps where these kids now learn the finer points of handling everything. We did it on our own, and we must have did okay.

My leg fractured my senior year in high school, so when I graduated and had a chance to go to University of Mississippi with an athletic scholarship, I delayed it for a semester for my leg to heal up.

I was a college man at Ole Miss *(University of Mississippi)* and during the summer vacation, when I came home, the Studebaker plant had semi-pro baseball. The people at the Studebaker plant organized the team. They made sure the people on the team were hired at the plant for these jobs. We used to play all these good teams. Especially the Negro teams, which at that time weren't being accepted into the major leagues, but they were terrific ballplayers. One of the teams I played against was the Kansas City Monarchs, which used to have all time hall-of-famer Satchel Paige.

At that time I visualized sometimes making it big, whether in football or in baseball. But my dreams were curtailed with my bad left knee. It hampered my style of play. I played as long as I could, but I never made the jump from "semi-pro." If I had been injury-free I think I would have been able to develop into something, but with bad legs you don't get far.... So, I was at Ole Miss when my injury was giving me problems, and I was thinking that I would eventually finish school and go into the teaching field, maybe coaching. But that all fell by the wayside when World War II broke out.

I was on the verge of being drafted. We had a big game against LSU *(Louisiana State University)*, and after that game I dropped out. I had everything prepared, packed to go home, and that's what I did. I didn't tell anybody I just got on the bus and went home.

I married Butch in 1943 while I was in service. I had met her in my senior year of high school. Butch was the cheerleader; I was the athlete. I had broken my leg in one of the games and she was able to catch me because I was on crutches. She says we were at the library in school when she first started talking to me. That's the area where they tell you to be silent, don't they? So Butch and I were talking about marriage and things were moving real fast, people were being assigned and going overseas so we had to move fast too.

I was shipped overseas just before D-Day took place. Luck was in my favor too at that point, because our company was assigned to a division which was supposed to meet overseas at one of the landing areas where D-Day was supposed to be staged, and with some mistake or something our company was assigned to go just directly to England. I was at the American Embassy—and that was at the time when the Germans were bombing London with the buzz bombs and the rockets. We were fortunate that nothing happened really. We pulled our duty there. I was discharged on January 1st, New Year's Day, 1946.

I came home and went to my usual job over at Studebaker's, and that was about it. I thought I would settle down and raise a family. Our only daughter, Tina, was born at that point. We bought our home, and we still have that home right now, and that's my little dream house.

I already was approaching my middle forties when Studebaker went out of existence, they went bankrupt. I took a job at Buchanan, Michigan, which was a hot forge shop. I worked there for 20 years. They were paying incentive, which I loved, so the more pieces you were able to produce, the more you got paid for it. The manual work there was awfully hard, but physical labor at that time didn't bother me. I loved it. It probably was good for me.

I've been retired from Buchanan Steel for the last 16 years and, about a month ago, they sent me a letter and told me that my health plan is being terminated. At this point in my life the health plan is the most important thing I need. In 1997 I had a bypass surgery, 1998 I had a pacemaker installed, and as the body keeps deteriorating there's no telling what is going to happen. And it was real easy for them to just say, "As of March 31st your health plan is finished." They claim that they have hard times, the economy is real low, and their business has been dropping. The easiest thing to do is to pick on the retirees. So any health plan I have now I acquired within the last month and it's costing me money.

But, I'm enjoying life, really. I always stressed the fact that if you can only maintain your health and raise a family the rest can take care of itself. Marrying Butch was a terrific choice. From there on in it was all gravy. It doesn't take much to please us. Just being able to get up in the mornings and perform our chores and do our little things is more then good enough for us. We have wonderful grandchildren. They've got so much on the ball. . . . They're liable to be doing a lot of things before they settle in and zero in on something more definite. Our daughter has been our one joy, a big joy, especially for me. I keep telling Butch that we're sitting on top of the world.
—Erin, grade 10

This final essay offers a much clearer introductory paragraph and better cohesion throughout. This time the essay clearly moves from football to family, and in fact Mr. Rzepnicki's wife becomes the focus—and the title—of the piece. The author accommodates her audience with a definition of *Ole Miss* and later of *LSU*. The piece is generally organized chronologically from past to present, with the last paragraph even nodding to the future. Sometimes it's helpful to find a strong last sentence to shape the whole piece. This author contemplated using "on top of the world" as a title at one point but thought it sounded too arrogant. Instead, the phrase anchors the essay at the end by showing the contentment this man feels with his American dream: achievements, setbacks, a lifetime of hard work, and the support of a loving family.

The Office Goddess

Valerie Guy is the operations coordinator for the Chicago Youth Symphony Orchestra and also teaches the flute privately. Referred to commonly by the orchestra members as "Val, the Office Goddess," she is characterized by her black wardrobe, her addiction to nicotine, and her ability to make the most boring of memos entertaining.

When I was in high school, I was going to either be a dancer or a musician, so I chose a school with a great dance program. Then, I ended up getting injured. The summer before I was supposed to go to Butler University, I was in a car accident and I injured my back. The doctor said that I really shouldn't dance anymore despite the fact that I had a *really* promising future. It was a crushing blow for me because the entire previous year, my senior year in high school, I was in a state of total emotional trauma about making the choice between classical music on the flute or dance. I was completely focused on two things and excelled in both of them equally. Then, I finally made the decision to dance and didn't go to Eastman or Curtis or any of those good music schools. After that, it was a little bit like fate slapping me in the face to get injured. It's so much harder to transfer to those music schools than it is to go in as a freshman. Overall, it was a pretty crushing blow.

Since then, I've had to form new dreams for myself, pretty much because, as you get older and financially independent, and all of that good stuff, all the doors are not open to you anymore. There is a certain window of time in music performance where you have to just kick ass and that's during college. Since that didn't happen for me, I went through a period about two years ago where I was sort of despairing over the whole administration vs. performance thing. I decided to chuck the administration and go with performance. Financially, though, it was virtually impossible for me to go back to school full time to get my master's in performance. In music, you can't do it part time. You can't just take orchestra this semester and take something else next semester and spread it out over twelve years. You have to do it all at one time and I couldn't. So, those external constraints served to definitely alter my expectations for my future. I have since focused on excelling in administration, which I *do* enjoy. In many ways, it takes a lot more brains than music does. It takes different skills and I'm very good in certain ways at what I do. I've never had huge dreams of huge financial success. Personal success, yes, but that is closely tied with artistic creation. I just really want to be able to make a living at something I love.

I have two groups of friends within my life right now. Half of these people are following what would be generally considered closer to "American dreams." Not necessarily in the historic sense of striving for 40 acres and a cow and all of that, but in working for financial success, family, and prestige. Their dreams are more centered on making their surroundings as comfortable as possible, not like poshy comfortable, but as comfortable as possible to make their lives easier and more pleasant so they can go on vacation.

My other group of friends, who are much closer to me, are mostly between twenty-five and thirty-five and they are all passionately following artistic dreams. Two of them are visual artists, some of them are dancers. Most of them are involved in rock bands or are classical musicians. They have McJobs. They serve coffee. They work for cleaning services. They do all of these really crappy jobs just to pay their rent and to keep as much time free as possible. It's not money that they want, it's time to create, time to do what they do best. Their dreams are primarily focused around creating something or expressing something. They have financial dreams also, but those are *so* distant in the future.

Nobody expects to make a million dollars. They are all in the stage where they are establishing themselves as artists and so they're really working more towards keeping their art pure as opposed to pandering themselves to whatever is wanted by the public right now, to get greater financial security.

Some of these friends are going to grow out of it. Some of them are going to give up. As you grow older, you can't help but think a little bit more about the future and security. With the state of things right now, especially in our country, it's in your face all the time. "There are *no* jobs out there. The economic situation right now is incredibly impossible to live in for *everybody*." You can't avoid that. I've known a few of my friends who have given up a little bit, gone safer routes. Many more of them are just going to keep plugging away, though, and they're never going to give up. Those are the people who I respect the most. It's very brave, don't you think, to keep going for your dreams despite lack of security. I would say that my parents always expressed a great concern about security. Having had that sort of a background, I really have a large amount of respect for people who are willing to go out on a limb for what they believe in. Even if they live in a hovel somewhere, in the boiler room of some building, but they are ecstatic about the song that they just wrote, or the painting they just created, then they are successful.

I don't think that it is possible for anybody to be 100% successful in their own eyes, though. There's always going to be the path not taken. There's going to be opportunities missed or screwed up. There are always going to be regrets. I think that the people that are the most successful in the end are the people who can live with those regrets and look beyond them. They have gone out and pursued their dreams instead of sitting, waiting, or hoping that everything is going to be OK, not wanting to rock the boat and not wanting to take chances. Even if something doesn't work out, I think that people are going to feel more successful if they have followed their dreams.

There is a certain amount to be said for living for the day, I think. I've been learning to do that. For a while, I was pretty full of regrets when I had a major dream crushed. I try to live in the moment and enjoy it and not put too much weight on tomorrow. I have many friends who are always looking towards tomorrow and I would say that kind of mentality is contrary to being happy in the end. If you are always looking towards tomorrow you are going to reach a point in your life someday where you're going to start looking at yesterday and wondering where did it all go. It's as if you were digging yourself out of a tunnel, trying to reach the stars in the sky.

If you're too focused upon just getting closer to the stars and that's where *all* of your joy comes from, you're just setting yourself up for a fall.
—Janina, grade 10

This author uses much longer paragraphs, perhaps because of the subject's philosophical introspection. In shaping a long transcript, Janina opens with a setback and then offers a redemptive arc of sorts as Ms. Guy moves from performer to administrator. The essay features two central oppositions—"the whole administration vs. performance thing" and the tension of doing "something you love" vs. "living comfortably." The title nicely captures these oppositions, and the ending of the essay, a decidedly short paragraph, is striking because both oppositions play out in the final image of "reaching for the stars."

Civil Rights Essays

One of the best reasons to work on civil rights interviews is to reinforce the idea that civil rights issues didn't end in the 1960s. This topic is so expansive that it can cover a range of related issues: immigration, gay rights, housing, equity in school funding, health care, etc.

The following interview with a retiree who works with an improv troupe to advance important social issues is the first oral history project I ever witnessed. I was a leader of a community service group in Philadelphia that tried to introduce young student activists to older activists. In that spirit, a student and I interviewed an older adult and produced the following essay.

Lillian Shirley—Acting for Change

We had just finished watching a woman named Lillian Shirley, a woman in her late sixties with enormous energy, do some wonderful improvisational acting with her best friend, and she seemed like an interesting person to interview. Her dress was nice and neat, pressed to perfection, deep black. It was accompanied by bright, beaded jewelry, lipstick, and earrings and topped off with a black beret. Her glasses were square, but rounded at the corners. On her feet were soft leather, black shoes. Her face was round, cute, and dark. She looked formal, but inviting. We situated ourselves across from Lillian on a bench, while she sat on a chair.

Unfortunately, when I was young, the lack of African-American hiring was widespread in Philadelphia and all over, and it hit the schools hard. I never actually saw an African-American school teacher, but I was blessed with great teachers nevertheless. They encouraged me to never stop learning and to continue on to college. It was those dedicated people, who looked past our black faces. One teacher stood out in my mind, a junior high teacher named Mrs. Babb. She encouraged me to read Bronte and Hawthorne, and even bought a ballet ticket for me.

A key element in my society was the family. The family was always together—there would sometimes be three or four generations in the same house (until World War II). Despite poverty, I stayed optimistic. My father bought a house and supported all four children in our family on forty dollars a week on two jobs, during the Great Depression. We didn't know we were so poor. We said grace, never stole or envied anyone else, and lived as comfortably as possible with the money we had. (We even had a cat and a dog.) Even though times were tough, we were taught to make do with what we had.

The father was the undisputed head of the family, but he listened to the mother and the family. Discussion was always held at the dinner table; we spoke of school and my father's expectations for us, his thoughtful encouragement. My siblings, along with the rest of the community's children, also received encouragement from the parents of the community. The community realized that, to make the community better, we had to work together. Parents looked out for other neighbors' children; when the kids were out of line, they would get scolded and put in place. The children learned values and morals from the community, and the community did its best to produce better children with a brighter future. This was no utopian situation, but times were simpler . . . life was much simpler then. People didn't pick things apart. Things were how they were. For instance, whereas interracial marriage is a taboo today, it was nothing then. My brother engaged in an interracial marriage, and there was nothing of it.

However, interracial workplaces continued to be a problem. I recall a specific incident. I was one of the first African-American saleswomen at John Wannemaker's in 1952, as there were none prior. The first day on the job, a woman came by and spat directly on my face. It is hard to imagine such hostility and hate.

I just stood there, too awestruck to move. My eyes scarcely blinked as the flowing tears trickled down my face in disbelief and sadness. Just then a rich, well-dressed woman walked by and helped me. She pulled out a perfumed handkerchief and used it to dry my tears. Hope was not gone.

This is the truth that I and millions of other live by. There are many races now. Every race has its downs. But maybe in our own little way, we can make the difference.

The civil rights movement wasn't a revolution by brute force, but an effective one nevertheless. There were powerful lectures at the church, demonstrations, sit-ins, and boycotts. Boycotts could be a powerful weapon at the time, because the African-American population was a large consumer group, and a boycott could be quite detrimental to a company's revenues. One of these boycotts stands out in my mind. In my day, the Tastykake Company was a leading producer in Philadelphia who employed few African Americans; the ones the company did hire were used for manual labor. The African-American population in Philly became angered at this, and staged a boycott. The company responded by hiring more African-Americans, and the boycott was cancelled.

Before World War II, African-Americans weren't really involved in politics. They were more or less removed—in some places, they could not even place their vote, and massive social exclusion was being felt. As a matter of fact, the ball didn't really start rolling toward civil rights until Truman integrated the troops. I had two brothers fighting in World War II, before integration, as part of segregated troops.

The massive oppression was deeply felt, but my strength allowed myself to fight it. It should have made me inferior . . . but it didn't. I have a brain. I have the equipment with which to work. I could use it. My intellect allowed me to rise above the stereotypes that I was supposed to feel. We knew it was wrong. However, this is the way it was.

The times were increasingly tough. I recall taking my five-year-old son to Washington D.C. North of D.C., the train was a comfortable ride. However, upon entering D.C. itself, Jim Crow came into effect, and I and my son were forced to walk the length of about thirty cars only to get to a bad car. My son was astonished. "Why mommy, why? Did we do something wrong?" he said. His innocence reflects the hardship every African-American child faced at the time: dealing with being punished for being born with dark skin.

It was terrifying to be so oppressed that one simply had to accept it. But I rose above this. I started fighting. I am now part of an improvisational acting troupe that deals with real life problems and issues, and hits them head on in real situations, all improv—never scripted. Straightforward. We're not entertainment—we tell it like it is. Unbiased, true, and real.

My family is also a big part of my life. I had one son, who is now retired after twenty-eight years with Philadelphia Electric. He is now fifty-one years of age and resides in Maple Shade, NJ. He has four sons. The oldest attends Drexel University and majors in robotics. The second works with Philadelphia Electric. The third attends Rochester University in Rochester, NY. The youngest is in training for the Olympics as a runner. He is a straight A student in school.

Lillian's story is a very special one. She gives an account that perhaps may not be found in textbooks. She is a real-life person with a real experience. We must learn from her and others who have experienced this country in a form quite different from our own. We hope her story has touched and enriched your life like it did ours.
—Ismail, grade 10

While I supervised this interview, I let Ismail edit and craft the script. The story takes on a powerful narrative arc, from discrimination to fighting back. The description of Ms. Shirley's successful grandchildren at the end of the essay supports the narrative swing of the entire piece by highlighting the reverberations of the civil rights struggles in successive generations.

The introductory paragraph in italics does a nice job of setting the scene, with visual descriptions of Ms. Shirley and the interview location. The final paragraph is less successful, I think, because it settles for generalizations ("special" and "real"). The author does, however, offer a striking contrast between this oral history he and his subject have crafted and the historical narratives offered in textbooks.

Vietnam War Essays

I was first given the idea to explore Vietnam War literature through oral history by Larry Johannessen. Larry was not only a superb teacher but also a military veteran, serving in Vietnam as a marine. His wonderful book *Illumination Rounds* is a model of teaching through inquiry.

Following Larry's lead, I tracked down Vietnam vets and invited them to speak to my classes. It was not difficult to find willing subjects, and as a first step I usually asked the class to interview a vet *as a class* so we could talk about the most surprising responses and the most revealing questions. Then together we considered how we could shape the responses we were given into a coherent essay.

When it came time to have students conduct their own interviews and craft their own essays, I allowed them to interview "anyone who had a significant experience during the war." This allowed students to interview conscientious objectors, protesters, government officials, etc., in addition to soldiers and others who actually went overseas. The result of this was a wide array of subjects that reflected the contentious spirit of the age.

As I do with every essay, after students have secured someone to interview I ask them to prepare a minimum of ten questions. Here are two sets of questions students submitted, along with my parenthetical comments after each:

1. Place, Job, How you got there (*not yet a question*)

2. What was a typical day like? (*potentially interesting but a little broad*)

3. What were your views on what was going on in Vietnam? (*too general — there was too much going on*)

4. Did you ever wish you were doing something else in the war? (*what, fighting?*)

5. Did you ever wish that you weren't there at all? (*Yes/No questions*)

6. Was there any crucial time or thing during the war that changed your views about what was going on? (*Interesting question, but ask more definitely: e.g., "What experience most changed your views about the war?"*)

7. How did your experience at war affect your life?

8. How did you change as a person? How did you look at life differently? (*The first of these two is too broad; the second is likely to elicit a story response.*)

9. How do you think your life would've been different had you not gone?

10. How were you alike or different than the other American soldiers? (*This last question is especially interesting, getting at the idea of normalcy.*)

Interview Questions

1. What is your most memorable experience from when you served? (*Nice*)

2. How did you feel when you came home? How were you treated?

3. What did you miss most (from home) when you were in Vietnam?

4. What was the reason you went to serve? (*These first 4 questions are strong and are likely to lead to story responses.*)

5. What do you think was your biggest accomplishment (either something you did or something you got out of the war)? (*Interesting*)

6. Are you happy you served in the war? Why? (*Is "happy" the best word? "Proud?" "Satisfied?"*)

7. Do you believe in war for solving conflicts? (*Y/N*)

8. Do you keep up with any men you met while you were in war? (*Y/N*)

9. If you were to do the whole experience again, is there anything you would have done differently? (*Y/N; force subject to identify something he or she would have done differently.*)

10. Did you keep in touch with people when you were at war? If so, who? Do you think that had an effect on you? If yes, how so? (*Interesting*)

11. What was an event that was a very big learning experience? What did that event teach you? (*What event changed your views most?*)

12. What do you think you gained / got from Vietnam? (*A little broad*)

13. Did you kill anybody? (*Too intrusive?*)

14. Do you think war caused you to become meaner or more ruthless? (*Too leading; I'd leave this more open-ended.*)

15. After dealing with people and death, were you able to move on quickly? (*Y/N*)

16. Has the war changed your view on things? If so, what? (*A little broad*)

17. Did the Vietnam War bring out racial issues between you and your colleagues? (*Great question, but Y/N*)

18. Were you always motivated to fight? (*Y/N*)

19. Was there any turning point for you in war? If so, what was it? (*In terms of . . . ?*)

20. Do you have any regrets? (*Quite personal. I'd only ask this if I sensed the person was extremely forthcoming.*)

At this point, it might be useful once again to follow the rest of the steps leading up to a finished essay. After identifying a subject and asking questions like those listed here, one student was left with the following transcript. It's full of powerful observations, but it's raw and rambling.

Raw Transcript

Well, uh, I was going to school and uh I was in my first year of college and at that time it was 196 ... 8 and if you dropped out of school it was almost guaranteed if you were 19 or older you'd get drafted and uh I guess I was sort of going through some philosophical changes or whatever, [*laughs*] as we used to say, and, uh, I decided to just take the risk 'cause I wanted to sort of discover life, I didn't wanna get drafted, but, uh, I dropped out of school, I was out about, uh, well, that spring I got drafted. So I was out less than a year and, uh, at that time the draft was for two years and you know it was pretty much guaranteed you'd probably end up going to Vietnam so, including people who sometimes, uh joined, instead of getting drafted because they thought they'd, see, then you could choose an assignment, like you wanna go to Germany, but they still would end up getting shipped to Vietnam, and you know after they were there, 'cause they had to sign up for four years, or whatever, so, uh, pretty much everybody Who went in at that time would end up going over there and, uh, I guess I scored fairly high on their test, they give you a battery of tests when you go in, and uh, they made me a personnel special-ist and, uh, I guess today that's called human resources, you know, and basically I had to go through two months of basic training which, uh, everybody didn't enjoy too much, of course nobody did and, then I had to go through two months of what they call AIT, which is Advanced Individual Training, that was in the, in the personnel specialist and, uh, it was kinda funny when you think, you know, you're in the army, you're being trained to type, uh, you know I guess they called the corps Remington Raiders, 'cause of the Remington typewriters, we didn't have computers or word processors at that time. So, uh, we basically sit there for I think it was like 6 hours a day, we did other things, but learning to get our typing speed up to thirty-some words a minute.

Where was this?

Uh, this was in the United States, still, you know and you could be assigned any-where, but I was assigned to Vietnam and then I think they gave us a month leave or so before we went over there. And, then, uh, I got assigned to a place called Long Binh and, uh, it turned out that that was the largest post in Vietnam, and it was about, I would say 40 minutes by highway from Saigon, say roughly like where Elmhurst is, let's say, from Chicago. And, uh, at that time, let's see, like there were what they call Quonset huts, I think, they are sort of like metal, uh, uh, I don't know, just houses, you know, and then there were beds all in, like rows, you know and you had a locker and stuff and, uh, so you had to definitely learn to get along with other people, um, and oh, by the way, where I was assigned was called the 24th evacuation hospital, that was very similar to M*A*S*H* and of course, M*A*S*H* was the Korean War and since I was a clerk, I didn't really watch M*A*S*H* very much, but I guess that would make me Radar. . . .

*   *   *

[In the interest of space, I'm cutting off the transcript here. It contains no paragraphs and includes a number of false starts and stammers, as with anyone— even the most articulate subject. These are difficult questions, after all. The following rough draft shows some of the whittling down process.]

Rough Draft: Where It Lands, It Lands

I was going to school and I was in my first year of college and at that time it was 1968. If you dropped out of school, it was almost guaranteed if you were 19 or older you'd get drafted. I guess I was going through some philosophical changes, as we used to call it and I decided to take the risk 'cause I wanted to sort of discover life. I didn't want to get drafted, but I dropped out of school. Well, that spring I got drafted. It was pretty much guaranteed you'd probably end up going to Vietnam so, including people who sometimes joined, instead of getting drafted. They thought that then they could choose an assignment, like they wanna go to Germany, but they still would end up getting shipped to Vietnam. Everybody who went in at that time would end up going over there. A lot of people went to Canada in order to flee the draft, I didn't want to do that. I even considered going to jail. About that time there was a cook county jail scandal that came out and revealed some of the stuff that was going on in the jail and that didn't sound real appealing to me. It sort of brought home the realities of jail and so I thought I'd take my chances with the war. Some of these guys had managed to get out of the draft by faking it, paying off a doctor, or whatever, sort of a little badge of something. It's strange: half of me; and I guess it is the same half of me that made me drop out of school and wanted to experience life, was almost a little excited about doing something like this. I was going to another country and doing something that people definitely didn't expect of me. I was one of the more artsy people and I was involved in music in school and I would've been way at the bottom of the people likely to be in the Army.

Edward Budzilowicz was in the American Army during the Vietnam War from 1967–1969. We sat at my house at a table near the window, while the sun shone brightly in. He was wearing a blue suit with a flashy blue tie, and turned his chair parallel to the table so as not to be bothered by the sun.

As a first step, this author has eliminated the stammers from the first line and also taken out unnecessary information. Although she has begun to shape the story chronologically, she isn't yet thinking in paragraphs, partly because she hasn't yet grouped like terms, sifting through the entire transcript (which was about ten single-spaced pages) for topics that might serve as paragraphs—time markers, job descriptions, attitudes. By the final draft, she has shaped the material much more clearly and creates a powerful portrait of Mr. Budzilowicz and his own understanding of his time in Vietnam.

Final Draft: Where It Lands, It Lands

At that time it was 1968. I was in my first year of college, and if you dropped out of school it was almost guaranteed if you were 19 or older you'd get drafted. I guess I was going through some philosophical changes, as we used to call it, and I decided to take the risk 'cause I wanted to sort of discover life. I didn't want to get drafted, but I dropped out of school.

Well, that spring I got drafted. It's strange: half of me, and I guess it is the same half of me that made me drop out of school and wanted to experience life, was almost a little excited about doing something like this. It was pretty much guaranteed you'd end up going to Vietnam, including people who sometimes joined instead of getting drafted. They thought that then they could choose an assignment, like they wanna go to Germany, but they still would end up getting shipped to Vietnam. Everybody who went in at that time would end up going over there.

A lot of people went to Canada in order to flee the draft. I didn't want to do that. I even considered going to jail. About that time there was a Cook County jail scandal—abuse of the prisoners by the guards—that came out and revealed some of the stuff that was going on in the jail and that didn't sound real appealing to me. It sort of brought home the realities of jail and so I thought I'd take my chances with the war. Some guys had managed to get out of the draft by faking it, paying off a doctor, or whatever. I was one of the more artsy people and I was involved in music in school and I would've been way at the bottom of the people likely to be in the Army.

They give you a battery of tests when you go in. I guess I scored fairly high, so they made me a Personnel Specialist. I had to go through two months of basic training, which everybody didn't enjoy too much. Of course nobody did. I had to go through two months of what they call AIT, Advanced Individual Training, that was in the personnel specialist. It was kinda funny when you think, you're in the Army and you're being trained to type. They called the corps the Remington Raiders, 'cause of the Remington typewriters. So, we basically sit there for I think it was like 6 hours a day learning to get our typing speed up to thirty-some words a minute.

I got assigned to a place called Long Binh and it turned out that that was the largest post in Vietnam. I was assigned to the 24th evacuation hospital that was very similar to M.A.S.H. I didn't really watch M.A.S.H. very much, but since I was a clerk, I guess that would make me Radar.

I worked for the personnel office, which was one of the few air-conditioned. At the time I got there, they didn't really have plumbing; they had outhouses and cold showers. The showers were cold water, and even though it was a hot country, it was uncomfortable to take a cold shower. I was only there 14 months, and by the time I was half way through there, they already had plumbing in. A lot of guys had built plywood walls around their beds to make rooms. From the P-Ex (Pacific Exchange), the store where you could buy things and you wouldn't have to pay any duty or tax, they would buy stereos and air conditioners. Sometimes you'd walk into this plywood door and there would be a carpet and an air conditioner and a stereo. It'd be like a little dorm room. It was very strange to think you were in a war and suddenly you'd step into the United States. Very home-like.

I liked it better though when it was open, 'cause I found that people actually got along much better. Once they started putting up those walls, it's like they say, fences make bad neighbors, people didn't relate as much.

I worked six days a week, I think, twelve hours a day starting at seven in the morning. Of course you always had to get up early. I would eat at the mess hall. The cooks were GIs; the help was Vietnamese. They'd check them every day to make sure they weren't carrying a bomb or something. Even though they were needy and certainly would take handouts, they did not want our food, because it had been refrigerated. They were used to having fresh vegetables, so they really didn't eat our food. The food wasn't that bad I thought or maybe I just got used to it.

One of the duties they gave me was handing out Purple Hearts to the wounded. It didn't matter what circumstances, as long as you were wounded by the enemy. They were kinda neat looking: hearts all lined in gold, rather large and heavy. They were made of plastic, but they looked like they were some kind of jewel on a ribbon in a jeweler's box. I'd get out a little scroll that I typed up with their name on it and I'd just find the guy, in whatever shape he was in. I'd have a guy who's been a dancer, literally, and he lost his legs, and that kind of thing. A lot of them basically said in words I won't use "keep your medal" and I understood that, and I understood that it wasn't a job that anybody else really wanted to do.

There were times that guys that I knew would actually ask me to give them one, even though they did no fighting, didn't even see any combat. Then there were some other cases where somewhere out in the field, an officer was asleep and they started getting attacked and he went to put his helmet on, hit himself in the head and knocked himself out. And for that, he got a Purple Heart. I didn't see how that deserved it, but they were under fire and he got wounded.

During the Tet (the lunar New Year), the action would heat up a lot and there would be a lot of attacks. They would have us help out with the helicopters bringing in the wounded. They told us there was this really bad head case that came in, meaning fragments from a grenade or mortar, so we rushed out to the helipad. They bring this guy out and he's in a bathing suit, and he's perfectly fine except he's unconscious. He had been surfing. They would send us on R and R (Rest and Recuperation) for two weeks every year, and he got hit in the head with his surfboard. Now, I don't think this guy got a Purple Heart.

But the rest of the time you just had to try to find something to do to keep sane. You're counting off the days that you're there. People have a misconception, like I did, before I went in, that you're in danger constantly when you're in a war. You can never relax. You carry a gun all of the time, but the reality is that for every combat person there are about four support people.

I would once in a while go to Saigon and that was the only time they did issue us a weapon. You would get issued a pistol or something and carry that. We'd have to return them in the daytime and they would lock them up, because they were more afraid of the GI's getting drunk and shooting each other over a card game. I'm sure in other areas of the country they carried them constantly.

I know a lot of the camps were further North. They would be basically constantly under attack. There was one time, it was during Tet. I was sitting out talking to somebody and suddenly we saw an explosion. These rockets started coming in. They would walk them in 'cause they weren't that accurate. They'd have to see where the first one exploded, then get closer and closer to the target. We started running to our barracks and yelling incoming. The sort of joke of this place is that it had gotten lax about security and the bunkers they had built out of sandbags had deteriorated over time. They weren't safe to go in 'cause probably if it got hit anywhere near by a rocket it would collapse and kill you, so you'd be more in danger. So what they told us to do was go up near our beds, so then if something fell it would fall on our beds. So that's what I did and it is very scary. I've heard this said by other people that you feel like the next one is going to land right on you and that's the way I felt. And there is nothing you can do about it. You can't fight a rocket. Where it lands, it lands.

Mr. Budzilowicz made me realize that I am one of the people that had a misconception of war. He showed me that though war is scary at first, one can be strong and simply look at his time in Vietnam as an experience incomparable to any other. Mr. Budzilowicz is currently back at school at Northeastern University in Chicago and

sings in the Chicago Symphony Chorus, Music of the Baroque, Chicago Opera Theatre and the Lyric Opera.
—Lee, grade 11

Among other notable choices here are the paragraph breaks to signal time ("by the spring") and topic (note how paragraph three contrasts the subject's own experience of being drafted with a description of other people fleeing to Canada—even though that description occurred near the bottom of the raw transcript). The final line—as with some earlier essay examples—is powerful. To some extent, the subject himself is like a rocket, propelled into service and, at least initially, not sure where he would land.

Fear

Zung Dao was born in Laos, North Vietnam, but was raised in Saigon, the capital of South Vietnam. He volunteered to join the South Vietnamese army when he was 19 years old. He volunteered for the Special Forces, at that time called the Technical Directorate, and fought against the communists from 1972–1975. After the war, he moved around a lot until he finally ended up in Chicago. Considering he has not been speaking English for his whole life, it is pretty good. Now he sits across from me at a table at his restaurant, The Edgewater Beach Cafe. His demeanor is pleasant, and he still looks fit, like he could be a soldier. Zung leans back in his chair and takes a sip of ice water, contemplating my first question; he pulls in a deep breath of air before he starts his story.

The first two years of my service I volunteered for virtually any mission that was volunteer only because in those missions you were probably going to die. Those first two years, fear never entered my mind. Anticipation, yes. But after that, I did feel. Yes there was a fear. You lose sleep. And you sweat. In the middle of the night, you get nightmares; so many things happened. The more involved and the more I served in the Armed Forces, the more disillusioned I got.

I saw the communist soldiers moving from the North to the South, in our border. In our land. And during that time, we did not have any lead battalion, lead division in the North. Only us. A team of six known as the Technical Directorate. We did the unconventional warfare. They'd drop us behind that enemy line past the 17th parallel to collect information; capture VIP high-ranking officers for interrogation purposes; destroy bridges and land mine the Ho Chi Minh trail to try to interrupt the flow of soldiers and weapons.

There is a fear, yes. Cold-sweated nights, yes. But when you touch the ground the fear and anticipation, everything disappears and you become like animal. Instinct. Your mind's too occupied on what to do next rather than being scared. You don't have time to be scared because every moment you calculate how to get from point A to point B. The training that you get, the experience that you have, diverts your attention from fear to what you have to do next. But we can't make any difference, six of us. They spit and we'd drown. So I got more scared and more disillusioned.

There was anticipation when I received a mission for briefing, because you knew it was only six of you against a thousand of them, and things can happen to you. One mission was to go into the Southeast of Hue [in the jungle]. There's an enemy's base. They have heavy artillery, tanks, clinics, and they grow their own vegetables. The number of enemies is roughly 2200. To confirm activity they dropped us, a team of eight, to capture anyone higher than Lieutenant Colonel. We spent six days studying the habit of their movement and activities. To pass the time you read. You still have to do your job; you still have to keep a log: the temperature, the soil, the surroundings, and whatever you think is out of the ordinary, note it. We have to take pictures and plan our own defensive. You're living in enemy territory, so you're always alert. We do not speak, we whisper. We used to carry magazines, or we'd play jokes on one another. We'd catch snakes, centipedes, scorpions, and we'd slip them to one another. It's isolated. We couldn't talk. A voice in the jungle carries. If you talk, you're dead.

One time we were fishing in the stream. We threw the hook in the stream and we caught a wild chicken. It started to make sounds. It was so scary. The jungle was so quiet and all of a sudden this bird was going "Yappity yap!" all over. I cut the line so fast. Oh boy, it was so scary. For a couple of days, we were completely silent.

Some of the most enjoyable moments are when we read the magazines (the tabloids). When we're sitting there, sometimes we'd laugh so hard (without any sound). We listened to music, we admired the orchids in the jungle.

At night, you can't even see your hand this close [holding his hand right in front of his face]. The dead leaves produce this luminescence, so that at night, you see this sparkle all over the place. We learned that dead leaves and dead animals actually produce a luminescence. It's like ghosts.

You start to hear things in the jungle. The rain and the leaves start talking to you. When the wind blows it's like a concerto, like a symphony. And at night, you can't shout, you can't cuss. You can't do anything.

On the sixth day we found a group of about 32 soldiers (a squadron). They moved every morning at 6 o'clock from where they live to the base of their daily activities. And in the group of 32 there's a colonel riding on a bicycle.

We learned for three days that as late as 6:05, they passed through where we stayed. We measured carefully how long the group of 32 soldiers was and how we were going to execute the ambush. So what we do is plant directional mine which is only pressure and no pellets. We had four in the middle to come out and capture the Colonel, two on each end to detonate the mines, and then start shooting with hand grenade launchers to stop the reinforcement.

From where we were to the road was about 15 feet. When six or seven pass by, we would click the detonator. The Colonel on the bicycle was thrown about 50 feet into a ditch. 31 people almost die. Some of them die, some of them are dying. Our job is to come out, get the Colonel, and we have to get rid of all the rest. We do mercy killing. We just put a shot in the head of the soldiers. They are Vietnamese too.

I felt so sad because I saw them as Vietnamese, as a human being just like any one of you. When people get hurt, you cry. I looked at them as one of my brothers. I understood what they were saying. I looked in their eyes and saw this fear, this pain, this misery. They would cry, calling their loved ones. Most of them call "mommy." I've looked down at a 16 year old kid and I saw him crying. He looked at me, crying he says, "Mom … hurt … hurt …" and smoke is all over. Blood is all over. Arms, legs, people. I was haunted. I couldn't do anything. I turned to my Sargent and said to him, "Do it. Do it for me" [the mercy killing]. I grabbed the hand-grenade launcher, ran and tried to shoot them [the reinforcement], and then went to contact the helicopter which was supposed to pick us up two and a half hours later at a predetermined site.

As the team leader at that time, I did not show any emotions because that is a sign of weakness. Don't feel anything. That is the objective of the mission. I did not feel very proud of it. But some of the members of my team feel very proud of it: the more you kill, the more captured; mission accomplished. Some of them told themselves, "Yes, I did OK." But not me. Not when I see a 16-year-old boy calling for his mom.

When I came home that night, I could not sleep for 10 days. Every time I closed my eyes, I saw those squirming Vietnamese soldiers, moaning and groaning, calling their loved ones. The things that happened are so vivid in my mind that sometimes I still have flashbacks.

After that, I really felt pretty scared, fear, disillusioned; even though we got a medal for that mission. But when your profession is a soldier, you have to eat it. You have to swallow it. And you have to digest it. Either you eat it and life goes on, you die of despair, or you kill yourself; eat your own bullet. Your conscience is for you to keep. But out on the battlefield, you can't show that to others.

If one out of us hesitates, one person makes a mistake, all of us will die. Our lives are intertwined. We have no choice. We live and die together. You only have x amount of time to live. One lifetime. There are certain things that scar your life. Your soul, your mind. These things will be there forever. Some things you wish you didn't have to do, but you have to do it.

I want to be a good soldier, but yet, I do not have a clear conscience of what I did. I'm still really confused. Sometimes I just seal myself for weeks without talking.

There is a long pause after Zung's last words. Although he seems to be coping just fine with his actions and involvement in the war, he is still bothered by the atrocities that occurred. When he first started out, there wasn't a fear; maybe due to his lack of experience with war, but as he became more involved in the war, saw and experienced the effects of the war, fear grew in him. Now, even though he doesn't regret his involvement in the war, he still feels sad about what happened to so many people. He wouldn't want anyone to have to experience something like he did, and have to live with it for the rest of their lives.

—Lisa, grade 11

One reason why this is an extraordinarily powerful essay is the author's decision not to change the subject's voice to Standard English. The broken English in places ("you become like animal" or "blood is all over") intensifies the pathos of the scenes the subject was forced to participate in and witness. The decision to open the piece with a description of the setting is also a terrific choice. The author helps us see how the subject readies himself to launch into the story. The revelation that Mr. Dao owns a restaurant is also interesting. It's a reminder that the people who populate our lives—even in the background—are complicated human beings full of their own stories.

Essays on Race

Race: How Blacks and Whites Think and Feel about the American Obsession is a brilliant collection of oral histories gathered by Studs Terkel. As my students and I quickly realized, however, race is never really "black and white." The first time I had students write a "race" essay, I asked them to interview someone of a race "different" from theirs because I sought to promote greater understanding across the races. My naïve idea exploded, however, when Sian asked whom she should interview since she self-identified as biracial. The simple-mindedness of my assignment was quickly apparent to everyone, but my naïveté at least became a useful starting point for our course. From then on, as in the following example, I asked students to interview someone on the *subject* of race.

Amanda Shackelford

I first saw her at a meeting for the Campaign to End the Death Penalty in the Hyde Park Union Church. She lives in a single floor house on the far South Side of Chicago where she has lived since her last year of high school. She says that she feels comfortable there. "The school I graduated from was mixed. And it was nice. I didn't see no prejudice." She has three sons, two of whom are incarcerated. Her youngest son Herbert is in jail for theft. Her middle son Gerald has been serving a term of life in prison since his arrest in 1992. She maintains that he is innocent and that he was beaten into giving a false confession by white officers.

I didn't know he had been arrested until Gerald had been in jail two days. In the transcript the police stated that they gave him one phone call to call me. I never got that call.

My youngest son Herbert called me from jail and told me "Mama, Gerald's been arrested." They arrested him and he's in prison on two counts of murder.

Gerald had gotten shot years ago in the leg with a hollow head bullet and when the hollow head bullet hits you it explodes; it just messed his knee up. So to put it back together they put a pin in it. He told me that the night they arrested him they beat him and broke that pin to get him to say he did that.

He was in so much pain he said, "I did it," just to get them to leave him alone.

After he was arrested he was going back and forth to court. They didn't have no proof, wasn't no witnesses to say that he did it. He tried to get the public defender to check at a shell gas station right at the corner of 69th and Wentworth *(to establish an alibi)* but she never did. There was a young man named Turner who was in jail at the time. They got this young man, in order to get out of jail, to say that he seen Gerald with the gun that had shot those people.

Gerald had made mistakes, he had did drugs. He might have gotten into fistfights.

But he was never the type of person to hurt nobody. If we had food in the house and he knew somebody who was hungry he would take some food to him. If he had money and somebody needed something he would give it to them. He was a helping one. I'm not saying it because he's my son; I'm just saying it because that's the truth.

One day when he had been in jail a year, or a year and a half, the other inmates beat him. Right there in prison, right there in Cook County. There was an officer there and he turned his back. That is wrong. You got a sign on your car that says "we serve and protect." What type of protection is that? How can you say you're protecting me?

When I went to see him in the county hospital I didn't know who he was at first. His face was swollen up so bad I had to ask. I don't really want to say there was a racial issue because I wasn't in the jail. I didn't hear the things that were said. I know the police that beat Gerald were white. But it's not just white that's beating the blacks. Some of the black officers are doing the same thing. They feel, "I am an officer. I can do this and I can get away with it. Nobody is going to be able to prove it because we back each other up."

But it's not fair for a person to suffer for something they did not do. When this happened Gerald was helping some people move, up on the North Side. Then the police took him from his friend's house over in Marquette. He's been in prison for almost eleven years for something he did not do.

I got a younger son, Herbert. He's in prison for something he actually did. He was stealing. He knows he did it. It's been time for him to get his act together. He has a daughter and she needs him. Every time she comes to my house he's in jail. He did drugs for I don't know how long, and it became a part of him. He stole damn near everything you could think of: anything that he could take to the drug man. One day I had a canned ham and he stole it. It was like he could smell money.

There are young men and women who got so much free time. They get that money and soon as you get the check it's gone. Even your [food] stamps. You took it to the drug man. If you've got kids who need to eat they can't eat if you don't give them no food.

My kids' father wasn't a lot of help to me. He wasn't the type of man to come home on payday with his paycheck and say, "Now here's so much and I'm going to go out tonight." He just stayed out until the money was gone.

I can't blame him for that because I was always there for them. Every now and then I went out but it wasn't a lot. My friends knew that if I went home, I wasn't going to come back out.

One night a couple of friends and I, we all worked together at the beauty shop, wanted to go out. They said, "Come on Armanda, come on let's go." I told them I don't want to go, my clothes are dirty. Debby said, "I got a blouse for you." I said I don't have no money. "I've got ten dollars you can borrow." It's good I did go because I did meet my husband. He passed four years ago. They wouldn't let Gerald out for the funeral. He was incarcerated, for something he did not do.

But it's not just my son, it's quite a few men. It's not just black people. There are poor white people who are going through the same thing but people that got money can get away with murder. Take two people. Two men get arrested. Both of them black. One is poor and one has money. The one who is poor, he's going to be in jail. Even if he didn't do it he's going to be in jail. They're going to think of some way to keep him there. Now the one who has the money, all he's got to do is pay that money, get him a lawyer and he's out.

So I can't always say it's a racial thing. Because I'm not a racist. I got white friends and we holding together. One of the young ladies that I pray with she's visually impaired and she always let me know that she's always praying for Gerald and that everything is going to work out. But my son still talks about hurting himself because he don't feel like he's ever going to get out.

I was feeling negative that there wasn't any hope, too. But the things that this group *(The Campaign to End the Death Penalty)* has done....You all don't have to do this. This is not your family. But just thinking that people care. Makes you feel good. It really does. It makes me believe that it is going to be ok.
—Derin, grade 12

This essay captures the subject's voice with great power and sympathy. The author is also adept at adding parenthetical information for his audience (offering the helpful phrase "to establish an alibi"; adding the name of the group to which Ms. Shackleford belongs).

◎

According to Donald Ritchie, a past president of the Oral History Association, oral history "[makes] history more believable by associating real people with historical events" (170). But more than that, oral history powerfully connects students to the world around them and to the idea that we are living in a historical time *now*. History cannot be limited to a few dates—July 4, 1776; September 11, 2001. Ours too is a historical age, and we are all part of that history.

And oral histories teach students a great deal about writing—how to organize ideas, why we use punctuation, the importance of voice in compelling writing. But perhaps more important yet, according to writing professor Don Graves, "Learning how to acquire knowledge from others brings more than life to the curriculum: It is an essential life skill" ("Bringing Life" 22). These skills and the life skills associated with any oral history project will inform students' writing and thinking throughout their lives.

In the next chapter, I return to the specific skills of asking questions and conducting interviews through a discussion of the exploratory essay.

10

Off the Beaten Path: Exploratory Essays

I will try
 to fasten into order enlarging grasps of disorder, widening
scope, but enjoying the freedom that
Scope eludes my grasp, that there is no finality of vision,
that I have perceived nothing completely,
that tomorrow a new walk is a new walk.

—A. R. AMMONS

These ending lines from "Corsons Inlet" assert a sort of *ars poetica* for Ammons. In this poem, the speaker announces his desire to accept the world for what it is—complex, chimerical, contradictory—rather than attempt to reduce it to a single precept. To accomplish, this he seeks "the wanderings of a mirroring mind," knowing that he must be "willing to go along, to accept / the becoming / thought, to stake off no beginnings or ends, [and] establish / no walls."

This is a goal state for both me and my students: to cultivate a mind driven by inquiry, a mind that refuses to foreclose on complicated truths by settling for facile answers. Sadly, this goal is not often realized in English classes. Instead, the dominant essay form remains the thesis-support model in which students demonstrate the validity of a proposition (usually one they held before beginning their writing) as though it were a simple syllogism.

A veteran writing teacher once told me that all he wanted was for students to show their work, like they do in math class. The problem with this goal is that most topics worth writing about resist simple algebraic proofs. This form is so commonplace that Sheridan Blau called for a resistance to "the hegemony of the thesis-argument essay." To Blau, the artificiality of the form is as alarming as its ubiquity:

> The unquestioned dominance in schools and colleges and the virtual absence of living models of such essays in the real-world reading experience of students have rendered it an ossified and ritually practiced form unlikely to be perceived by students (or their teachers) as having much authentic social or intellectual purpose, even if it will produce a respectable score on an Advanced Placement test or on similar assessments of competence in writing about literature. (175)

The narrowness of the range of assignments in many English classes is a problem, Blau suggests, since "the form becomes so fixed for many students as a model for writing that they can't imagine how to think about any topic they might write about through any other frame" (179)—even when writing about their own experiences.

William Zeiger's "The Exploratory Essay: Enfranchising the Spirit of Inquiry in College Composition" articulates some of the epistemological limitations of thesis-argument essays as the sole writing paradigm. Such essays, he says, create "a logically exclusive, linear progression to a pre-determined end" (456) while refusing to "recognize and weigh alternatives." By offering students a steady diet of thesis-argument essays, he continues, "we are implicitly teaching that the ability to support an assertion is more important than the ability to examine an issue" (458). As I noted in Chapter 8, such assignments favor monologue over genuine intellectual conversation.

Organizing courses around thesis-argument essays also limits the interpersonal dimension of classrooms. "For when the aim of an essay is to prove or 'win' a point, the projected audience members become not co-inquirers or even neutral attendants, but critical opponents. The students see the audience as an antagonist" (Zeiger 458). This rhetorical stance runs counter to any notion of the classroom as a community of learners and potentially creates hostile relationships that result from a discourse predicated on winning and losing.

Getting Started

I always ask my students to explore the reasons why they live their lives the way they do. One year, however, I wanted to drive the point home as never before, so I hit them with some eye-opening stats: The average life expectancy for an American man is seventy-two years. If we sleep eight hours a day (or one-third of every day), that means we are asleep for twenty-four solid years. Talk about your hibernation! Add to this the extraordinary statistic that Americans on average spend an additional four and a half hours a day watching television. That's the equivalent of an additional thirteen and a half years of constant TV watching. In total, we spend thirty-seven and a half years—more than half our lives—either unconscious to the world around us or focused on the tiny rectangle of a TV set. Rather than view this math as an exercise in cruelty, it seemed to me a reminder that we had better make good use of our time.

"So how do you spend your time?" I asked. As it happened, the first student to volunteer a topic in class was a runner. No one else in his family ran, yet he ran at least five miles every day. He further admitted to being "obsessed with times"—even outside of running. I asked some questions for him to think about: When did you start running? Why do you run? What do you get out of running? And then some harder questions—think about running as a metaphor in your life: What are you running toward? What are you running from? The answers to these questions may not be fully answerable, but it seemed worthwhile to think carefully about what he called "the central activity" of his life.

The student sitting next to the runner said he was a hunter, an activity no one else in the class participated in. I asked similar questions about hunting and the class joined in. Their questions were a mix of genuine interest and gentle parody of me: What are you hunting for in your life? And this continued with the next student, a wrestler: What issues are you wrestling with? What else in your life are you attempting to pin down?

This line of questioning didn't work with every student. Lisa claimed not to have a dominant activity. What do you spend your time *thinking about* then, I asked, reminding the class that thinking is also an activity. "That's easy," she replied. "My grandmother lives in our house and we just found out she has Alzheimer's disease." What a great exploratory topic, I thought. Even scientists are stumped by the causes and treatments; there is no clear consensus on the treatment of the disease or the ways in which families might cope. Far from generating a slam-dunk thesis statement, this topic seemed exactly right for our next assignment: to write about the significant activities and concerns of our lives, plumbing the depths of these topics by approaching them from a variety of angles.

Here is the assignment sheet I pass out:

Exploratory Essay

Most school writing is thesis-driven: a claim is made and evidence is found to support that claim. This is especially true in "research" papers, where sources are often consumed to "prove a point." This is perhaps useful to polemicists but not to writers interested in discovery.

This approach to writing clearly runs counter to everything we've studied this year, so we'll approach our next essay as a hybrid of personal writing and research—but not in the service of a predetermined conclusion. Rather, we will care about exploration.

THE TOPIC: Start by picking three topics that define you: subjects you care about, sports/activities you participate in, issues/problems you are confronting. I'm happy to help you choose a topic once you've made a tentative list. NB: These topics should come from major activities in your life and should relate to major themes therein.

THE RESEARCH: You'll need to read outside sources on your topic—books, stories, essays, articles. The number and length of these will differ from topic to topic. I will give you a list of resources and books that might be helpful **after** you choose your topic. In addition, visit the library, consult librarians, and search databases such as ProQuest, Questia, and CQ Researcher.

A second part of your research is an interview you'll conduct with someone else who is interested in the topic you've chosen. Preferably, this person should not be someone you know well or someone with whom you've already spoken on the topic.

THE PERSONAL: Write a scene or two about your personal experience with the topic. As we've discussed all year, pay special attention to focused moments and character development.

THE ORGANIZATION: We will explore a number of different organizational strategies. Since we're using several different writing genres here—interview, written texts, personal story—we'll work on blending sections where we can and demarcating segments where blending won't work.

I usually give students several days to brainstorm topics and to hand in proposals for their explorations. It's important that students write about significant topics they have a personal stake in, either a defining activity in their lives or a subject they are unusually passionate about. I have allowed students to investigate topics such as space exploration, criminal punishment, and immigration, for instance, especially if they can establish a personal connection, such as a visit to an anti–capital punishment rally or a naturalization ceremony. Almost any topic works as long as students write about big issues in their lives and frame their research with a "why" question.

Here is a list of some of the most successful topics students have written about recently:

Why do I enjoy playing poker for money?

Why does my grandmother have dementia?

Why do I (a skinny, nerdy kid) enjoy lifting weights so much?

Why do I "bomb" (spray paint) public spaces?

Why do I stutter?

Why do I fish? (And why do I no longer fish with my father?)

Why do I care so much about physical beauty, even after I stopped competing in beauty pageants?

Why do I suffer from anorexia?

Why am I clinically depressed?

Why do I box?

Why am I so interested in water conservation?

Why am I going to college?

Why do I run long distances every day?

Why do I star gaze?

The various parts needed to assemble the final essay can be written in any order. But I caution students to secure interviews as early as possible (see Chapter 9). As I insisted with the oral history interviews, I want students to interview an expert on their topic with whom they have never previously spoken. It's important to help students find possible interviewees by identifying people and organizations they might consult. Students have had incredible success by cold-calling local professionals. Other people in the school building who have contacts in various fields have also been invaluable. For one of the papers reprinted in this chapter, for example, a student interviewed an eating disorder specialist recommended by a social worker in our building. (For more information on interviewing, I again recommend Chapter 9, in which I discuss interview strategies in detail.)

The amount and kind of research for these papers depends on the topic. Again, if I am unfamiliar with topics, I rely on my colleagues and our librarians to guide the research. One thing I insist on, however, is that students read excellent writing and first-class research, so we look for books, essays, and articles that students can read in the approximately three weeks we spend on this assignment. We are after authentic research—which is to say, reading that is appropriate for students' abilities and the time they can devote to the project. I never want students to pretend to read books simply to pad their works cited pages. Additionally, I encourage them to consult a variety of other sources they might use in their essays, such as movies, pamphlets, short stories, poems, and songs.

For the sake of narrative inquiry, I usually require two personal stories for this assignment so that students have an additional means of incorporating their own lives into their writing. Students almost always use personal stories to lead off the final essays since starting with the history of a topic or the science behind it might be off-putting to readers. Personal stories invite readers in and allow the different sections that follow to change the texture and tone of the essay without leaving the subject at hand.

While students are writing, reading, and interviewing, we look at professional and student models. For professional models, I use Howard Dully's "My Lobotomy," a twenty-five-minute radio documentary originally aired on NPR by a man who explores the results of a lobotomy he was given as a teenager; Kyoko Mori's "Yarn," which explores the author's interest in knitting, but also offers fascinating information on the history of yarn, gender, and the connection between yarn and stories; and Lee Zacharias's "Buzzards," which intertwines stories of the author's fascination with these birds and stories of her relationship with her father. These last two pieces come from the annual Best American Essays series, which offers great examples of exploratory essays every year. Student examples follow. Let's start with an initial draft of an exploratory essay.

Exploratory Essay

It started with the food. The intricately folded tortellini that my grandmother made by the thousands every month for eighty years suddenly began to warp and fall apart. We blamed her hands, saying that she had become too old to make the familiar yet tedious fold on the pasta dough. Brownies came out of the oven hard as bricks because she forgot to put the eggs in. Senility, we said. Everyone gets old, right?

There is a very blurred vision among people as to what exactly happens when our bodies start to finally give in and creep slowly towards death. Senility, sometimes used interchangeably with dementia, is no disease. Senility is the mental and physical deterioration associated with aging. Everybody falls apart. Our bodies are as perishable as the gallon of milk in the grocery store, only with a longer expiration date. Eyesight worsens, knees cramp up, backs crack, bowels clog up—like it or not, these things happen when you grow old. They are not, however, the same thing as dementia, which is defined as the "deterioration of intellectual faculties, such as memory, concentration, and judgment, resulting from an organic disease or a disorder of the brain. It is sometimes accompanied by emotional disturbance and personality changes." Everyone's body shuts down. The difference is that in some people the brain shuts down at a quicker rate than their body. It is estimated that as much as half the population over eighty suffers from dementia. Given how commonplace it is today, what is the future of dementia?

The next step was not as subtle as a waning ability to prepare food. Standing at the kitchen sink while gently washing a plate, my grandma would stare out the window, smiling and laughing slightly. All we could see was the bleak autumn sky and the neighbor's garage. "Look at those children dance," she would tell us, pointing to the garage roof. "Look how long their legs are! They dance with the leaves." Needless to say this was the point at which we knew something was wrong. The doctor confirmed it. Lewy Body Dementia.

Defined as an overlap between Alzheimer's disease and Parkinson's, Lewy Body Dementia composes 10-15% of all diagnosed dementias. People with this type of dementia experience repeated falls, fluctuating cognition with variations in attention and alertness, and recurring hallucinations which are usually experienced early on in the disease.

The dancing children soon seemed to blow away with the leaves, and for a period, no more strange beings were seen by my grandmother. But soon, our optimism disappeared. Mysterious and malicious, men in black began to appear around my grandmother's house. In the kitchen, in the backyard, in the bedroom—these men stalked my grandmother with the intent of killing her. "They're trying to kill me," she would tell us, despite our comforting.

Hallucinations are common in every type of degenerative disease, but in my grandma's case they were extreme. Delusions affect 30-70% of patients, and the most common are delusions of persecution, theft, and a "phantom boarder," or someone staying in the house. If you had talked to my grandma without knowing her situation, you would have thought that she ran a boarding house. Every night was a party, and she would always tell us how busy she was cleaning the house for the party. Dead brothers, cousins, aunts, uncles, and friends were all on the guest list to my grandmother's parties. As much as we tried to avoid saying, "Grandma, Joey wasn't there, he died forty years ago," we had to eventually. Did this change anything? No. Past events meant nothing to my grandmother; what she saw was what she knew, and nothing anybody else told her could change that.

—Mary, grade 12

The potential in this essay is clear even though the draft is rough. The author powerfully describes the harrowing specter of dementia and the disturbing symptoms of warped memory and hallucination that accompany her grandmother's disease. When I showed this draft to my class, though, they pounced on the lack of attribution for sources. The author offers some fascinating information—some of which is even quoted—yet no source is cited. This is fine for a draft, but sources must be provided in the final draft as a courtesy to the reader. The single biggest issue, however, is organization. "Group like terms," I always say—just as we did in sifting through transcripts to create oral history essays (see Chapter 9)—and I ask the class to identify the mini-sections present in this early draft excerpt. This essay alternates between personal reminiscence and research material with little regard for transitions. Sectioning material off would help the author to develop the grandmother's character and condition gradually while offering the scientific material in a more coherent and linear fashion.

Here are several complete drafts of exploratory essays.

Man of Steel

I

As the blazing May sun beat down on my neck, I thought to myself, "I'll never finish this race."

I had long dreaded this day. As the warmer months approached, I feared the possibility of being put through such a demeaning and humiliating exercise. It was Field Day. Field Day was a special day at Sears School, the day where all the athletes and, for lack of a better word, jocks of our school got to shed their worries of algebra and history in order to celebrate their athletic superiority over nerds like me.

Field Day was made up of a variety of track and field events, and every student was required to participate in at least one. I chose the 800 meter race, on the idea that being soundly beaten in a longer race was far less humiliating than being slaughtered in a short sprint. From the moment the race began, I deeply regretted my decision.

I was not built for physical activity. My mother showed her love to me in the way only an Italian mother would: food. Being a late bloomer, I did not have the luxury of a growth spurt to shed my extra pounds, and thus found myself competing with taller, faster, and fitter classmates.

I finished the first lap just as the other competitors had finished the race. I had another agonizingly long lap to go, 400 meters of expectant parents and snickering classmates. As I rounded the first corner, my eyes became cloudy with a salty mixture of sweat and tears. By the second turn, I was flat out sobbing, unable to live with the pathetic spectacle I must have presented the spectators. Every step felt agonizingly slow, each footfall reverberated throughout my entire body, both jarring and tormenting. My shirt was soaked with sweat. By the time I had finished the race, the runners of the 1600 had already lined up and were waiting for me. I was devastated.

I wandered off, crying silently and shuddering at the thought of being handed a trophy for participating; I knew that participation prizes were for losers only. "Hey Bullet, nice race," B., star quarterback of the Sears football team, yelled across the blacktop. Through years of poor athletic ability, I had gained the nickname "the Bullet," an allusion which was hardly lost on me. Being compared to Superman, my childhood hero whose physical capabilities dwarfed anything I could have imagined, hurt far worse than B. could have guessed. I stopped. I was going to do something about this. I was going to change. I would build myself a new body.

II

In the world of bodybuilding, no name is more revered than Dave Draper, the bodybuilding god who took bodybuilding from the basements and boiler rooms of the United States onto the stage and into the magazines. A generation of pimply-faced teens grew up worshipping his Herculean image, including the son of a German police chief named Schwarzenegger. Known as the Blond Bomber, Dave made an indelible mark in the world of bodybuilding, even if he never achieved the competitive success of other bodybuilders. For Draper, success took him to places he could never have dreamed of as a wet-behind-the-ears kid from New Jersey.

"I walked into the picture about the middle of the Twentieth Century when I wrapped a skinny, child's hand around a Hercules hand gripper," Draper muses in his bodybuilding manual cum memoir, *Brother Iron, Sister Steel: A Bodybuilder's Book*. From the gripper, Draper moved on to the three-spring chest expander, the five-spring super expander, and a wall-mounted bungee-pulley contraption which hung on his kitchen wall. Soon Dave got into barbells and dumbbells; although he was forced to lift in the boiler room of his local YMCA with a few other bodybuilding pioneers, experimenting with rickety bench presses and dilapidated barbells, he was on his way to greatness.

Draper was discovered by Joe Weider, head of Weider Barbell Company in Union City. Soon Draper found himself in Muscle Beach doing photo shoots with beautiful women and the ocean at his back. Weider pushed Draper more and more, pressuring him to compete in body-building competitions while still featuring him in all of his magazines. The pressure proved too much. In 1970, Draper disappeared from the world of bodybuilding, retreating into his own world where he focused on making furniture, his new passion. He also began to descend into a darkening world of alcohol and PCP. His ultimate ignominy occurred when he almost blew up his house trying to manufacture PCP. In the world of bodybuilding, Dave Draper's name seemed all but forgotten.

Dave cleaned up and prepared for a comeback. The weights had never left him, "no more than an old sheepdog leaves a gritty sheepherder tending the south forty." When Dave returned, he did not find the bodybuilding he had left, made up of a few strong men focused on building their body. The bodybuilding world had expanded since he had left, had grown tentacles and become something of a monster. When he finally decided to return in 1985, it was chemical warfare. Steroids were the name of the game, to the detriment of solid discipline and steel. Draper was appalled, and opened up several gyms as well as a muscle magazine of his own, preaching a retro-style philosophy of high protein and all-natural workouts, gaining him the credibility he had once left behind, almost 20 years earlier. His return brought new life to the sport, inspiring another generation of body-builders.

III

"Fuck. I am so busted," I thought, panicking as Ms. S. and Dr. K. walked over to me.

I tried my best to put on a composed, sober façade but to no avail. I could barely stand; I couldn't even find my ass with both my hands. I had to lean against my hotel room door as they walked towards me (it surely didn't help that I hadn't lifted a weight in 3 months). "Ronnie," Ms. S. said. "We need to talk. We know that you've been drinking and, although it pains me to say this, you are going to undergo some serious consequences. When you decided to come to Italy with the Latin class, you signed an agreement stating that you would not engage in this kind of behavior, and you have broken that agreement. I'm sorry."

They turned to leave, and I slammed the door before falling onto the bed, numbed by a combination of vodka and cold-blooded fear. "How could this happen to me?" I thought. But I already knew the answer; this had been coming all along. Surely it had something to do with my weight-lifting, but in the beginning I could never then have dreamed that such honest hard work could have brought me so low.

Like Dave Draper, I first started lifting weights because I was fascinated by men with muscle. I had grown up and slimmed down since middle school, but was now stick-like in stature. A fellow twig named M. shared my fascination, and being of German descent felt that there was an Arnold Schwarzenegger in him which he had to unleash. So during the first weeks of sophomore year we ventured down to the Cage (aptly named, since it seemed that the enclosure which surrounded the weight-lifting area was the only thing keeping the hulking beasts inside from escaping and wreaking havoc on the general populace). Every day in the cage we worked, shirts soaked with sweat by the time we stumbled home. Soon we saw results and before long both gained a new confidence. M. had a straight head about him and bulked up humbly, but I was filled with pride. And pride does indeed come before the fall.

My new muscles gave me a confidence I had never felt before. I even felt my preternatural shyness diminish as my muscles grew. I was a new person, and I felt like I could take on the world. My headstrong confidence caused me to one day take up drinking, then smoking. The discipline faded, the focus left me, and daily visits to the gym became visits every other day, and those workouts soon were only once a week. It didn't faze me; I could remain confident and outgoing with just a couple shots and a quick puff. M., who knew nothing of my debauchery, noticed that I had changed. "What's wrong with you, Ronnie?" he asked me in the hall. "You got me into lifting, and now you don't come anymore. I mean, look at you!"

It was true. The months of hard work were rapidly becoming for naught; in fact, I was in worse shape than I had been before I started lifting. But I didn't care. "I don't need to do this anymore," I said before walking off, leaving M. speechless. I continued like this for months, recklessly abusing my body and my soul as I was sucked into a dark world, culminating in that night during the summer after sophomore year. Looking back on it, how else could it have ended? I had only wrought what I had sown.

IV

I returned to school my junior year with my head hung low. I had lost the respect of my parents, peers, and teachers; but most importantly, I had no more respect for myself. In a school of thousands, surrounded by friends who were thrilled to see me after months of vacation, I felt more alone than ever. As the dismissal bell rang, I didn't feel much like going home; so, purposeless, I wandered the halls.

For some reason, I wandered down to the Cage (I think I was looking for someone, but I don't exactly remember). As soon as I saw it, it began to draw me back, with the same fascination and excitement it had when I started lifting almost a year earlier. Each weight was a solid steel friend which I could trust: the 40 pound barbell would never switch and become 50, and just knowing this gave me a strange feeling of safety. These weights spoke my language. It was a language of numbers, of movement, of certainty and of success. I put on my gym uniform, racked up the weights, and all of a sudden things just felt *right*. Nobody else was down there (I had to ask a trainer to open up the cage, which he happily did), and the silence was beautiful. No dividing my attention, no self-consciousness, nobody to impress; just me and the weights. I finished my workout and stumbled home, feeling the same elation I had felt a year earlier after a particularly hard workout. No. It was not the same. I was older and wiser, tempered by the mistakes I had made and the lessons I learned. I felt great. Only one thing left to do.

The next day I waited by M.'s locker after school. When he first saw me, he was shocked; I had all but disappeared from his life after I stopped working out. "You wanna, maybe, come lifting after school?" I asked, sheepishly.

"You better with your sorry, outta-shape ass," he said. "I'll see you down there in 5."

I have often wondered why lifting is such an important part of my life. I now realize that weight-lifting offers me the one thing we all seek so desperately in our lives: control. I cannot control my family or my friends, nor can I control much of anything that goes on around me. Many people feel the same powerlessness, wondering why they are thrown into a world where everything seems to be outside of their power. But there is one thing we can all control, and that is our selves. It's really ironic that there is such an enormous weight loss and fitness industry telling us what to do with our bodies. We all have the good fortune to live in a time and place free of slavery, and that is why we can truly claim ownership of our bodies. The human body is a wonderful, beautiful piece of art which can be molded by the mind; eating right, running those extra miles, lifting those extra weights, all things we can do to control something, however small it may seem. This same sense of control inspired Dave to start bodybuilding 50 years ago, before it had become a multi-billion dollar chemical war. "I could enjoy a basic oneness of the activity," he said, "where you were in control of being controlled."
—Ronnie, grade 12

In the opening section of this piece, the speaker creates a strong ethos by revealing his own vulnerability, his inability to play sports with "the jocks." The transition between sections is smooth. Note the deft turn of phrase between "I would build myself a new body" and "Dave Draper, the bodybuilding god." The biographical material on Draper he offers may seem to veer off course, but the author hopes to draw a parallel between his own life and that of his weight-lifting role model. Not only do they both lift, but they also both nearly destroy what they have built for themselves through substance abuse. By exploring his own personal choices, Ronnie comes to see "control" as an underlying motive for weight lifting. This insight doesn't answer all his questions, as evidenced by the oxymoronic quote from Draper that ends this piece, but Ronnie has come a long way toward scrutinizing a major activity in his life that he had never given much thought to before. What's not in this essay as of yet is Ronnie's interview with a former Mr. Olympia. Although he did not write up the interview, it is a testament to the power of the assignment that Ronnie went ahead with the interview even after the essay due date had come and gone.

Higher Power

1

"Mommy, what's going on?" My mother quickly responded, "Don't worry honey, David will be back. Go back to sleep." It was another terrifying phone call in the middle of the night. My brother was missing again; there was no telling where he could be. As I crawled back under my green comforter, I remembered how just two days ago David and I were playing tag. Neither of us had a care in the world. What was wrong? I love him so much.

For much of my life I have walked through school halls, cities, and airports not sure whom I can trust. If one person, a well liked, stable, poster boy could be a ticking bomb ready to become my worst nightmare, couldn't just about anyone else? I had seen our once happy home become a place where the unyielding feeling of terror reigned. Where we had to walk on eggshells to avoid setting off an alarm. I recall walking home from school wondering what would greet me at the door. Would there be yelling, violence, police, an ambulance? Would my mother be crying, or would there be silent depression waiting to explode?

For a while, this fear paralyzed me. It prevented me from living my life. I remember hovering in the fetal position in my room for hours too afraid to open my eyes—afraid of what my life looked like. But eventually, I came to see that it wasn't all about my life, and that my actions were not helping him, and they certainly weren't helping me. I started to separate his issues from mine. The uncertainty and my lack of control over the situation taught me how to rely upon myself. I learned to complete a meaningless homework assignment even though my house was in ruins, or to be a good and cheerful friend even though my best friend, my brother, was no friend to me. I learned how to have a smile on my face even though my life events seemed to conspire to turn it upside down. I learned the effects of mental illness, depression, and drug addiction on an individual and their family.

If only there was a higher power to help each individual affected to reach stability.

2
1, 2, 3, 4, 5, 6, 7, 8, 9, 10, 11, 12

David has attended more than 12 various centers for drug and behavior problems. A twelve-step program is a set of guiding principles for recovery from addictive, compulsive, or other behavioral problems. The people who started

AA—recovery from alcoholism—initially started the 12-step program. The 12-step program has been incorporated in other programs such as: <u>Narcotics Anonymous</u>, <u>Overeaters Anonymous</u>, <u>Co-Dependents Anonymous</u>, and <u>Emotions Anonymous</u>.

The first twelve-step program was founded in 1935. <u>Bill Wilson</u> and <u>Dr. Bob Smith</u> (Bill W. and Dr. Bob) established the program in Akron, Ohio. In 1953 AA allowed Narcotics Anonymous to use its Steps and Traditions. Drug addicts who do not suffer from the specifics of alcoholism involved in AA hoping for recovery are not welcome in meetings for alcoholics only. David, like all other addicts, abides by these rules. As a consequence, while I am playing tennis four nights a week, David attends various AA and NA meetings daily. (12STEPSTATS)

These are the original Twelve Steps as published by <u>Alcoholics Anonymous.</u>

1. We admitted we were <u>powerless</u> over alcohol—that our lives had become unmanageable.

2. Came to believe that a Power greater than ourselves could restore us to sanity.

3. Made a decision to turn our will and our lives over to the care of <u>God</u> *as we understood Him*.

4. Made a searching and fearless <u>moral inventory</u> of ourselves.

5. Admitted to God, to ourselves, and to another human being the exact nature of our wrongs.

6. Were entirely ready to have God remove all these defects of <u>character</u>.

7. Humbly asked Him to remove our shortcomings.

8. Made a list of all persons we had harmed, and became willing to make <u>amends</u> to them all.

9. Made direct amends to such people wherever possible, except when to do so would injure them or others.

10. Continued to take personal inventory and when we were wrong promptly admitted it.

11. Sought through <u>prayer</u> and <u>meditation</u> to improve our conscious contact with God *as we understood Him,* praying only for knowledge of His Will for us and the power to carry that out.

12. Having had a <u>spiritual awakening</u> as the result of these steps, we tried to carry this message to alcoholics, and to practice these principles in all our affairs.

A sponsor is a more experienced person in recovery who guides the less-experienced candidate through the program. Everyone going through the program should have at least one sponsor. There are a variety of approaches to recovery available that may or may not emphasize spiritual solutions. (12STEPSTATS) David has tried almost every solution in the book.

> "Sponsors share their experience, strength, and hope with their sponsees. . . . A sponsor's role is not that of a legal adviser, a banker, a parent, a marriage counselor, or a social worker. Nor is a sponsor a therapist offering some sort of professional advice. A sponsor is simply another addict in recovery who is willing to share his or her journey through the Twelve Steps."
>
> —*from NA's Sponsorship*

Over 45% of the men enrolled in the inpatient professional twelve-step programs were still clean one year after they were released, compared to 36% of those treated by cognitive-behavioral therapy. Although, no one is ever "cured." It's a lifelong struggle.

3

This journey began for me when I was 8. Too young to understand so much. My parents' words were censored. Censored to the point where certain information had disappeared. Too many missing links. How can I be satisfied with an incomplete description of my brother's life? What in fact happened? Why does *he* suffer from this disease? Is there a common thread between all addicts? Why David?

Now another journey begins. To figure out what those late night phone calls were about. Early morning wakeup calls from unknown numbers. Soothing words but then sudden weekend trips. A strong pressure to go to a friend's house when a conversation got heated.

Those same old days now reveal their nasty truths. . . .

"Oh, I didn't know David was coming home today!" I exclaimed while opening the wooden front door to our home in Glencoe. He looked extremely ragged and tired. Yet nothing could compare with my excitement to see him. Right then I heard footsteps racing down the stairs. The petrified look on my parents' faces did not match my enthusiasm for seeing my older brother for the first time in a month and a half.

Looking back, how could I have been so naïve? How could I not have noticed the constant state of hysterics my parents were in for *four* days? David had been in Oregon at a program called TREX for drug and behavioral problems. A sort of outdoorsy rehabilitation center—a place we hoped would cure his problem. One day David picked up and left, only leaving behind a short note which can be summed up by saying, "Screw you, I'm leaving." With not even a penny, only his genius street smarts, David made it across the country in four days. For those four days no one knew where he was. No one knew if he was dead or alive. Starting in the desert, ending up at our house. David has revealed tidbits of his journey to me over time—hitchhiking and coming across a friendly meth addicted truck driver that drove him all the way to the Ohio border. Dozens of puzzle pieces like this are still filling into my mind. Scenes that once seemed like happy times meet the reality of the trauma and horror that accompanied them.

Why did this happen to David? There is no trace of addiction in my family for as long as our knowing family tree goes back. He's a good kid, with a good heart. He has a brilliant mind that could be put towards so many amazing items other than drugs. If I *needed* an *answer* I'd be stuck pulling my hair out—I will never get a concrete answer to why. Studying the root of addiction offers a better understanding yet leaves my emotion and love for David still confused.

4

Addiction is a chronic, often relapsing brain disease that causes compulsive drug seeking and use despite harmful consequences to the individual that is addicted and to those around them. As of 2003 30.3% of 8th graders partook in illegal drug use. Of 10th graders that number was 44.9% and 12th graders 52.8%. What is causing these numbers to rise? What kids fall into these traps? What is the difference between the occasional user and the person whose life revolves around drugs? (DRUGSTATS)

Many believe that drug use is more common among lower socioeconomic levels but is it not true that famous people, friends, family of affluent stature fall into the addictive trap? This disease cannot be confined to one ethnicity or economic status.

According to Megan Kursawe, David's current therapist in New York, there is no clear-cut description of what an addict can be. No matter what their social or economic status is they can too suffer from addiction. There is a common thread that *most* patients show—"the fact that they have a poor self image and self esteem" contribute to their drug abuse problems. A common addict would exemplify signs of not being able to cope with life. Everything Megan said to me about her experience practicing with addicts made sense. David fits the mold of this so called "addict" along with thousands of others that appear nothing like him. They have trouble coping with emotions. They put the weight of their issue 100% on themselves . . . they need to give it over to someone else. This other thing can be god, or any kind of higher power.

The thing that struck me the most about my great conversation with Megan was when she said, "drug dependent people are usually very bright, unusually bright." This sentence resonated with me. I had heard it before. I recall, "Andrea, David is so smart…" This was my mother reassuring me that David will be ok.

"Their intelligence can be an addict's worst enemy," stated Megan. These genius people can end up rationalizing anything to make it seem right in their mind. Their mind can rationalize drugs to be positive until the drug has taken over the mind all together.

5

For many years no one knew how this story would end. Happily, things are looking good for everyone. I learned that the problem was his to solve. I could not fix him with my love, nor could my parents. We could only offer the tools. Watching, horrified as my parents told David he could not sleep in our house broke my heart, but they were right. I learned the limits of what a person can do for another even though the love is limitless.
—Andrea, grade 12

Andrea's essay is almost as illuminating for the reader as it was for her. By writing about her experiences as a young girl living with an addict, she comes to see herself, and her role in the family, in an altogether new way. Andrea threw herself into the research for this paper with all her heart. She was not just looking for a grade; she was looking for understanding. Her decision to interview her brother's therapist (after getting her brother's permission) was an inspired choice. It not only provided her with insight into addiction, but it also opened up new conversations with her brother that she had not been able to broker before. As I mentioned earlier, this author's other brother, Eric, wrote a memoir I offered as a model in Chapter 5. While Andrea wrote about David several times that year, Eric never did. This doesn't mean that the brothers weren't close. On the contrary, Andrea often wrote about how close her brothers have always been. But I mention this fact here to underscore the importance of allowing students to write about whatever they are comfortable with. Andrea's final paragraph offers a telling line: "For many years no one knew how this story would end." In authoring her life story, she has come to understand the narrative arc her family has traveled. In so doing, she has become a hero of sorts—not the kind who "saves the day," but someone who seeks understanding of her life through her writing.

Why I Care about New Orleans: A Search for Meaning
Preface

Men are from Mars, Women are from Venus, and if you like to eat alligators, suck crawfish heads, dance in spontaneous parades, tell dirty jokes, and clap your hands to jazz music … you must be from New Orleans.

About two weeks ago, I began a voyage aboard American Airlines flight 743 from Chicago O'Hare to Louis Armstrong International Airport. While the two great American cities are only separated by around 750 miles, the cultural and historical differences would lead you to believe that they are on two separate planets.

Of course, only New Orleans could have been founded in 1682 by a French man of the name Rene-Robert Cavalier Sieur de la Salle. Only New Orleans could have secretly switched ownership from the French to the Spanish, without anyone knowing for six months. Only in New Orleans of 1812 would Andrew Jackson lead a group of soldiers, Indians, farmers, and pirates in defeating an attempted British invasion. Only in New Orleans would there be over 4,000 freed people of color before the Civil War, and only in New Orleans would 25% of them own slaves.

It is a city unlike any other, with its own food, music, unique history, culture, and people.

Before I began my voyage, I sat in the comfort of my family room, watching Spike Lee's documentary "When the Levees Broke." The footage of Hurricane Katrina tearing everything in her path to shreds is familiar to all of us. She flooded the entire Crescent city, some parts with over 18 and 20 feet of water. The natural disaster shocked a country that until 2001 had seemed so invincible, but it was the days that followed Hurricane Katrina that made it even worse. Each night, people like me watched thousands of low-income families wailing for help on CNN nightly news, trapped among human feces and dead bodies in the Superdome and Convention Center. Only two years ago, I sat in the same leather couch, watching a middle-aged white woman with dirty brown hair clutching a naked baby that had passed out in the sun, dangerously close to death. Holding the baby up to the camera she wailed, "Why isn't anyone helping? Where is the help? Are you going to let us die here?" The scene of our fellow Americans seemed almost too terrible to be true.

Today, there is an important question that we all must be asking ourselves. Do you know what it means to miss New Orleans? I am not a native of New Orleans, nor have I moved to the Crescent City, or even visited its beautiful buildings along the banks of the Mississippi for an extended period of time. I did, however, recently mosey on down to the birthplace of Jazz about a month ago, and it is through a series of essays regarding my observations and experiences that I hope to share with you my newfound interest, love, and appreciation for this vibrant city.

> *"Have you ever been to New Orleans? If not you'd better go.*
> *It's a nation of a queer place; day and night a show!*
> *Frenchmen, Spaniards, West Indians, Creoles, Mustees,*
> *Yankees, Kentuckians, Tennesseans, lawyers and trustees ..."*

Spirit

The first time I took New Orleans seriously was on Easter Sunday at the black Baptist Church. In contrast to all the images of Mardi Gras and big partying in a city that knows how to live, and live good, the drive to the church was painfully eye-opening. It was the first time that we could look out of the bus window into daylight, and the amount of destruction was overwhelming. Questions sprouted in my mind like spring flowers: Where had all these people gone? How come we don't hear about New Orleans anymore? Where was all the help, the cranes, the construction crews?

Home after home was destroyed. Business after business was completely gone. I couldn't stop thinking about how screwed the people of New Orleans were, especially the poor, black, New Orleans residents of the Lower 9th Ward and St. Bernard's Parish. By the time we got to Church, I had a list of questions for God that was longer than the bus.

But as the Church service started, I slowly began to understand why the people of New Orleans had not given up the fight. Packed like sardines in hard wood pews, the whole neighborhood spilled into the Church, most wearing the finest suits and Easter dresses that I had ever seen. Then, without notice, they began to hold hands in prayer and sing. I looked for a hymnal, but there was none. Instead I found the people of this wrecked community smiling! Their voices rebounded off of my chest, so powerful that they could have blown the roof off. I was not one person in an ocean of people, I was a brick in a wall of soul, and we were a strong wall.

Towards the beginning of the service a middle-aged black woman made her way to the front of the room, and took hold of the mike. Over the groove of the house band, and shouts from spirited community members, she asked us to bow our heads in prayer. It was her words that would set the tone for the entire trip. Her words erased any questions that I might have had, and doubts that I may have contained.

"Dear God, you are a gracious and forgiving God. Oh God, I said, you are a gracious and forgiving God."

I raised my head and watched as she continued.

"We have been through a lot in this community."

"Amen," shouted the old women in the front rows.

"We've had a hurricane destroy our homes, divide our families, and take our loved ones!"

"Yes we have!!!" An elderly man to my left rocked back and forth.

"We have debts to pay off, our schools are in terrible shape, and our neighborhood isn't safe ... and yet ... we're still here! We're still here, aren't we?"

I couldn't believe my ears. Was I really about to hear these people thank—

"Oh God, thank you for your blessings! It is only for the Grace of God that we are here, and isn't that a beautiful thing!!! Look at all that we have to be thankful for!! Look outside. Isn't it a beautiful day to be alive?"

I struggled to hold back the tears. We were surrounded by people who were in some of the most desperate situations in the whole country. They were short on cash, out of homes, stuck in gang violence, and tied down with debt, and yet they had more hope than any group of people I had ever encountered. Not only did they have hope, but they gave thanks for the little that they did have, and it was these two startling facts that brought tears to my eyes.

> "... Negroes in purple and fine linen, and slaves in rags and chains.
> Ships, arks, steamboats, robbers, pirates, alligators,
> Assassins, gamblers, drunkards, and cotton speculators;
> Sailors, soldiers, pretty girls, and ugly fortune-tellers;
> Pimps, imps, shrimps, and all sorts of dirty fellows ..."

Jazz

"Basin Street is the place to be, where all the honey's meet...." I attempted to sing along with my very first Louis Armstrong recording in my Chicago living room, imitating his scratchy, deep voice.

"Mickey?" my mom turned her head around the room to see me parading with my fake plastic toy-trumpet, squirming like a worm, and singing along. "Do you have to use the potty?"

And then, perfectly in time with Louis, I let out a big belly laugh, disproportionately large when compared to my body.

It was through the music of Louis Armstrong, an iconic symbol of New Orleans, that I learned what it meant to experience joy, and especially joy through music.

"Jazz music belongs to all Americans," historian Ken Burns writes, "and it has come to be seen by the rest of the world as the symbol of all that is best about us." A music rooted in African rhythms and folk harmonies, and wrapped in a warm blanket of soul, Jazz music is the music of our people, and of course, the people of New Orleans. As Ken Burns writes in *Jazz*, "It (Jazz) grew up in a thousand places but it could only have been born in New Orleans."

It's true. There is something special in that New Orleans second-line beat. You must start with the pulse of the group, the jump and jive feeling that is created by the clunkity-plunk of the bass, the rat-a-tat-tat of the drums, and the short, percussive strokes of the banjo. The rhythm section sets the tone and mood for life in New Orleans, a happy and motion-filled dance that we as Americans have treasured for decades. As a jazz musician myself, I love playing with a good rhythm section, because it creates a groove that as a horn player, I can just wrap myself up in and enjoy the feeling.

Then you add the main melody, usually carried by the trumpet, supported by the fluid improvisation of the clarinet and trombone. The trumpet is the leader of the band, just as Louis Armstrong and his trumpet were the leaders in Jazz. But these different instruments only make their most beautiful sounds while living in harmony, just as the Creoles, whites, blacks, aristocrats, and alligators do in Southern Louisiana.

In the Big Easy, there is jazz music everywhere. In restaurants, clubs, bars, barbecue joints, neighborhoods, corner stores, everywhere. It is the music of this city that traveled up the Mississippi, until it became America's music. It is my favorite music. It is a music that doesn't set the rhythm for a moment, but a tempo for life. And what startled me the most, despite Katrina, despite all the damage that remains, and despite all the skepticism towards New Orleans, there is one thing that remains constant. The beat goes on.

"…A progency of all colors—an infernal motley crew;
Yellow fever in February—muddy streets all the year;
Many things to hope for, and a devilish sight to fear?
Gold and silver bullion—United States bank notes,
Horse-racers, cock fighters, and beggars without coats …"

Swamp Boat

The long strands of Spanish moss lay all around me, wandering in the afternoon breeze. Their braided hair swayed from side to side, dangling from the tops of the trees, tickling my head. All that could be heard were the soft whispers of the Spanish moss, gossiping in the wind.

I looked over the side of our swamp boat into the stagnant clear pool. Sprinkled with what seemed to be endless amounts of green parmesan cheese. I sat not in a reflecting pool, but a pool of reflection.

Time seemed to slow to a halt. There was a great egret standing erect across the way, safely hidden in the shade of a banana tree. A snake slithered through a branch, sunning itself in the warm Southern Louisiana sun.

It was so quiet; deathly quiet. Imagine a world of natural beauty that lingers in time. A world that is half-real and half imaginative, a world that can be found with your eyelids half open and half closed. Imagine sitting for hours, days, years, solving the world's problems in such a serene setting, with only a community of alligators and shrimp to weigh in their opinion.

"…Snapping-turtles, sugar, sugar-houses, water-snakes,
Molasses, flour, whiskey, tobacco, corn and Johnny-cakes,

Beef, cattle, hogs, pork, turkeys, Kentucky rifles,
Lumber, boards, apples, cotton, and many other trifles ..."

History

New Orleans was established in 1718, in a mosquito-infested swamp. It has been ruled by France, Spain, and the United States, and until recently, has been the South's busiest seaport. Because of its location near the Gulf of Mexico, and its location near the mouth of the mighty Mississippi, It is understandable that New Orleans is a city of diverse backgrounds. Even in 1860, over forty percent of the people of New Orleans were foreign born. It is also a city of contrasts. Before the emancipation proclamation, New Orleans was the home of the largest number of slave auctions. But of course, it was the home of the largest number of concentrated free colored people in the country. Today, New Orleans consistently ranks among the country's top ten cities in poverty and crime, and yet neighborhoods such as the Uptown area have some of the highest concentrations of this country's wealthiest people. The miracle is that all these people, from different racial, financial, and social backgrounds, coexist with a shared vibrant spirit. The color of your skin or size of your pocketbook do not really matter in New Orleans. What I observed, is that what truly matters is the size of your heart. (And stomach.)

Food

"Now, grab that little sucker, and rip it's tail off. O000hhh, that look mighty fine, ain't it ... ?"

Mr. Pickles stood there, his two hundred pound belly jiggling in pure joy, as he heartily taught me how to eat boiled crawfish. He was a king in his own court.

"Now, get at dat meat in the tail, gobble it up." From the head of the table, he wolfed down three crawfish tails as I struggled to find the correct angle to attack my first one.

Mr. Pickles was the bus driver for our trip to New Orleans. He was a man with an immense sense of pride. He kept his bus clean, and each day he wore a clean-pressed shirt, the starch white uniform a stark contrast to his dark black skin, and shiny bald head. He was serious as he drove around the neighborhoods, solemnly contemplating the level of devastation that still remained two years after Katrina. But, Mr. Pickles was a hearty man, and a man who knew how to live right.

"Now pinch that sucker's little beady eyes, and SUCK THE HEAD!!!"

I was hesitant to suck the crawfish's head, its slimy little body seemingly staring at me straight in the eye as if to say, "I know I may not look like food, but this is New Orleans, man, eat me." I looked up to see Mr. Pickles smiling right back at me, with that smile that could melt an icicle. "Har, har, har," his big belly laugh shook the tent at the St. Bernard Parish's annual crawfish festival. "Come on, buddy, just suck that juice! Ain't it spicy. Welcome to New Orleans. If you wanna stick around here, you've got to learn to eat right!"

I had quickly realized that food in New Orleans is like food nowhere else. I had just eaten alligator on a stick, tasted my friend's shark sandwich, and now was about to suck a crawfish. The food was spicy, thick, and . . . sooooo gooooood. "Living in New Orleans is like drinking blubber through a straw," literary genius Andrei Codrescu writes. "Even the air is caloric."

But it's not just about the good food. It's about the people too. In his book of essays, *New Orleans Mon Amour*, Andrei Codrescu describes the scene at his house just a day before a big hurricane was about to hit New Orleans in 1985. "At my house, Jimmy Nolan cooked four-star meals, because as he said, 'I will not have the apocalypse without style!'"

I pinched the head of the "bawld" (boiled) crawfish, stuck its butt in my mouth, and sucked. The spicy juice and blood slowly invaded my oral cavity. I could hear my taste buds screaming in excitement as the crawfish juice dripped past my tongue and down the back of my throat. There was something liberating about eating something I would usually call the exterminator to get rid of . . . and loving it.

"Mr. Pickles," I shouted out to my new friend, "toss me another one of those crawfish!" And the big man let out another hearty chuckle.

Boom Boom Room

"Thank you so much everybody for coming out tonight, I have to tell you, we have had an incredible time in New Orleans this week, and being able to play here tonight in Ray's Boom Boom Room is an incredible honor. . . ."

I stood in front of the Big Band at Ray's Boom Boom Room, a jazz club/BBQ joint/meeting place/hole in the wall/living room/community center/watering hole on Frenchman's Street. As I stood in front of the band to introduce one of the tunes in the middle of our jazz band's set, I looked out into the audience and made note of what I saw: tourists, natives, blacks, whites, overweight, not so over-weight, young, old, drunk, really drunk, not drunk yet. There was Mr. Pickles over at the bar, laughing it up with the bartender. It was as if they had known each other for 20 years, and knowing New Orleans, they probably had known each other for that long.

The room was a long narrow room that opened up to the bustling French Quarter. From my vantage point in front of the band I could see everyone in the room, hear everyone, and smell everything. Oooohhh, did that barbecue smell good.

The Parade

The beads fell from the sky, like wildly colored drops of rain. The bright sun reflected off each bead, magnifying the vibrant sun's rays. Green beads, blue beads, magenta beads, pink beads, large beads, small beads . . . the sky was an ocean of beads.

"Toss me some beads, mistah!" A little girl standing beside me on Decatur Street jumped up and down, shouting to the old white man expelling beads from atop his float. It was the Easter Sunday parade, a grand excuse for a party in this Catholic city, and the street was filled with floats, brass bands, fancy cars, and people in elegant costumes. It was my first afternoon in New Orleans, and my quartet of friends had clumsily stumbled upon this grandeurs spectacle. . . .

"Ouch," a bead necklace dropped from the sky, knocking me across the head. I picked them up, and placed them around my neck, and turned down the street to watch the marching Dixieland band.

"Can you hear that trumpet?" my friend Colin shouted. "Damn, do they sound good!" The trumpet player led the band in a stroll down the street, then the clarinet, the bass drummer, the tuba, all dancing as they played. A woman cackled with glee besides me, as she too broke out in dance.

I was surrounded by pure joy.

My friends and I ran along the parade, catching beads and candy, and shouting along with the adoring crowd. It was as if the parade was a series of waves and we were bobbing among them, along the muddy banks of the Mississippi.

Beads continued to fall from the sky. But this time, I noticed that it was not the bright sun's rays that were reflecting off the beads. Instead, the smiles of me, and of the people on Decatur Street, wider than the Mississippi itself, were reflecting in the falling beads. It was those smiles that reflected light warm enough to fry a shrimp or broil a crawfish.

—Mickey, grade 12

Mickey was a star trumpet player in high school and already admired New Orleans horn players like Wynton Marsalis, but when his jazz band played a benefit show for Hurricane Katrina victims, his newfound love for the region encompassed much more than music. By reading books, watching movies, and reporting on conversations he had, he came to appreciate the buoyancy of the people and the startling variety of food and culture in the city as well. This essay doesn't come to a neat conclusion and there is no obvious moral to draw here. Instead, the exploration—of the city and of himself—allows the author to reflect on his experiences and his natural affinities, even providing him with some life direction he might achieve through his music. Mickey offers subheadings to separate the various sections of his essay and effectively uses excerpts of a poem to highlight his impressions of New Orleans as well.

The Sky's the Limit

The time on my phone read 12:15 am. Praying that my parents wouldn't wake up and realize that we were gone, Laura, Eliza and I continued trekking down the beach. The wind whipped our hair in our faces and the ocean water crashed dangerously only feet away from us. Looking out on the water, I could see the lights of Fort Myers ahead as we made our way down the shoreline of Sanibel Island. Behind us, the stars shone brightly in a cloudless night.

Pausing briefly, we turned around and watched as the vast dark sky seemed to grow closer. The stars filled the night sky, appearing to almost touch the surface of the water, eliminating the need for us to look up. The stars were popping out of the sky just like a giant Lite Brite put together by a young child who only used the white pieces. Never before had I seen so many stars in the same place. The feeling was overwhelming, but in a good way. Laura's laughter broke my trance. I turned my back on the stars and jogged to catch up with my friends as we continued to make our way along the beach. The island was complete darkness save for a few lights shining from homes along the shore. The stars and the moon were the only things lighting our path.

Wake me up, shake me up.
Race me to the stars.
Too much to know, so far to go.
The galaxy is ours.
—The Galaxy is Ours by Proto Zoa

Sanibel Island has one of the strictest outdoor lighting ordinances in the world. These restrictions have restored night to this small island off the south-west coast of Florida. There are no streetlights anywhere on the island, making the island almost entirely dark at night. The only lights that shine in the evening are from houses. And despite tremendous development pressure, Sanibel still has protected wildlife preserves that cover forty percent of the island. Sea turtles are a main focus of these preserves and are also most affected by light pollution. Sea turtle hatchlings instinctively head towards light, and before electric lighting, bioluminescence and the reflection of the moon on the water made the ocean brighter than the land (The New Rules Project). But when there is light pollution, the hatchlings often head for land because it's brighter than the ocean. This is obviously very dangerous. The strict limits on the street lighting on Sanibel have been put in place to remedy the imbalance between the unnatural brightness of the shoreline and the natural bioluminescence of the sea.

Not only does light pollution affect wildlife like sea turtle hatchlings, it also interferes with the work of astronomers, both professional and amateur. Amateur astronomy, once a backyard activity, is becoming an expensive pursuit, requiring a great deal of travel. Instead of spending time enjoying the night skies, amateur astronomers are spending their hours traveling to remote places like Nebraska and Australia where the skies are still dark.

The night sky has also become lost to millions of people. Under ideal conditions, 2,500 stars should be visible. This sight is now granted to less than ten percent of all Americans (The Amicus Journal). Along with that startling statistic is another: an estimated two-thirds of Americans cannot see the Milky Way from their homes. Researchers with Italy's nonprofit Light Pollution Science and Technology Institute estimate that by 2025 "no dark locations will be left in the continental US from where to watch stars" (The Providence Journal).

The International Dark-Sky Association, founded in 1988, is working to find and publicize solutions to the problem of light pollution. They estimate that the light shining above the horizontal plane makes up approximately one-third of the total nighttime illumination while also costing Americans $1 billion annually. Fixtures like a 50-watt metal halide lamp with a reflective shield are much better than most streetlights in use today. They cut down on glare, making night driving safer as well as improving vision for pedestrians. The Illuminating Engineering Society of North America is recommending products like these and is making them more accessible. San Diego has saved $3 million annually by creating light-pollution laws and Connecticut will save $10 million annually assuming the law they are working on now passes.

> Paint the sky with stars,
> Only night will ever know.
> Why the heavens never show,
> All the dreams there are to know.
> —Paint the Sky with Stars by Enya

It was raining. My best friend, Claire, and I were standing outside the movie theater entrance to Northbrook Court after seeing *Tarzan*. Protected from the rain, we stood under the overhang waiting for our ride. The tires of a 1995 blue-gray Toyota Sienna splashed to a stop beside the curb. We saw Mr. Rogerson's smiling face through the window and made a mad dash for the van.

As was usual in GUG 808, Claire and I headed to the third row of seats and strapped ourselves in. Then she pulled the lever on her side of the bench seat that lowered the back so it was parallel to the ground and we were staring up at the sky. The rain eased up as we pulled out of the parking lot, revealing a clear sky above us. And so our hunt for constellations began. Having studied the constellations in the Star Lab this past year as second graders, we considered ourselves experts. We found Orion's Belt, the Big Dipper, and Pleiades, also known as the Seven Sisters. Then we moved on and created constellations of our own: a rabbit, a boot, a spoon and a dog, possibly Snoopy. Even through the back window, the stars shone brightly. Completely reclined, we were transfixed by the dark beauty of the sky. Claire decided right there and then she wanted to be an astrophysicist. I had no idea what that was, but it sounded really cool. I then declared I wanted to be one too. I'd figure out what it was later.

> *Look up in the sky.*
> *It's a bird it's a plane*
> *Nah baby girl,*
> *That's a shootin' star with your name*
> —*Shooting Star by David Rush ft. LMFAO, Pitbull, and Kevin Rudolf*

Professor David Meyer is the Director of Astrophysical Studies at Northwestern University, aka an astrophysicist. "Whenever I'm sitting on a plane next to someone and I tell them I'm an astrophysicist, they always want to know more. No one wants to know more if you tell them you're an investment banker," he told me. He continued to explain how astronomy was a really unique subject. "Not many fields of study have both active professional and amateur communities. You aren't likely to find someone doing genetic testing for fun in their basement. And I'm glad that's the case," he finished with a laugh. Curious about the growing community of amateur astronomers, I asked him how he became interested in the subject. He told me that he grew up and was attending grade school in the 1960s which was when the Apollo Program was taking place. Watching the various take-offs and landings in school intrigued him. "I loved watching the rockets blast off. I decided then that I wanted outer space to be a part of my future."

As a member of the Astronomy and Astrophysics department at Northwestern, Professor Meyer gets access to the incredible Dearborn Observatory. I asked if light pollution was an issue for them since Evanston is right near Chicago, a city full of bright lights at night. "At Northwestern, light pollution isn't really an issue. We use the Dearborn Observatory for teaching, not research. We can see the moon and planets like Saturn just fine. We run into trouble when we want to look at galaxies and very faint stars." Unfortunately, galaxies and faint stars are an important part of research for professional astronomers. "To get a clear night sky, you'd have to go out to where the cows are, like Woodstock. Or else Mauna Kea, Hawaii or to McDonald Observatory in Texas, which is basically in the middle of nowhere. Researchers are running out of options, creating major problems for our future."

Mystical lights,
Magical nights,
A chance to place new trails,
Open your eyes travel the skies.
Your spirit major prevails.
—The Galaxy is Ours by Proto Zoa

Fabulous influences may well lead to one or two lucky breaks today and even if *there are any minor obstacles to overcome, the planets are nicely configured to give you that extra little push. It's definitely a day where you should take the longer term view and believe that anything is possible!* The planets are nicely configured. Really? How would horoscope.com know what the planets were doing? I have friends who check their horoscope daily, and I just don't get it. There doesn't seem to be anything factual involved with these "predictions." While looking up my horoscope to include in this paper, I looked at multiple websites, all of whom had different opinions about how my day was going to be. So I decided to figure out the secret behind them.

The study of the stars was started by the ancient Greeks, who used the skies as an effective way to know when to plant and harvest their crops. It then evolved into the belief that a person's life was pre-determined by the positioning of the sun and moon and constellations present at the time of a person's birth (dailyhoroscope.org). Throughout the years, scientists like Plato, Galileo, and Copernicus studied the skies and drew their own scientific conclusions, none of which had anything to do with the stars or planets predicting the future of a person's life.

During the Middle Ages, the practice of astrology went underground as the Christian church became the leading voice of the new world. In the 1600s, an astrologer named William Lilly started to call astrology "Christian Astrology" to make it more acceptable. Another astrologer, Alan Leo, came in the late 1800s with a large fan base. He was followed by Paul Clancy who published his own magazine in 1923 called "American Astrology," which was instrumental in popularizing astrology and horoscopes as we know them today (dailyhoroscope.org).

When the moon is in the Seventh House,
And Jupiter aligns with Mars.
Then peace will guide the planets,
And love will steer the stars.
This is the dawning of the Age of Aquarius.
—Aquarius by The 5th Dimension

Stars, according to Pumba, the warthog from *The Lion King*, are "balls of gas burning billions of miles away." He is correct, especially in comparison to his buddy Timon, a meerkat, who thinks that the "sparkly dots" in the sky are fireflies: "Fireflies that got stuck up on that big bluish-black thing." Here's a more technical description: "A star is a large celestial body composed of gravitationally contained hot gases emitting electromagnetic radiation, especially light, as a result of nuclear reactions inside the star" (cartage.org). For those of us who aren't astrophysicists like Professor Meyer, Pumba's definition will do. There are 8,000 stars visible to the naked eye, 4,000 in the northern hemisphere and 4,000 in the southern hemisphere. Half are visible at night and the other half would be visible during the day, but are obscured by the brightness of the sun. With the exception of the sun, the stars appear to be fixed, while in fact the stars are in rapid motion, but their distances from Earth are so great that their relative changes in position become apparent only over hundreds of years.

> *Cause you are the brightest star,*
> *I'm in love with who you are.*
> *And you are the brightest star,*
> *I'm lost without your love.*
> —White Lines and Red Lights by Between the Trees

There was a giant snow globe in the library. *Wait, it's not a snow globe. And I can't see inside of it because the outside is covered with tinfoil. And there's a tunnel. That's cool.* I was in second grade and we were just about to start our unit about constellations. And as a tool to help us learn, they had set up a "Star Lab" in the middle of the library. The tunnel entrance was kept closed by a vacuum effect and a burst of cool air greeted us as we crawled in. Emerging from the tunnel on the other end, we found ourselves inside a giant dome with a projector in the middle, shining the images of stars on the ceiling and walls around us. It was like being in an igloo, but better, because it wasn't cold. We sat in a circle around the edge of the dome, leaning gently against the soft walls, and stared up at the stars being projected. Ms. Heilizer, our teacher, used a red laser pointer to show us different stars.

Things I Saw in the Star Lab

The North Star	The Pointer Stars	The Big Dipper
Orion and His Belt	Cassiopeia	Scorpio
Andromeda	The Gemini Twins	The Scales of Justice

During our week and a half in the Star Lab, we studied constellations, wrote new stories about constellations, and learned about our Zodiac signs. We also learned how the Native Americans used the stars in their culture. At the conclusion of our study, we had a "Star Lab Night" where our parents came to hear us read our stories about the constellations. And according to the packet I have included, I took away three things from the study: 1) Orion has a blue star and red star, 2) The Pointer Stars point to the North Star, and 3) I learned a lot of new constellations. Really deep, I know.

Next year I will be heading to college as an engineering student. My major of choice is biomedical engineering, but maybe I'll end up studying astrophysics. It's unlikely, but as we all know, our futures are written in the stars.

—Blair, grade 12

Before Blair even got started, our class had fun riffing on possible sections for a paper on stars: celebrities, astrology, constellations, fate, navigation and direction, starlight, light years and time. Going in any of these directions might have provided an equally interesting essay. Blair's essay showcases a lifelong fascination with star gazing that she reveals through personal stories from elementary school to the present. Her interview with a local astronomer was "incredible," she told me. Not only did she learn a great deal, but she also got to visit a huge telescope only a few miles from her home that she never knew existed.

Disthintegration

The worst decision I ever made was an attempt at self-improvement.

I wake up early to the smell of pumpkin bread from last night's Thanksgiving feast. Quietly I tiptoe into the bathroom. The stark white scale innocently stares at me from its corner. I step on. With a dull boing, the needle swings up to 117. An all-time high. "That's it," I tell myself. "You've got to do something about this."

I scamper back over the cold bathroom tile to my room. Shuffling through my desk I unearth a little while notebook dotted with pink hearts. It was a party favor from my 6th birthday (though I am a junior in high school). The pages are rainbow-colored pastels: pink, blue green, and purple. I tear out a childish doodle of a stick figure with a bouquet. "I'll use this to record the calories in everything I eat. I'll make sure to get those numbers down."

And down it went from there.

About three percent of Americans are estimated to have eating disorders. One percent of adolescents suffer from anorexia nervosa, but these numbers vary drastically across gender, race, and social class. Given that anorexia was hardly recognized as an illness until two decades ago, research is relatively new and incomplete. Yet eating disorders are an increasing problem, a "silent epidemic" (Anorexia Nervosa and Related Eating Disorders).

As of yet, no one has identified one single cause of eating disorders. Experts agree, however, that a mix of biological, environmental, and psychological factors contribute to the disease. I believe the primary causes rest in the patient. Society's pressures will always be present; whether or not an individual succumbs to these expectations depends on her chemical makeup and self-concept.

Certain personality traits, for example, almost always appear with anorexia: perfectionism, low self-esteem, and reductionist black and white thinking (good versus bad, fat versus thin). There is no healthy ambiguous gray area. Eager to please and fearful of conflict, anorexics often hide their feelings. This has a two-fold effect: the anorexic hopes to please others by losing weight and losing weight often becomes an outlet for suppressed emotion. Hence the name "good girl's disease" (ANRED).

In contrast to most mental illnesses, anorexics typically come from tight-knit, perhaps overprotective families. Because of family support and pressure, anorexics are often high achievers but seek control and independence. Shedding pounds is a way to veto whatever physique nature has in mind. It's also a way to dodge impending womanhood—no hips, no bust, no period, no hormones. Some psychologists interpret anorexia as an attempt to forever remain a child (Bellwood).

I think my biggest issue was confidence. The previous spring my best friend lost her visa and abruptly moved away. I didn't have a social network besides her. Socially I was floundering and mentally I was overwhelmed by school. Although I was managing, the junior year workload was taking its toll. Further I had quit ballet that year and was displeased with recent weight gain. Needless to say I wasn't feeling too good about myself that fateful day when I decided that something about me needed to go.

"No, I don't want to go!"

"What do you mean? You picked this concert out of the program. You said these were your favorite cello pieces—and it's not like you have any homework. You're on spring break," my mother shouted, holding two off-white tickets in her hand.

I turn my swivel chair so that my back faces her. The chair groans in disapproval. "I just want to stay here."

"And do what?"

"Read."

"You've been reading all day. C'mon."

True, I remind myself. I have been reading all day. After months of calorie counting, my appetite has vanished. Today I had an apple for breakfast and peppermint tea for lunch. Now I can read all day without getting hungry.

"If you insist, Mom." I lift myself out of the chair and set down *Walden* on top of *Tuesdays with Morrie* and *Man's Search for Meaning*. I'm having an existential crisis: what causes happiness? Why do people have a will to live? Why are people so interested in socializing?

The onset of anorexia is a tricky point to determine, but researchers have linked it with low levels of thiamin and zinc. Julie Ross, a local specialist in eating disorders, states that chronic dieting depletes thiamin levels into "the danger zone," where anorexia sets in with a loss of appetite. (Personal interview with Ross). Preceding zinc and thiamin depletion are low levels of amino acids. As L-tryptophan, an amino acid, is found in few foods, dieting frequently causes tryptophan deficiency which in turn lowers seratonin levels. Seratonin regulates mood, so depletion can cause depression, irritability, anxiety, and low self-esteem. Sadly, in an attempt to boost her self-esteem, an anorexic will intensify her diet and therefore worsen her mood. Ross also hypothesizes that low seratonin levels lead to the obsessive-compulsive behavior of anorexics: calorie counting, excessive exercising, self-criticizing, obsessing over food preparation, and controlling eating schedules.

I wince at the crushing squeeze of my left arm, and the nurse frowns as she takes my pulse. Before working in a hospital laboratory, I had to get checked out. Her white coat brushes against my hand as she leans over for a double take of the reading. "Um . . . 80 over 60?" An abnormally low blood pressure. She loosens the Velcro strap on my arm, and I breathe in a gulp of sterile, alcohol-scented air. She hesitates, shifting in her leather swivel chair and then continues down her checkup list. "What's your weight?"

"95 pounds." The nurses's eyes flicker. She knows.

I am unaware that I have passed the threshold for diagnosable anorexia: I am more than 15% below my original healthy body weight, and I am obsessed with keeping it off. I have lost my period, but I am convinced I need to lose a few more pounds.

In 10 minutes I will be home, devouring my 800 daily calories. I can picture the yellow box of Oat Flakes cereal in the corner of the bottom shelf. Yes, I'll have Oat Flakes soaked in boiling water.

It is characteristic of starvation to demand nothing but warm, soggy food (Garner). Typically anorexics are cold due to their lack of insulating fat. They suffer from low blood pressure and slowed metabolism. With weakened immune systems, they are frequently ill. They lose interest in socializing and have dramatic mood swings (Simon).

Despite the overt social, emotional, and physical pressure, anorexics often escape detection. An anorexic typically is secretive and in denial about her problem. Being a hard-working student, few will suspect she has serious issues. I hid my figure in oversize sweaters and baggy jeans so that no one saw the physical toll of my disease. My family only saw me when I was binging at home—who would guess that I was "purging" by fasting the rest of the day? My friends never saw me because I skipped lunch every day. "It's the work," I explained. "Those damn college applications."

Prompt: Write a note to your future college roommate relating a personal experience that reveals something about you.

Dear roommate-to-be,

Roommates end up sharing a lot, but there's one thing we probably won't share: our taste in food. I'm vegan, but don't worry! I'm a decent cook, so no one has ever minded my vegan ways ... no one aside from my older brother, that is. A few months ago, he returned from college while I was preparing dinner. Hearing keys jangle at the door, I turned off the stove and ran to welcome him. He greeted me with a horrified expression. He sniffed the air and groaned. "What on earth have you been doing?"

"I made dinner ... why?"

"What is that, cat food?"

"No, it's a garlic veggie burger." Cautiously he sampled a bite. He pronounced it edible and finished his meal.

So, roommate, I promise there's no need to fear my tofu or meat substitutes. If you're doubtful, I understand, but I am always happy to share.

I originally became a vegan because I thought it would help me slim down. It resulted in nutritional disaster as I eliminated fat and several essential minerals from my diet. The human brain is over 60% fat, so in periods of starvation, the body depletes fat stores and later will literally cannibalize the brain. A wide variety of personality changes and mental disorders ensue.

Tears splash down on my empty dinner plate. "I'm such a pig. I ate too much. I have no friends. I hate school. I don't want to go to college." We've been having this conversation for 10 minutes now. It's Sunday night. Sunday night is my breakdown night.

Mom sets down her fork, metal clanking against china. "What else would you do?"

"I don't know. The world would be a better place without me."

For one of the few times in my life, I see my mother's eyes turn red and watery. "Why would you say something like that? You have so much going for you!"

Her voice cracks.

"I ate too much!" I bawl. I had a plate of spaghetti and green beans.

My mom gives an exasperated sigh. "We've been through this already. You didn't eat too much. What else is going on with you this year?"

The answer comes by mail. The Monday after Thanksgiving, *Newsweek* features a cover story on anorexia. A somber looking girl stares from the front page. "Fighting Anorexia," the headline reads in bright yellow letters. My parents recognize my symptoms. So, fight we do.

My growling stomach jolts awake in math class. The overhead projector seems to blur, a smeared numerical Picasso. I try to focus, but something inside my chest shudders and skips a beat.

Anorexia depletes levels of ions in the blood, ions that are necessary for the heart to function. An electrolyte imbalance can cause cardiac arrhythmia, an irregular heartbeat. Anorexia is the most fatal mental illness because it breaks hearts. Most anorexics die not of starvation, but of heart attacks and suicide (Simon).

My brother and I recently talked about eating disorders. He does research in an abnormal psychology lab and has studied mental illness. "An eating disorder is the result of a choice, a persistent urge to lose weight. So, don't people essentially choose to have these problems?"

He replied with a definition. A disorder is something that cannot be controlled, and an anorexic can't control her distorted body image. "She just sees things that aren't there." When an anorexic looks in the mirror, she perceives someone fatter, uglier, and stupider than the rest of the world sees. It might be thought of as "perfectionism off its rocker." My brother also cited something called cognitive dissonance theory, which states that we always try to align our thoughts and actions. So, once a dieter starts slimming down, she convinces herself that losing weight is worth it. The vicious cycle continues from there.

And why does anorexia not only wreak havoc on the body, but also on relationships? "Depression frequently accompanies eating disorders and slows down the brain, causing low rates of [mental] image production and hyper-attentiveness to those images." Essentially, the brain dawdles as it fixates on self-defeating ideas. The decreased brain metabolism "kills" spontaneity and humor, the "stuff of conversation and socializing" (Simon).

If I could take back two Thanksgivings, I would chuck that white notebook in the trash without hesitation. But eating disorders opened my eyes to the value of relationships, to the importance of confidence. To the role of emotion in self-preservation, to the connection between misery and illness, happiness and health.

Anorexia nervosa has the highest mortality rate of any mental illness. Roughly half of people with eating disorders never recover, either fluctuating between recovery and relapse, chronically disintegrating or dying. The other half does, miraculously, return to life (Simon).
I feel blessed to consider myself one of them.
—Annie, grade 12

Annie's essay is moving because of the way she combines her personal story alongside her research on her disease. Writing about her recent struggles might easily have caused her even more profound pain than the suffering she details here. A scientific mind by nature, she delves into complicated biochemistry matters to try to understand the basis of her disorder. Her personal stories and her interview point her to examine psychosocial factors as well. Annie was grateful for the opportunity to explore her mysterious recent past, a scary time that remained hidden to almost all of her classmates and teachers. Using her family members as a sounding board reinforced the power of personal relationships in maintaining health.

What all of these models have in common is a synthesis of the skills we've worked on in earlier assignments. The personal writing relies on skills detailed in early chapters, the analysis of texts was important in writing op-ed essays and writing about inexact and irresponsible language (Chapters 6 and 7), and students were familiar with interviewing from their oral history writing (Chapter 9). Each essay in this chapter braids personal writing with research, and, since all of this work is on topics that represent significant issues or episodes in students' lives, the essays hold a powerful intrinsic interest. Because these essays explore complicated subject matter with no easy answers, the project also encourages students to think about the nature of knowledge and the kind of arguments they have written throughout their school lives. This will be the subject of the final chapter as students examine what they have learned, how they know they have learned it, and what these experiences suggest about the directions their lives will move in the future.

What Did You Learn in School Today? Reflections on Education

11

What did you learn in school today, dear little boy of mine?
What did you learn in school today, dear little boy of mine?
I learned that Washington never told a lie.
I learned that soldiers never die.
I learned that everybody's free—
That's what the teacher said to me.
That's what I learned in school.

—TOM PAXTON, "What Did You Learn in School Today?"

Paxton's protest lyrics are both ironic and profound. What *do* our students actually learn in school? This is not a question that only teachers might obsess over. It's also a question that students are genuinely fascinated by.

As Tim O'Brien mentions in *The Things They Carried*, "We get our material from the intersection of the past and the present" (34). Who we are is, to some extent, what we know and what we've experienced. But some knowledge is transitory. One year, in an exercise as masochistic as it was cruel, I visited teachers all over the school and asked them if there was a critical concept or idea they had spent a good deal of time on that they were pretty sure none of their students would remember. Luckily, no one was offended. Rather, my colleagues became kind of giddy at the task. Ask students about the Agrawator from *A Tale of Two Cities,* an English teacher said; or Owl Eyes in *The Great Gatsby* said another. And it's not just English class. A chemistry teacher suggested I ask, "What is stoichiometry?" A math teacher told me to ask, "What is Hero's formula in geometry?" or "How can you determine the surface area of a sphere?" A biology teacher offered these questions: "How is protein selected for, and what are the consequences of this selection for the production of DNA?" or "How does a fetal pig's digestive tract differ from yours?" A social studies teacher asked,

"What is the Sixth Amendment to the Constitution?" A Spanish teacher told me to have my class name two words in Spanish that end in *o* but which carry a feminine article. You get the idea. These are all topics that students had spent at least a couple of days (in some cases a couple of weeks) on within the last two or three years.

At about this point in my class, I reassure students that memory loss doesn't get any prettier with age! But does this mean that students haven't learned anything, or that the human mind is a sieve? Of course not.

So what *have* students learned? Perhaps these topics are just quiddities (*Hamlet* 5.1.102, remember?). As a lifer in education—the students all graduate, but I'll go back to school again next year—I continually struggle with the value of education. And I want my students to think critically about knowledge and about their education too, so I say, "You've learned millions of pieces of information, hundreds of processes, explored myriad issues, wrestled with many ethical and philosophical dilemmas, but what did you really learn?"

The Assignment

Here's the assignment. As you'll see, it invites students to create knowledge through narrative inquiry, a process at the heart of this book.

> As a final writing assignment, write an essay (let's say 3–5 pages) in which you look back on your four years of high school—not just English—and reflect on what you've learned, how you've changed, how you've grown. You can decide on the format—essay, dialogue, poem sequence, whatever. Interview teachers, friends, classmates if you'd like. Just make sure you think carefully about what you know, what you've learned, how you've learned it, how you know you know it, and how you've become the person you continue to become.
>
> In writing the essay, here are some questions you might consider: What is your purpose as a student in school? What did your school see as its purpose for your education? What were your parents' expectations for what you'd learn? When, if ever, did these purposes/emphases diverge? If you or the school fell short, how might you or the school have done things differently? What are you most proud of having done/learned? What kind of knowledge was prized in class? What is the knowledge most worth knowing? Did you learn more in school, or in some extracurricular activity, or even talking among friends outside of class?

This is your chance to tell the story of your high school life, and in so doing you might consider how other people—school administrators, your parents, colleges, teachers—would tell your story.

Include a minimum of four artifacts from the past four years and embed these artifacts in your final essay. You'll also bring these artifacts (or representations of these artifacts) in to class for a series of presentations that will end our class. Together we'll share all we have learned in a sort of Knowledge Museum on the last day of class.

I can't wait to find out what you learn in writing this final paper. Have fun!

This assignment calls for a great deal of synthesis and, as Howard Gardner points out in *Five Minds for the Future*, "the synthesizing mind" that can "knit together information to form a disparate whole is vital today" because "sources of information are vast and disparate, and individuals crave coherence and integration" (46). Here the synthesis is also metacognitive, and as in Chapter 1, I invoke Peter Elbow and Pat Belanoff, who have argued that "[t]he most important kind of learning in school is learning about learning. The most important thinking is thinking about thinking" (18). This essay gives students the chance to practice exactly this sort of thinking. The vast majority of young people spend more time in school than anywhere else. Perhaps this is why students love to wax philosophical discussing education and the nature of knowledge: how do we know what we know, and to what extent does this knowledge define us?

One student blogged about the anxiety he felt over letter grades in school that did not reflect his actual learning. Greg further resented the fact that he was scrutinized by colleges who had to accept the shorthand of a grade as proof of knowledge. Andy complained that he consistently said "No" to invitations to dances or rock concerts because he was too wrapped up in résumé building. Sarah told me she felt embarrassed that she breezed through essay tests that cared only about form. "Give them a clear thesis, no matter what the topic, and they'll be happy" she wrote. A boy named Dhruba, who won numerous writing awards in school, confessed that every single paper he wrote in high school argued that a character moved from innocence to experience. "Why change a winning hand?" he wondered. Mary, a teacher friend, told me that her biggest regret in college was not taking a Shakespeare class taught by a dynamic instructor whom all her friends had said was the best teacher they'd ever had. She chose not to take it, however, because she feared it might lower her grade point average.

The discussions are lively and students quickly generate powerful examples. With this assignment, I try to get out of their way as much as possible, imposing very few restrictions on the final products they produce. The assignment itself is clearly an expression of my own values as a teacher. I don't privilege any one form over another here as long as students are clearly wrestling with questions of knowledge and learning, and I don't grade these pieces, yet students usually invest themselves fully in this assignment, probably because this is clearly a dialogic enterprise in which, to paraphrase Patricia Lambert Stock, students and teachers work together to construct an understanding out of their experiences, images, languages, traditions, values, and motives (14). Such research, Stock suggests, helps students better understand "their experiences and how those experiences have been shaped into stories by [students themselves] and by others" (14).

Here are a few examples of my students' recent work. The first of these was excerpted in Chapter 1.

Four Years in These Walls

To the nurses office I'm a red folder full of old immunization records and my temperature from the one time I actually needed their services. To the IT department I'm 20060916@ ...—it's a mouthful, I know. To the Dean's office I'm parking pass 224 with a '95 maroon Volvo license plate 6718748. To the College Board I'm 329-XX-2222 and 13 penciled-in computer-read bubbles that spell my name, as if it even matters. To the college counselors office I'm a 5.26 GPA AP student on the Honor Roll—all of which turn out to be meaningless distinctions in the real world, but I guess the school community never got that memo. To many of the teachers I'm just another brain, waiting to be filled with insignificant facts that I'll never remember, and even if I did remember, I'd never use. But hey, that's just the way the system works. It's impossible for every student to have a personal relationship with every faculty member. Nevertheless I'm not willing to let my school define me entirely by the overwhelming mountain of folders and numbers tucked away out of sight among the thousands of other files from students current and past. It's my responsibility to find a way to be remembered years after I walk down the central aisle at our commencement ceremony. My education is a two-way relationship—my school has left its mark on me but recently I've discovered that it's my duty to leave my mark on my school in return.

As the doe-eyed fledgling of a freshman that I was, I entered high school wanting to be molded by my teachers. I wanted to absorb everything my teachers told me from magnetic fields to the Ming Dynasty. And what's more, I wanted to repeat all the information right back to my teachers to gain their approval. I wanted to know everything and I wanted everyone else to know I knew everything, too. I loved school, I was eager, I was enthusiastic—who am I kidding, I was obnoxious and naive. School was the end all and the be all of my future. I didn't want to think of life after my school years because it was too scary. The New Trier world was safe, it was comfortable, it allowed me to be passive. I was told what I had to know and was then assessed by predictable written regurgitation tests— information comes in, I spit it back out on paper and bam! the A's practically earn themselves.

Those A's stare me in the face every morning as I pour myself a glass of milk, my transcript held firmly to the slick white surface of my refrigerator by a giant "Kiss the Cook" magnet. From freshman year all the way to 1st semester of senior year, it's been one long line of A's. So I must have learned a ton, right? Yeah, of course I did! I can tell you the area underneath any curve, I can define *shibboleth* and *eleemosynary*, I can write a cookie-cutter five-paragraph essay with my hands *and* feet tied behind my back, I can explain why the Populist movement failed, I can walk you through every step of cellular respiration *with* diagrams included, and I can even calculate my weight on the moon, give or take a few pounds of course. Well that's all fine and dandy except that about all I can do with that information is sound intelligent at parties, cool trick huh?

Knowing all those things doesn't change the fact that I still don't know how to change a tire, I'm incapable of driving to Chicago without getting lost because I rarely leave the suburban bubble, I'm convinced balancing a checkbook means putting it on a scale, and up until about a week ago I thought a pound of pasta might not be enough for two people. It's sad, I know, but it's also very very true— not to mention a huge waste of some delicious spaghetti. So if such everyday activities baffle me, just what have I been committing my mind to, because it's obviously not inquiry? What have I been doing?! It's absolutely terrifying to think that my past 13 years of education have been for naught, but fear not friends, for there is a spotlight at the end of the tunnel: theater.

I used to cringe whenever I heard the word theater. It meant men in tights, bad acting at cheap community theaters, and chatty old women with walkers at a Sunday matinee. So when my theater-enthused friend Abby suggested I get involved in stage crew I couldn't help but laugh in her face.

"Just do it, you'll have fun," she would plead with me regularly. My curiosity and desperation got the better of me sophomore year. I hadn't made many friends freshman year and I needed a way to meet new people so I agreed to do stage crew for the fall show.

Theater made its impression on me too. It was in the Gaffney basement that I met my first serious boyfriend. I learned how to build a magical world out of a disorganized stack of 2x4's and plywood. I built friendships, too, with people that I'll stay in contact with for life. Theater taught me about social dynamics and how to work in a group. I learned problem-solving, humility, individuality, and teamwork. Most importantly I learned how to try something new, push my comfort limits, and break into a new world.

Once I'm gone from New Trier, I won't be remembered in the classroom, my email will be obsolete, someone else will have my parking pass. I'll be forgotten to the New Trier community at large, but I'll live forever in the theater. In the back shop on a load-bearing pillar, I am remembered by a small patch of white and black paint. "Alexa 'Shorty' CoProducer '06!" it says. It doesn't look like much, but I know that when I come back for my 50th reunion, my name will still be there, maintained by students to come, who will also sign their names, and become part of the everlasting history of theater.

I'll be graduating from this school in less than two weeks, and then I'll just be a memory at this school. I won't be walking down the halls every day, seeing familiar faces of students and teachers with whom I've forged tremendously strong relationships. But I won't be forgotten. I'll be remembered by my teachers as a hardworking student, a friendly face who always said hi in the hallways. I'll be remembered by my friends as the short comedian who spent every waking minute trying to make people laugh. I won't let myself become a ghost, just a number in a file. I'm not just a tuberculosis shot, an email address, an ID, or a GPA. Even after I'm gone, I know I'll be remembered, and I'll remember what I learned here.
—Alexa, grade 12

In prewriting discussions, Alexa argued powerfully for self-determination. She wanted to be in charge of her own story and laughed at the idea of institutions defining her by a series of numbers (easy for a straight A student to say, some of her classmates added), yet how few students can really laugh at such reduction? I love how Alexa has begun to make story-sense out of her schooling through her humor and her creation of character and scene—notably her friend Abby talking her into the theater. Returning to the introductory list of numbers in the conclusion is also a nice touch. Through the stories she tells, Alexa implicitly argues for interpersonal knowledge (an ideal time to talk about multiple intelligences) over received knowledge, and it's that knowledge she is sure she will always remember. For teachers, this essay represents an interesting challenge: how do we see our students, how well do we know them?

Here's a decidedly different response from another student, one who implicitly draws a sharp distinction between schooling and education:

Why?

The bright light blinds me.

"Ughh," waking up to guttural screams is never a good way to start your day, especially when you're the one making them.

I had no choice, the light was on; my mom was standing in the doorway; and she wasn't leaving until I showed some signs of life. I screamed again as I sat up. My feet hit the cold floor and the frigid shock ricocheted through my entire body.

"Why?" I cried as I sat holding my head in my hands.

"It's time to go, Nick," she said to me, still standing in my doorway.

I couldn't win. She was a skilled adversary, and I didn't even know if it was possible to beat her. But, at this point, I knew she had already won. So, I trudged into the shower and began another weekday.

"Why do you fight me every morning?"

"Because I hate school," I mumbled between bites of oatmeal.

"But you've been going for 11 years now, you'd think you would have gotten used to it by now."

"Yea, you'd think, wouldn't you?" The truth is I still don't know why I go....

What is the point of school. Why do I go? These questions are so complicated that the only possible answer must be a single sentence, so I'll turn to the school motto: "To commit minds to inquiry, hearts to compassion, and lives to the service of humanity."

So and at the end of my four years has my mind been committed to inquiry, my heart to compassion, and my life to the service of humanity? I'm not so sure.

What I *am* sure about is that I bought a whole lot of books that I never read; I scribbled a whole lot of unintelligible junk in workbooks; and I bought a lot of notebooks that I didn't write a whole lot in. And at the end of it all, I am sure that I will be going to a top ranked engineering school.

So, it seems that the question is, what, exactly, was all that stuff that happened in the middle?

Frankly, I don't remember much of the specifics. I mean with all of the classes I took, how can I be expected to remember every single piece of information from every single class? You try taking Chemistry, English, US History, Physics, Latin, and some other major that obviously was not important enough to make the cut of my memory.

———————

But wait a second, before I get lost in my own memories I have a question. I thought my teachers acted like they wanted me to remember every single morsel of information presented in their class? I mean that's why they had tests and finals, right?

And they clearly evaluated my performance in the class based on how well I was able to remember inane facts on a specific test.

I can't remember if I got every fact right on the tests, but I do remember that I did pretty well in terms of final grades. So, my question is if I did well in the classes, and the point of school is to commit my mind to inquiry, why don't I remember all of the stuff I learned?

I want to explore how a teacher would go about committing a student's mind to inquiry.

Let's just assume for a second, that all of the people who enter this high school are completely and totally extrinsically motivated in regards to learning. So in this (not so) hypothetical situation, the goal of the teacher is to develop some sort of intrinsic motivation in the student. So, the teacher begins to bombard the student with ideas, and to make sure that the student at least acknowledged the fact that the teacher is presenting ideas to him; the teacher has to give some sort of comprehension assessment. But remember that, the point of the class is not to pass the comprehension exams but to commit the student's mind to inquiry.

So, if the student understands the material being presented to him, how does his mind become committed to inquiry and intrinsically motivated towards learning? The best way to accomplish this is to present the student something he disagrees with, or doesn't understand the workings behind. Belief is the most important part of the learning process, because if you challenge a student's belief he will have motivation to challenge the teacher in an attempt to reaffirm his belief, or realize that his belief is flawed and modulate his views with the ones presented by the teacher.

Now, looking back as a student, this process of teachers challenging my beliefs has been the most important part of my learning, because of the reasons mentioned above. But, we are left with a slight problem. The grades you receive for the class are not based on how often your beliefs were challenged and how often you had to create independent thought to defend them; but they are based on how well you comprehend the information the teacher has presented you.

So if that is indeed the truth about the education system, how did I manage to do so well without remembering anything about the War of 1812 or redox reactions? Interestingly enough, it happened through the same process through which my mind became committed to inquiry.

I started high school with no regard to my grades, all I cared about was if I enjoyed learning in the class, whether that learning was in the form of arguing with my teacher or doing a lab in a science class. So naturally, I didn't do very well in classes I had no interest in. So after a semester of this, I quickly realized that other people did not judge me by how much I learned in the class, or how well I enjoyed the class, but simply by one of five letters I received at the end of the class.

This challenged my beliefs, to say the least. I wanted to be happy in the classes I took, and the people around me wanted me to get this letter "A" from the classes. So, to reconcile this challenge to my beliefs I did some research, as I would to settle any dispute.

After a long time spent meditating, I realized that making other people happy was much more important than making myself happy in the short run, because other people will be deciding my path to eventual happiness in life. Other people decided where I would go to college, what job I would get, and how much I would get paid. And most of the time these other people based their decisions on one of five letters and a few assorted numbers.

So to achieve my goal of eventual happiness, I had to pretend like I cared about *Pride and Prejudice*, and pretend like I knew a lot about the Treaties of Versailles. I had to do a lot of pretending to do well in school, but occasionally there were those rare moments where true learning took place. And I believe that those moments have shaped me into what I am today.

"Do you think you'll ever like school?" my mom asked. "Because we'll be paying $30,000 a year to send you to school for the next four years, and if you don't like it, we won't pay for it."

"Mom, you know the only reason I'm going to college is to drink beer, do drugs, and have sex," I smiled. "It's gonna be a four year vacation! Learning isn't the important part."

I walked out the door, on my way to another day at school.
—Nick, grade 12

Just as he had been all year long, Nick's final paper is irreverent, the work of a subtle thinker and a total smartass. His voice emerges as powerfully as Alexa's; each produced a paper that only she or he could have written. For the first time in his life, Nick said, he examined how much time he spent "pretending to read" and "pretending to care" and how much time his teachers spent administering assessments that pretended to account for learning in the classroom. Insights like this offer a powerful intrinsic argument for the role of personal writing in school. Reflective teachers must also wonder about the extent to which classroom assessments measure genuine learning. Wayne Booth's wisdom obtains: "our students give [us] the work we ask for."

How sad is Nick's "epiphany" that in the short term it is better to make other people happy, and what an indictment of school life (my own class included, of course). Unlike Alexa, Nick sees teachers and schools as exerting enormous control over his life, and he feels his education is very much a one-way street. Still, this final essay is terrifically honest and features a lively voice, something that Nick also told me was almost entirely absent throughout his school career.

Let me offer one last example, a student named Ned, who wrote his final essay as a personal letter to me. Ned quoted a Jeff Tweedy lyric, "Candy left over from Halloween / A unified theory of everything" as a sort of implicit justification for his final paper. Unable to offer such a "unified theory," he offered instead a sort of random collection of short pieces. It reminded me of Tim O'Brien's observation in *The Things They Carried* that "what sticks to memory, often, are those odd little fragments that have no beginning and no end" (36).

So Ned offered some thoughts on classroom geography ("how circular rooms promote out-of-the-box thinking"), on school standards ("that limit our ability to create"), on important people in his life (a character sketch about a boy with special needs named Georgia who wore a "black cowboy hat" and "clicking cowboy boots"; Ned adds, "if there were a stable to keep his imaginary horse at school, I'm sure Georgia would ride"), a poem about leaving for college (since Ned "never writes poetry"), and a hand-drawn self-portrait ("for every art class I never took"). The paper is a bit of an organizational mess, yet Ned is clearly thinking deeply and imaginatively about many important issues. And most of all I love the risks he takes throughout the piece, especially the challenge of experimenting with the various genres he had, for some reason, never tried in school.

Is this essay a success? I'd like to argue yes. It was the fourteenth paper Ned wrote that year, and it shows rather than tells of the many sentence strategies and skills he has learned. The frame of the personal letter supplies the essay with structure.

With this final paper, I hope to give students a chance to reflect on their writing and more generally on what they have learned in their lives. The essay also provides me with an opportunity to reflect on my own writing beliefs. Here is the statement of beliefs I wrote a few years back that I mentioned in Chapter 1. On the last day of class, I give this to my students as a course evaluation:

My Goals from the Beginning of the Year

1. To offer assignments unlike any papers you've written before.
2. To offer assignments that insist on originality—assignments that no one else could have written.
3. To get to know you as individual people and fellow writers.
4. To reinforce the idea of writing as a creative process.
5. To demonstrate connections between writing and other arts/disciplines (history, journalism, film, photo, painting, music).
6. To offer only "real world" assignments, those with audiences and purposes beyond the English classroom.
7. To bring in voices other than my own!
8. To welcome all views but also to insist that all positions (including my own) are supported by example.
9. To ensure that you will help determine the shape of the course (leading discussions, presenting projects and positions) and the direction of your writing.
10. To help everyone understand the importance of writing for its own sake, not just for the grade (since we are not reducible to a grade).
11. To allow everyone the chance to revise.
12. To ensure that you are genuinely proud of having written at least one piece of writing (maybe more!).

I leave it up to my students to decide whether I have achieved these goals in our class. I leave it up to you to decide whether I have achieved these goals in this book. As a writing teacher for the past twenty-five years, allow me to add a personal declaration about personal writing. If our students have a stake in the subjects of our courses, they will more fully invest themselves in their inquiry. In an age of inane standardization, it is important that we insist on humanization. Students can sense whether we value them as individuals. The story of our classroom life cannot be told by a test or by a single teacher's voice. The polyphony of voices in a classroom is what brings a class to life. But we teachers also need to insist that we are valued as individuals. We are not accountants filling up a grade book, but teaching artists whose art is the collective work of our classes. Our art is always a work in progress—never ending, unreachable, and utterly worthwhile.

Bibliography

Ammons, A. R. "Corsons Inlet." *Collected Poems: 1951–1971*. New York: Norton, 2001. Print.

Blau, Sheridan D. *The Literature Workshop: Teaching Texts and Their Readers*. Portsmouth, NH: Boynton/Cook, 2003. Print.

"Blogging Helps Encourage Teen Writing." *e School News* 30 Apr. 2008. Web. 1 Nov. 2008.

Boling, Erica, et al. "Collaborative Literacy: Blogs and Internet Projects." *Reading Teacher* 61.6 (2008): 504–6. Print.

Booth, Wayne C. *Now Don't Try to Reason with Me: Essays and Ironies for a Credulous Age*. Chicago: U of Chicago P, 1970. Print.

Boyd, Danah. "Blogging Out Loud: Shifts in Public Voice." Paper presented at the Library and Information Technology Association Conference. San Jose, CA. 1 Oct. 2005. Web. 17 Aug. 2011.

Brainard, Joe. *I Remember*. 1975. New York: Penguin, 1995. Print.

Brooks, David. "The Medium Is the Medium." *New York Times*. New York Times, 8 July 2010. Web. 16 Sept. 2011.

Bruner, Jerome. *Making Stories: Law, Literature, Life*. Cambridge: Harvard UP, 2003. Print.

Cazden, Courtney B. *Classroom Discourse: The Language of Teaching and Learning*. 2nd ed. Portsmouth, NH: Heinemann, 2001. Print.

Clausen, Tom. "Middle Way." *Contemporary Haibun: Volume 4*. Ed. Jim Kacian, Bruce Ross, and Ken Jones. Winchester, VA: Red Moon, 2003. Print.

Clemetson, Lynette. "The Racial Politics of Speaking Well." *New York Times* 4 Feb. 2007. Print.

"Common Core State Standards for English Language Arts and Literacy in History/Social Studies, Science, and Technical Subjects." Common Core State Standards Initiative, 2010. Web. 14 July 2011.

Csikszentmihalyi, Mihalyi, and Reed Larson. *Being Adolescent: Conflict and Growth in the Teenage Years*. New York: Basic, 1984. Print.

Darwish, Mahmoud. *Unfortunately, It Was Paradise: Selected Poems*. Trans. and ed. Munir Akash and Carolyn Forché. Berkeley: U of California P, 2003. Print.

Dewey, John. *How We Think*. 1910. Mineola, NY: Dover, 1997. Print.

Dunphy, John. "Facing the Wall." *Stone Frog: American Haibun and Haiga, Vol. 2*. Ed. Jim Kacian and Bruce Ross. Winchester, VA: Red Moon, 2001. 18. Print.

Elbow, Peter. *From Grades to Grids: Responding to Writing by Criteria*. Marist College Writing Center. N.d. Web. 2 Sept. 2011.

Elbow, Peter, and Pat Belanoff. *A Community of Writers: A Workshop Course in Writing*. New York: McGraw, 1989. Print.

Gallagher, Jamey. "'As Y'all Know': Blog as Bridge." *Teaching English in the Two-Year College* 37.3 (2010): 286–94. Print.

Gardner, Howard. *Five Minds for the Future*. Boston: Harvard Business School P, 2007. Print.

Goodlad, John. *A Place Called School: Prospects for the Future*. New York: McGraw-Hill, 1984. Print.

Gorman, Michael. "Revenge of the Blog People!" *Library Journal* 130.3 (15 Feb. 2005): n.pag. Web. 14 Sept. 2011.

Graves, Donald H. "Bringing Life to Learning." *Educational Leadership* 57.8 (2000): 19–22. Print.

———. *Writing: Teachers and Children at Work*. Exeter, NH: Heinemann, 1983. Print.

Gutkind, Lee, ed. *The Best Creative Nonfiction, Vol.1*. New York: Norton, 2007. Print.

Hartwell, Richard. "Our Writing Lives: How I Evolved as a Writer." *The Voice* 6.2 (2001): 20–21. Print.

Hass, Robert. "On Visiting the DMZ at Panmunjom: A Haibun." *Time and Materials: Poems 1997–2005*. New York: Ecco, 2007. Print.

Hillocks, George Jr. "The Focus on Form vs. Content in Teaching Writing." *Research in the Teaching of English* 40.2 (2005): 238–49. Print.

———. *Teaching as Reflective Practice*. New York: Teachers College P, 1995. Print.

Hurlburt, Sarah. "Defining Tools for a New Learning Space: Writing and Reading Class Blogs." *Journal of Online Learning and Teaching* 4.2 (2008). Web.

Johannessen, Larry R. *Illumination Rounds: Teaching the Literature of the Vietnam War*. Urbana, IL: National Council of Teachers of English, 1992. Print.

Keller, Josh. "Studies Explore Whether the Internet Makes Students Better Writers." *Chronicle of Higher Education*. Chronicle of Higher Education, 11 June 2009 Web. 15 Sept. 2011.

Ketchek, Michael. "Birthday Haibun." *Up Against the Window: American Haibun and Haiga, Vol. 1*. Ed. Jim Kacian and Bruce Ross. Winchester, VA: Red Moon, 1999. 55. Print.

King, Stephen. *On Writing: A Memoir of the Craft*. New York: Scribner, 2000. Print.

Kristof, Nicholas D. "Et Tu, George?" *New York Times*. New York Times, 23 Jan. 2007. Web. 14 Sept. 2011.

Kundera, Milan. *The Art of the Novel*. New York: Perennial-Harper, 2003. Print.

Lenehan, Michael. "The Terkel Rules: Translating from Speech to Prose." *Chicago Reader* 31 Oct. 2008. Web. 14 Sept. 2011.

Lopate, Phillip, ed. *The Art of the Personal Essay: An Anthology from the Classical Era to the Present*. New York: Anchor, 1997. Print.

Macrorie, Ken. *Telling Writing*. Upper Montclair, NJ: Boynton/Cook, 1985. Print.

Mandelbaum, Paul, ed. *First Words: Earliest Writings from Favorite Contemporary Authors*. Chapel Hill: Algonquin, 1993. Print.

McAdams, Dan P. *The Stories We Live By: Personal Myths and the Making of the Self*. New York: Guilford, 1997. Print.

Michie, Gregory. *Holler If You Hear Me: The Education of a Teacher and His Students*. New York: Teachers College P, 1999. Print.

Morris, E. (Producer/Director). (2004). *The fog of war* [DVD]. Culver City, CA: Columbia TriStar Home Entertainment.

Mueller, Lisel. "Why We Tell Stories." *Alive Together: New and Selected Poems*. Baton Rouge: Louisiana State UP, 1996. 150–51. Print.

Murray, Donald M. "All Writing Is Autobiography." *The Essential Don Murray: Lessons from America's Greatest Writing Teacher*. Ed. Thomas Newkirk and Lisa C. Miller. Portsmouth, NH: Boynton/Cook, 2009. 205–17. Print.

National Council of Teachers of English (NCTE). *NCTE Beliefs about the Teaching of Writing. National Council of Teachers of English* [Guideline]. 2004. Web. 7 Sept. 2011.

Nye, Naomi Shihab. "For Mohammed Zeid of Gaza, Age 15." *You and Yours*. Pittsburgh: BOA, 2005. 54. Print.

O'Brien, Tim. *The Things They Carried*. New York: Houghton, 1990. Print.

O'Connor, John S. *Wordplaygrounds: Reading, Writing, and Performing Poetry in the English Classroom*. Urbana, IL: NCTE, 2004. Print.

Orwell, George. "Politics and the English Language." *A Collection of Essays*. San Diego: Harcourt Brace Jovanovich, 1981. Print.

Paley, Vivian Gussin. *The Boy Who Would Be a Helicopter: The Uses of Storytelling in the Classroom*. Cambridge: Harvard UP, 1991. Print.

Radiolab. "Who Am I" [Podcast]. *Radiolab*. Alfred P. Sloan Foundation. 7 May 2007. Web. 15 Sept. 2011.

Richardson, Will. *Blogs, Wikis, Podcasts, and Other Powerful Web Tools*. Thousand Oaks, CA: Corwin, 2006. Print.

Rief, Linda. "Writing Matters." *Voices from the Middle* 11.2 (2003): 8–12. Print.

Ritchie, Donald A. *Doing Oral History: A Practical Guide*. 2nd ed. New York: Oxford UP, 2003. Print.

Romano, Tom. "The Power of Voice." *Educational Leadership* 62.2 (2004): 20–23. Print.

———*Writing with Passion: Life Stories, Multiple Genres*. Portsmouth, NH: Boynton/Cook, 1995. Print.

Root, Robert. *The Nonfictionist's Guide: On Reading and Writing Creative Nonfiction*. Lanham, MD: Rowman, 2008. Print.

Rose, Mike. *Lives on the Boundary*. New York: Penguin, 2005. Print.

Ross, Bruce. *How to Haiku: A Writer's Guide to Haiku and Related Forms*. Boston: Tuttle, 2002. Print.

Rozmus, Lidia. *My Journey*. Evanston, IL: Deep North, 2004. Print.

Rushdie, Salman. *Haroun and the Sea of Stories*. New York: Penguin, 1991. Print.

———. *The Wizard of Oz*. London: British Film Institute, 1992. Print.

Salinger, J. D. *The Catcher in the Rye*. 1951. New York: Bantam, 1986. Print.

Schaafsma, David. *Eating on the Street: Teaching Literacy in a Multicultural Society*. Pittsburgh: U of Pittsburgh P, 1994. Print.

Schaafsma, David, Gian S. Pagnucci, Robert M. Wallace, and Patricia Lambert Stock. "Composing Storied Ground: Four Generations of Narrative Inquiry." *English Education* 39.4 (2007): 282–305. Print.

Scholes, Robert. "Mission Impossible." *English Journal* 88.6 (1999): 28–35. Print.

Smith, Michael W., and Jeffrey D. Wilhelm. *"Reading Don't Fix No Chevys": Literacy in the Lives of Young Men*. Portsmouth, NH: Heinemann, 2002. Print.

Sophocles. *The Three Theban Plays: Antigone, Oedipus the King, Oedipus at Colonus*. Trans. Robert Fagles. New York: Penguin, 2000. Print.

Stock, Patricia Lambert. *The Dialogic Curriculum: Teaching and Learning in a Multicultural Society*. Portsmouth, NH: Boynton/Cook, 1995. Print.

Sullivan, Andrew. "Why I Blog." *The Atlantic* Nov. 2008. Web. 16 Sept. 2011.

Swenson, Janet, et al. "Extending the Conversation: New Technologies, New Literacies, and English Education." *English Education* 38.4 (2006): 351–69. Print.

Terkel, Studs. *Race: How Blacks and Whites Think and Feel about the American Obsession*. New York: New Press, 1992. Print.

——— "Studs Terkel: Winner of the 1997 Distinguished Contribution to American Letters Award." Acceptance Speech. National Book Foundation, 1997. Web. 19 Aug. 2011.

Thoreau, Henry David. *Walden: Or, Life in the Woods*. 1854. New York: Signet Classic, 1999. Print.

Turchi, Peter. *Maps of the Imagination: The Writer as Cartographer*. San Antonio: Trinity UP, 2004. Print.

Vargas Llosa, Mario. "Why Literature?" *The Best American Essays 2002*. Ed. Stephen Jay Gould. Boston: Houghton, 2002. 295–308. Print.

Watson, Don. *Death Sentences: How Clichés, Weasel Words, and Management-Speak Are Strangling Public Language*. New York: Gotham, 2007. Print.

Witte, Shelbie. "'That's Online Writing, Not Boring School Writing': Writing with Blogs and the Talkback Project." *Journal of Adolescent and Adult Literacy* 51.2 (2007): 92–96. Print.

Wolff, Tobias. *This Boy's Life*. New York: Grove, 2000. Print.

Zeiger, William. "The Exploratory Essay: Enfranchising the Spirit of Inquiry in College Composition." *College English* 47.5 (1985): 454–66. Print.

Zinsser, William K., ed. *Inventing the Truth: The Art and Craft of Memoir*. Boston: Mariner-Houghton, 1998. Print.

Author

John S. O'Connor has an AB in philosophy and English and an MAT (English) from the University of Chicago. He also holds a PhD in English from the University of Illinois at Chicago. He has taught English for the past 25 years in a wide variety of settings (public, private, parochial, independent, alternative schools; a maximum security prison; an adult literacy agency) and every level from grade 6 to college classes. He currently teaches at New Trier High School outside of Chicago.

O'Connor is the author of *Wordplaygrounds: Reading, Writing, and Performing Poetry in the English Classroom* (2004) and two books of poems: *Things Being What They Are* (2011) and *Room Full of Chairs* (2001). He has written on English and education in periodicals such as *English Journal, Shakespeare, OAH Magazine of History,* and *Schools*. His most recent essay for *Schools,* "Once More to the Ocean" (which, in modified form, appears as Chapter 1 of this book), was named a Notable Essay in *Best American Essays 2011*.

As a poet, O'Connor has published poems in places such as *Poetry East, River Oak Review,* and *RHINO*. He has also released a CD of well-known poems he set to music called *Evenings and Other Beginnings*. He has written radio commentaries on education for NPR affiliate WBEZ and has served as guest blogger for the Poetry Foundation website.

O'Connor speaks frequently at national and local education conferences and at schools and universities. He is a member of the NCTE consultant network.

This book was typeset in TheMix and Palatino by Barbara Frazier.

The typeface used on the cover is Bernhard Modern Standard Roman.

The book was printed on 50-lb. Opaque Offset paper by Versa Press, Inc.